# Language and Gender in Childre

Disney and Pixar films are beloved by children and adults alike. However, what linguistic messages, both positive and negative, do these films send to children about gender roles? How do characters of different genders talk, and how are they talked about? And do patterns of representation change over time? Using an accessible mix of statistics and in-depth qualitative analysis, the authors bring their expertise to the study of this very popular media behemoth. Looking closely at five different language features – talkativeness, compliments, directives, insults, and apologies – the authors uncover the biases buried in scripted language, and explore how language is used to construct tropes of femininity, masculinity, and queerness. Working with a large body of films reveals wide-scale patterns that might fly under the radar when the films are viewed individually, as well as demonstrating how different linguistic tools and techniques can be used to better understand popular children's media.

CARMEN FOUGHT is Professor of Linguistics at Pitzer College. She is the author of *Chicano English in Context* (2003) and *Language and Ethnicity* (2006). Her research on language and gender in children's films has been discussed in several major news outlets such as *The Washington Post* and a special issue of *National Geographic*.

KAREN EISENHAUER is the Head of Research for People Nerds, a human insights blog published by dscout. She has an MA in linguistics from North Carolina State University. Her research with Dr. Fought on language and gender has been featured in major publications including *The Washington Post*, the *BBC*, and *Time Magazine*.

# Language and Gender in Children's Animated Films

Carmen Fought

*Pitzer College, Claremont*

Karen Eisenhauer

*North Carolina State University*

# CAMBRIDGE
## UNIVERSITY PRESS

University Printing House, Cambridge CB2 8BS, United Kingdom

One Liberty Plaza, 20th Floor, New York, NY 10006, USA

477 Williamstown Road, Port Melbourne, VIC 3207, Australia

314–321, 3rd Floor, Plot 3, Splendor Forum, Jasola District Centre,
New Delhi – 110025, India

103 Penang Road, #05–06/07, Visioncrest Commercial, Singapore 238467

Cambridge University Press is part of the University of Cambridge.

It furthers the University's mission by disseminating knowledge in the pursuit of
education, learning, and research at the highest international levels of excellence.

www.cambridge.org
Information on this title: www.cambridge.org/9781108841672
DOI: 10.1017/9781108894586

First published 2022

A catalogue record for this publication is available from the British Library.

ISBN 978-1-108-84167-2 Hardback
ISBN 978-1-108-79503-6 Paperback

Cambridge University Press has no responsibility for the persistence or accuracy
of URLs for external or third-party internet websites referred to in this publication
and does not guarantee that any content on such websites is, or will remain,
accurate or appropriate.

This work is dedicated to every young scholar out there who has a passion, especially queer folk, women, and people of color. Don't let anyone tell you what you can or cannot do. And if you don't think your idea is good enough or serious enough to be meaningful, take it from two grown women who have spent a decade watching Disney movies: it is.

# Contents

# Figures

# Tables

# Preface
## Real-World Tips from Auntie Carmen and Auntie Karen

This book did not come into existence by magic, or through some mysterious process that is kept highly secret in the towers of academia. We often treat academic books as if they are produced in an objective, detached way, like boxes of cereal on a machine-run assembly line that doesn't really involve "people" at all. But academic authors are, in fact, verifiable people. We have lives and lived experiences, friends, mentors, pets, worries, hopes, like anyone else.

To that end, we have allowed our voices as individuals to come through in this book, more than is typical of academic writing. We believe that rather than weaken our authority, this approach strengthens it: we acknowledge who we are, what we think about, what angers or upsets us. There can be no real objectivity where humans and societies are involved, even in the presentation of facts and data that we hope will clarify and illuminate some aspect of the social sciences. So the best we can do is to be honest about where we're coming from.

We also hope to demystify slightly for students and others the idea of writing a book, which can seem daunting and alien, especially to those who come from marginalized communities or other social spaces where the academic world seems like a very far off place.

Over our years of conducting the research for this book, lots of things other than the book took place in our lives: Karen began as an undergraduate student, then got a Master's degree, and became a co-author. Carmen's husband was diagnosed with Alzheimer's and later passed away. Karen moved to Chicago, began a new job, and experienced the end of a long-term relationship. She got a cat.

We received a contract from Cambridge toward the end of 2019. In March 2020 we got together to make a definitive plan for finishing each chapter on time, with Karen flying out to California. As we were working through our plan, a frightening new virus emerged in the world, and the country began to shut down. People overbought toilet paper. Karen scrambled to change her travel plans and fly home. In Minnesota, a police officer knelt on George Floyd's neck for nine and a half minutes. People marched, around the country and around the world. For most of the late summer and fall, California, where Carmen lives, was on fire. Climate scientists released increasingly dire predictions.

There were times when we stopped and thought about the fact that the world was definitely. Not. Ok. It felt strange to be moving ahead, writing this book about cartoons, as so many unprecedented and alarming events were taking place around us. We kept writing, though. We asked for, and received, an extension on our original deadline. We agreed to be compassionate toward ourselves and each other. We had moments, individually and collectively, when we were discouraged, felt inadequate. We struggled. But we were also incredibly fortunate to be on a team, with each other and with an extended group of people who supported and encouraged us.

That's how the book came to be. It's not a secret. But as much as it was a challenging, arduous, and ultimately very human process, we still feel blessed by having met each other and by the friends, family, colleagues, collaborators who supported us through this process. So actually, maybe there was a little bit of magic, when you think about it.

# Acknowledgments

Because this project has been the result of a decade of work, we find ourselves with a decade's worth of people to thank. Though we cannot possibly hope to recognize every person who has made this project come to life, we do want to call out some in particular.

Firstly, we have had many assistants who have helped with collecting and analyzing data over the years. This book has almost 10,000 hand-collected speech tokens (!) and we couldn't have done it without them. Thanks to all of them, and to the Pitzer Research and Awards, Doman, and Davis research funds that helped us employ them:

Zoe Bauer  
Liam Brooks  
haley brown  
Ricky Canton  
Laura Casaregola  
Anna Hall  
Savannah Jett  
Olivia Landgraff  
Brendan Ly  
Shalina Omar  
Sam Resnick  
Alex Samuels  
Emma Wenger  

There are also many peers, editors, and mentors who have helped us create and strengthen our work. Thanks to Robin Dodsworth, Agnes Bolonyai, and Richard Shafranek for help in conceiving our analytical approaches, both qualitative and quantitative; Mary Paster and Robin Queen for help with our proposal; Armand deAsis and Rupert Deese for their assistance in automating some of our more tedious tasks; Lindsey Brinkworth, Katie Conner, Ari Janoff, Emily Pearl, Robin Queen, and Emily Safford for their valuable feedback during editing. Thank you to our anonymous reviewers for careful consideration of our manuscript. And a special thanks to Brendan Ly and Olivia Landgraff for helping us bring it over the finish line by polishing, standardizing, tracking down references, and just generally being cheerful and awesome even when we were a mess.

As is traditional, we absolve anyone we've thanked here of responsibility for any of our mistakes. The nice thing about being co-authors is that we can just each blame the other for any big screwups. We hope there aren't any, but just in case.

Of course, a huge thanks to Cambridge University Press for publishing our work, and to Andrew Winnard and Izzie Collins for working with us.

We also appreciate beyond measure those who have supported us emotionally through this process, past and present. Carmen wants to thank her awesome friends, especially the ones who provided food (Angela, Mita, Yolanda) or advice (Cliff, haley, Kathy, Louis, Mark, Patti) or took her to Disneyland (Monica and Mario). Also her mentors, John Rickford and Walt Wolfram, who taught her that you can be an academic and also a damn good person. And finally and forever, John Fought. *El amor nunca muere.*

Karen wants to thank her parents for always being supportive of her, and the many mentors over the years who helped her learn, including the faculty at Pitzer College and NC State, especially Carmen, for believing in her and giving her such an incredible opportunity. She also wants to thank Emma, Erin, Allison, Emily, Grae, Sara, Lindsey, and all her loved ones near and far who helped make 2020 into a year of surprising growth and community. And a special thank you to Richard, for lending his gentleness, creativity, connection, and coziness to her little Chicago studio.

Lastly, to our readers, thank you! More so than ever in this world of ubiquitous technology, we know you have choices about what to read, and so we are grateful and humbled that you picked our book.

# 1 Introduction

## A Whole New World?

I think of a child's mind as a blank book. During the first years of his [*sic*] life, much will be written on the pages. The quality of that writing will affect his [*sic*] life profoundly.

Walt Disney, cited in Giroux and Pollock (2010)

### The Power of Children's Media

*What's Your Favorite Disney Movie?*

We ask this question of our audiences all the time and get a wide range of answers. It's surprisingly rare, though, for anyone to say *I don't have one*, much less *I haven't seen any Disney movies*. And it's very common for the students we meet (or teach) to report having watched their favorite hundreds of times. As a child, the first author's favorite Disney movie was *The Aristocats* (1970), a movie she had *never actually seen*. She just knew it featured a white cat (for which she had glimpsed the plush reproduction toy on a rare visit to the park) and that other little girls were talking about it. Such is the power of Uncle Walt.

When we first began presenting our research, we discovered almost immediately that anything with the word *Disney* in it drew a crowd. Talking about the Disney Princess films was like ringing a Pavlovian bell that brought a surge of interest from fellow linguists, journalists, and our friends and family (including some who had had very little interest in our work before). After we presented our first paper at the Linguistics Society of America annual meeting in 2016, there was an explosion of interest from the popular press. The initial spark was an article by Jeff Guo in the *Washington Post* ("Researchers have found a major problem with 'The Little Mermaid' and other Disney movies"), which led to numerous articles across a variety of internet sites, as well as two notable accolades at more or less opposite ends of the media spectrum: (1) publication of our charts in a special edition of National Geographic on children and their situation across the globe

(Nowakowski 2017), and (2) a brief reference in the Weekend Update section of a *Saturday Night Live* episode.[1]

We mention this trend, not to prove that we are the popular girls and you should sit with us at lunchtime, or that this attention shows how impressive our research is. In fact, very few of those who talked to us about the project were particularly interested in the scholarly quality of our work. Rather, the point is that Disney itself has a tremendous amount of power and influence in the media and beyond. Each new addition to the Disney/Pixar canon seems to be a lightning rod for political commentary by everyone from film critics and mass market authors to YouTubers and Mommy-blogs.

So now it's our turn. This book presents the culmination of over a decade of research on language and gender in children's films. And the period of filmmaking that we cover is much longer than that: exactly 80 years, from *Snow White and the Seven Dwarfs* in 1937 to *Coco* in 2017. We have conducted an analysis of the 31 films included here using sociolinguistic methodologies. Our analysis begins with some basic facts – like who speaks more in the films, and by how much – and then focuses more closely on a number of specific speech acts in the films, including compliments, directives, insults, and apologies. We use quantitative methods to find broad trends in data and then use in-depth qualitative analyses to explore more nuanced aspects of our findings. By combining different techniques of linguistic analysis in this way, we are able to give an overview of a large section of the animated media landscape and to document patterns that might not be evident from analyzing an individual film. We also will be looking at these linguistic trends in their full context, though, by exploring how they work in specific scenes, where characters interact with specific aims and motives.

### Have You Checked the Children? The Influence of Media

Children's media matters a great deal when it comes to how children understand their world. We know that kids are watching bucketloads of TV and movies and learning important lessons from them. A 2019 report by Common Sense Media found that kids aged 0–8 spend, on average, close to two hours per day watching TV (Rideout & Robb 2020). One study showed that by the time kids entered kindergarten, they knew more fictional characters than they knew real humans (Liebert & Sprafkin 1988), and that study was from back before the advent of portable screens. Martin and Kazyak (2009) looked at the 20 top-grossing G-rated films for the years 1995 to 2005 (17 of which were from Disney, by the way). They report that:

---

[1] Debuted April 16, 2016.

In a 2006 survey of more than 600 American mothers of three- to six-year-olds, only 1 percent reported that their child had not seen any of the films we analyze here; half had seen 13 or more [Martin, Luke, and Verduzco-Baker 2007]. (2009: 318)

One percent? But if you're one of the many adults we know who has all the words to "Let It Go" memorized because your kid or grandkid insists on watching *Frozen* over and over, you're probably less surprised than we were.

These films reach far and wide and not only that: their importance can extend far beyond a single screening. Kids don't just see a movie once, talk about it over drinks, and go home. Kids obsess. Children are much more likely to rewatch the same pieces of media over and over (e.g. Mares 1998, cited in Martin & Kazyak 2009), and they also absorb characters into their lives in the form of toys, stories, and imaginary play. They use play to literally act out the narratives and social scripts they absorb, and in doing so, practice enacting social roles and values (see e.g. Wohlwend 2009). All this contributes to the claim that Giroux makes in his influential book *The Mouse that Roared* that children's films "operate on many registers, but one of the most persuasive is the role that they play as the new 'teaching machines' . . . these films possess at least as much cultural authority and legitimacy for teaching roles, values, and ideals as do more traditional sites of learning, such as the public schools, religious institutions, and the family" (1999: 84).

This growing role of mass media in kids' daily lives has been the subject of study (and concern) for grown-ups starting back in the 1970s. Scholars have produced an impressive body of literature on the influence of media consumption on children. We share below a few key insights from studies that have looked at gender roles specifically:

- Elementary school kids who watched more TV were more likely to have affinities for toys and clothes that reflected stereotypes about their gender (Frueh & McGhee 1975).
- Increased TV consumption was associated with increased acceptance of sex-role stereotypes throughout adolescence (Herrett-Skjellum & Allen 1995).
- Young girls who watched more feminine-coded "teen movies" tended to have more gendered (and negative) interpretations of peers' behavior (Behm-Morawitz & Mastro 2008).
- Kids with higher media exposure were more likely to feel dissatisfied with their bodies: boys wanted to have buffer torsos, and girls wanted to lose weight (Ata et al. 2007; Coyne et al. 2016; Grabe et al. 2008).
- Girls who had higher media consumption were significantly more likely to develop habits or beliefs related to disordered eating (Ata et al. 2007; Grabe et al. 2008).

The research discussed here confirms that consuming more mass media significantly impacts viewers' gender ideologies, usually moving views and

Figure 1.1 Dolls from Disney and Pixar in locations around the world.
Clockwise from top left: Shanghai, Tokyo, Moscow, and London
Reproduced by permission of www.gettyimages.com

behaviors to be more traditionally gendered, and in some cases, more harmful or toxic. No wonder Peggy Orenstein chose to name her bestselling 2011 book on so-called girl culture *Cinderella Ate My Daughter*.

### Disney's Media Empire

Having decided that we wanted to look at gender in children's media, we immediately turned to Disney and Pixar. It is difficult to overstate the power that the Walt Disney corporation and its affiliates wield in our modern media landscape. In addition to its more well-known fare of branded movies, TV shows, live events, and theme parks, the Disney company has been steadily acquiring an astonishing amount of the media we consume, including the Fox network, National Geographic, ABC, FX Networks, Lucasfilm, Marvel Studios, and ESPN. Reading the full list of the company's assets is a staggering experience, one which makes it slightly less surprising to learn that they pulled in $69.6 billion in 2019 alone, and were responsible for a full 30 percent of all film revenue earned in the US that year.[2]

The cornerstone of this massive media empire is, and has always been, feature-length animation. Disney currently produces films from two separate studios, Walt Disney Animation Studios and Pixar, and together they dominate the landscape of animated films both in the box office and in critical reception. Of the 10 top-grossing animated films of as of 2019, seven came from Disney/ Pixar. (*Frozen II* took the top spot, previously held by, of course, the original *Frozen*). And it seems like their momentum is only building; in 2019 the studios' major hits (*Frozen II* and *Toy Story 4*) took in $1.4 billion in ticket sales, outstripping every other animation studio in the market.

Disney and Pixar also hold a combined 15 of the 21 Academy Awards given for best animated picture since the award's inception in 2001. Between the two studios, the Disney Corporation has a crushing presence in the world of children's media that far transcends any of its competitors. Disney has built itself a reputation for being the gold standard of children's cinema – a reputation that has been in the works since Disney's first feature film in 1937.

### Gender Ideology in the Magic Kingdom

The dominance of these studios isn't inherently a bad thing. Disney and Pixar have some great messages about how we should tell the truth, be vulnerable with friends and family, stand up for what we believe in, and always give cooking rats the benefit of the doubt. The problem occurs when social factors become intertwined with more abstract moralizing in problematic ways. Children's stories are short and they're simple; they don't have time for nuance or complicated character development. Kids (in the US at least) just don't have that kind of attention span. So children's media, and cartooning in particular, ends up relying on a lot of cultural shorthand to sketch in character and plot as quickly as possible (Lippi-Green 1997). We expect animation to be a fanciful mode of production, and we expect children's media projects to be fast and fun, more than we expect them to be realistic. With those expectations comes a lot of freedom.

That freedom can be dangerous. In children's media, animators are allowed and even encouraged to construct worlds that are dictated more by ideology than by reality. As animator Tim Burton explains:

Precisely because of their assumed innocence and innocuousness, their inherent ability – even obligation – to defy all conventions of realistic representation, animated cartoons offer up a fascinating zone with which to examine how a dominant culture constructs its subordinates. As non-photographic application of photographic medium, they are freed from the basic cinematic expectation that they create an "impression of reality" ... (Burton 1992, cited in Lippi-Green 1997: 85)

---

[2] We don't have numbers yet on how 2020 affected them, but we're also not super-worried.

The issue here is that the alternative to reality that is being created is almost always predicated on dominant social ideologies, many of which are harmful. Pandey argues that, as a result, movies tend to "uphold mainstream values by according positive attributes to characters who function as prototypes of the dominant culture, while simultaneously ascribing negative values to characters from non-mainstream social groups" (2001: 2).

Here is one specific example: the freedom from reality that children's media enjoy allows Disney writers to set a movie like *Aladdin* in a fictional Middle Eastern city of Agrabah without necessarily having all or even any characters speak like they're from a Middle Eastern country in the real world. They don't need to speak an Arabic-influenced variety of English, much less actual Arabic. But mix that with common cultural stereotypes, and you end up with rough and mean background characters speaking with vaguely "Middle Eastern" accents, a fast-talking sidekick who speaks like a New York Jewish man, and the two romantic leads speaking like they're from Southern California[3] (Lippi-Green 2013). Intentionally or not, this leads audiences to link the (white, SoCal) standard variety of English with heroes, even in a Middle Eastern setting. As the creators pick and choose what they represent "realistically" and what to ignore or replace, they promote dangerous dominant ideologies.

We're certainly not the first scholars to consider that Disney and Pixar are worth studying. *Au contraire*, we pick up this thread from a long line of researchers, coming from an impressive range of academic fields, from media studies to marketing to social work.[4] And within that tradition, gender in children's films has been a particularly hot topic, especially with respect to the Disney Princess movies.

In terms of ideologies around gender, previous research has documented how Disney embraces gender-stereotypical characters and behaviors. Numerous studies report that the female characters in Disney tend to end up in domestic and/or romantic roles, such as mother or wife (e.g. Lippi-Green 2013; Towbin et al. 2004), while male characters have more choices. Female characters also exhibit stereotypically gendered qualities such as:

- passivity (Junn 1997)
- helplessness (Towbin et al. 2004)

---

[3] Which they literally are: Linda Larkin (voice of Jasmine) was born and grew up in Los Angeles, and Scott Weinger (voice of Aladdin) was born in New York but moved to Los Angeles when he was young.

[4] A sample of relevant fields on the list includes: media studies (e.g. Gillam & Wooden 2008; Junn 1997), gender studies (Brydon 2009; England et al. 2011; Martin & Kazyak 2009), marketing (e.g. Cook & Main 2008; Wilde 2014), sociology (e.g. Forman-Brunell & Eaton 2009), psychology (e.g. Coyne et al. 2016), and social work (e.g. Towbin et al. 2004). Disney is the ultimate interdisciplinary field.

- open affection (England et al. 2011; Junn 1997)
- being valued for conventional beauty over other traits (Junn 1997; Lippi-Green 2013; Towbin et al. 2004).

Male characters also conform to some unsurprising stereotypes, for example being shown as:

- physically strong/dominant (England et al. 2011; Towbin et al. 2004)
- assertive (England et al. 2011; Towbin et al. 2004)
- sexually aggressive (Junn 1997).

In other words, while Disney could take advantage of setting a film "under the sea" or in a mythical kingdom to try new things in the area of gender and gender roles, by and large, they don't. They reproduce the same ideologies.

There is also some evidence that Disney may be specifically to blame for some of the attitudinal and behavioral effects on children that have been documented. As we'll explain in Chapter 2, the 1990s created a lot of (rightful) concern about the gender lessons we teach young girls. It was at that point that scholars began looking at Disney Princesses, and they haven't really ceased since.

One key study of Disney's influence on children is Coyne et al. 2016. We appreciate this one particularly, because it was done longitudinally, to test the effects of exposure to the media in real time. The researchers report that:

Disney Princess engagement was associated with more female gender-stereotypical behavior 1 year later, even after controlling for initial levels of gender-stereotypical behavior. Parental mediation strengthened associations between princess engagement and adherence to female gender-stereotypical behavior for both girls and boys. (2016: 1909)

In other words, they found some good evidence that it is in fact *not* just entertainment; children who watched more of the Princess films were more likely to pick up gender-stereotypical behaviors. So whatever it is that children are seeing on the screen has measurable, real-world implications for how they understand and embody gender. That means that the language in these films is something we definitely need to know more about.

### Linguistics and the Media

*Studying Language in the Media*

There have been multiple full-length works dealing exclusively with representation of various groups in Disney. Books like *The Mouse that Roared: Disney and the End of Innocence* (Giroux 1999; Giroux & Pollock 2010), *From Mouse to Mermaid: The Politics of Film, Gender, and Culture* (Bell et al. 1995), *Tinker Belles and Evil Queens* (Griffin 2000), and *Diversity in Disney Films: Critical Essays on Race, Ethnicity, Gender, Sexuality and Disability*

(Cheu 2013) are examples of the many fine critical qualitative works that have been written in the past three decades. And that's on top of the vast number of articles from many corners of academia that have weighed in. But despite all of this research, linguistics has yet to make a significant contribution to the topic of gender in children's media – a fact we hope to change.

Linguists have historically been reluctant to use scripted media as a source of linguistic data because it's "not real." Sociolinguists, especially, have prided themselves on studying real people and communities, while looking askance at syntacticians who theorize about ideal speaker-hearers and spend their time considering hypothetical sentences like *What was the thing you bought Mary a book and?* that one is not likely to hear in the real world. Linguists who do venture into the world of media tend to do so by looking at unscripted film, like reality TV or political broadcasts (e.g. Mullany 2011; Sung 2012), which Queen points out is explained by the "assumption that the language of scripted, imagined media is somehow less authentic than either unscripted language in the media or real-life communication" (2015: 20). The goal of sociolinguistics is to describe how real people "do" things with language, based on how they wish to present themselves in a particular situation. So we expect that for many sociolinguists, the idea of conducting a sociolinguistic research project in which all of the speakers are fictional characters makes them understandably uneasy.

However, there is a growing body of work from scholars who believe that scripted media can be a rich source of linguistic data. Queen argues in her book *Vox Popular* (2015) that scripted media has vast untapped potential for analyzing social variation, both in terms of how variation contributes to characterization and narrative action, and in terms of how media assigns new social meaning to variation. Dynel (2013, 2015) similarly argues that language in scripted media shares enough in common with unscripted speech to be valuable, and that "fictionalized reality can reveal social processes more clearly than lived reality" (Coupland 2004: 258, cited in Dynel 2015: 339). Other scholars have backed this point up by showing the many similarities between scripted and unscripted speech (e.g. Culpeper et al. 1998; Quaglio 2009).

Some studies have gone even further and have begun to analyze social variables such as gender, ethnicity, and class as they appear in the media (e.g. Al-Yasin & Rabab'ah 2018; Fägersten 2016; Lauzen & Dozier 2002). Two interesting studies that apply some linguistic analysis to Disney specifically are Pandey (2001) and Lippi-Green (1997/2013). Interestingly, both of them focus on the use of standard vs. vernacular varieties of English.

Rosina Lippi-Green is the person who first brought the potential for studying Disney into the view of linguists as a chapter in her seminal book *English with an Accent* (1997/2013), and who inspired our own work. She showed that standard dialects of English correlate with "good" characters, whereas nonstandard dialects are usually used to voice villains or side characters. She also takes a critical look at gender roles, albeit from a general, not linguistic perspective (e.g. focusing on job titles available to female characters). Pandey similarly looks at how characters who use a standard variety are granted more leeway in using strategies of rudeness than those who use a nonstandard variety, reinforcing the hierarchy of power between the two varieties.

These studies demonstrate that linguistics can reveal patterns in ways that other methods of critical analysis might miss. Pandey's study, though, is wholly qualitative and based on individual scenes; Lippi-Green's has quantitative elements, but on an extremely broad level (i.e. counting the number of characters with a given dialect). Our project takes all of this a step further by applying traditional sociolinguistic methods to media sources, to parallel studies of sociolinguistic variables in real-world communities. With these methods, we want to address what we would argue is a critical (and missing) piece of the puzzle: language and gender in children's films. We are excited to take up this challenge, because we think our research can add some new and important viewpoints to the world of media analysis. We also hope to model methods for doing sociolinguistic analysis on speech communities that might include mermaids and talking teapots instead of ordinary humans. In our ideal world, great swaths of linguists and other social scientists would take up the baton and do this type of analysis more broadly on anything from movies that have won the Oscar for best picture, to bodice-ripper romance novels, to popular YouTube or TikTok videos.

### *Qualitative or Quantitative? Peanut Butter and Jelly*

A linguistic approach to media analysis also provides a unique scope and scale of research. Most previous studies of Disney have used qualitative methods or quantitative methods (leaning towards the former) but not both. The qualitative analyses we have seen (and cited throughout this book) bring valuable insights, but are often limited in scope. Many researchers focus tightly on individual movies or scenes, or choose different movies to answer each question. We get a snapshot of something very interesting, interpreted through a particular disciplinary lens.

While these narrower viewpoints can provide an excellent level of detail, we also wanted to look for patterns beyond individual movies or Princesses, the types of patterns that can go undetected because they only matter when you zoom out and look at the whole picture (in our case, 80 years of filmmaking). Male characters talk more than female characters in a movie? Not a problem. But male characters talk more than female characters in *all* the movies? That would be something to think about. Doing large-scale quantitative work can allow us to take a broader view (including chronologically) with the questions we ask about a set of films. Then, when we turn to qualitative analysis, we will have a general context from which to ask more targeted questions.

On the other hand, the quantitative studies that have been done on children's films span a broad range of movies and provide an interesting backdrop for tracking some general patterns in gender roles, particularly over time. Content analyses, e.g. England et al. (2011) or Hine et al. (2018), have documented a decrease in the proportion of some gendered behaviors in the most recent Princess films, for example. Again, they don't look at language at all. But beyond that, these purely quantitative methods don't provide a way to see how these behaviors actually function in context. In other words, they are missing the piece that is so critical in sociolinguistics: How are these behaviors (linguistic or otherwise) being used in the construction of an identity, specifically, for our interests here, a gendered identity?

We are prepared to address this question by combining quantitative and qualitative methodologies. This approach will allow our research to work at a scale that's at once both very wide (covering 31 movies) and very granular (on the level of individual words), which can contextualize previous findings in new and interesting ways. We use the quantitative approach to look at the bigger picture: trends that hold over the entire set of films, or patterns that we see changing over time. How do the features we are analyzing work together to create an ideology about masculinity or femininity overall? We use a qualitative approach to focus in and see how these features are being used in a particular context, by a particular character, to create a particular type of gendered linguistic performance.

Our goal is for this book to provide a model for those who want to apply linguistic methodology to media analysis, particularly with the aim of (1) looking at relatively large groups of films or other media, while (2) combining quantitative and qualitative methods in fruitful ways, and (3) tracking the dissemination of hegemonic ideologies about gender, race, or other social categories.

## Language and Gender

### Constructing Gender through Language

Since gender is our focus here, and not everyone reading this book will have a background in language and gender, we want to provide a quick overview of some of the key concepts that form the basis of sociolinguistic theory in this subdiscipline. Historically, some of the models that have been proposed to account for gender-linked differences in language have included the following claims:

- Men's language is the norm and women's language is an inferior or deviant version of it (*deficit model*).
- Men and women come from different subcultures and have differing/ opposed but equally valid ways of speaking, almost like two separate languages (*two cultures model*).

- Men and women speak differently as a fairly direct result of social imbalances which grant more social power to men than to women (*social dominance model*).

All of these theories have been criticized as having serious flaws. All of them, for example, presume a binary division between men and women, and ignore or downplay various types of intersectionality. We will return to the two cultures model in a moment, though, because it is quite relevant to how the discourse of gender is presented in Disney and Pixar.

Contemporary scholars of language and gender, in contrast, take the theoretical perspective that gender, like all social categories, is socially constructed. It is not something we are born with but something we learn to do, to perform. Gender interacts with other social categories like age, social class, ethnicity, etc., and is dynamic and mutable over our lifetimes or even across daily contexts and interactions. It exists on a spectrum (at least) or on some plane much more complex than a binary. In this model, language is one of the tools that people use to construct, play with, and challenge social ideas about gender.

The social construction model avoids conclusions like "men talk this way and women talk that way" (which were associated with the older models mentioned earlier). Instead, the focus is on identity, style, and how speakers choose to position themselves socially. This model recognizes the agency that each individual has in making linguistic choices about how to present themselves, as well as the external social forces and ideologies that affect those choices. This approach means that even a study of a single speaker can be enlightening in terms of how their language choices shift as they perform their identity in different contexts (see e.g. Podesva 2007). Social construction also requires researchers to ask more nuanced questions, such as: *How does this individual highlight certain aspects of gender identity in different contexts by using gender-linked language styles?* It's certainly more cumbersome and less pithy than *How do men and women talk differently?* But gender isn't pithy.

### Construction from the Outside: Linguistic Expectations and Policing

Many modern language and gender researchers focus on how gender is constructed from the *inside*, that is, the gendered linguistic performances that an individual creates in the course of a day or in the course of a lifetime. However, a central principle of this kind of scholarship is that our identity performances draw on larger social ideologies, and that speakers don't just create from scratch what it means to be a man or a woman. Speakers use language to position themselves in *relation to dominant ideologies of gender*, meaning that their construction of gender (linguistic and otherwise) must necessarily be accountable to "available gender identities" (Kiesling 2005).

The fact of the matter is that very few linguistic features actually directly and straightforwardly speak to (or *index*) masculinity or femininity in English, the language we are concerned with here. There are pronouns like "he" or "she," or gendered words like "stewardess." But in most other cases, the process of understanding linguistic performance is more indirect, as Bucholtz (2004) explains:

At the level of direct indexicality, linguistic forms most immediately index interactional stances – that is, subjective orientations to ongoing talk, including affective, evaluative, and epistemic stances (cf. Du Bois 2007). At the level of indirect indexicality, these same linguistic forms become associated with particular social types believed to take such stances. It is at the indirect indexical level that ideology comes most centrally into play, for it is here that stances acquire more enduring semiotic associations. Over time, the mapping between linguistic form and social meaning comes to be ideologically perceived as direct, and the connections to interactional stance may undergo erasure or be backgrounded (cf. Irvine and Gal 2000). For example, a mitigated interactional stance may be ideologically associated with women, and hence linguistic forms used to take such stances may come to be seen as inherently "feminine." (Bucholtz 2004: 148)

We have shared assumptions about what masculine and feminine behaviors look like (or perhaps more correctly, *should* look like) and we use those assumptions to be "read" in the way that best benefits us as speakers.

The natural next question is what those assumptions actually *are*, how they're created, and how they're maintained and enforced societally. These are aspects of the construction of gender from the *outside*: the ideologies that exist in a particular society, and the ways that society attempts to impose them on individuals. Because it's here that the rubber really meets the road, gender-difference-wise. We want to state in big, bold letters here one of the most important truths we can offer:

> The biggest differences in language related to gender are not in things that men and women **do** differently. They are in how the language used by male-presenting vs. female-presenting individuals is **evaluated** differently.

For example, a paragraph of text will be interpreted differently based on whether people are told the author was a man or a woman. Eckert and McConnell-Ginet (1992) discuss in detail the way that gender is done "for" children at first, until they can take over the performance themselves. In doing so they give several examples of experiments showing that boys and girls are evaluated differently including this one:

From infancy male and female children are interpreted differently, and interacted with differently . . . Condry and Condry (1976) found that adults watching a film of a crying infant were more likely to hear the cry as angry if they believed the infant was a boy, and as plaintive or fearful if they believed the infant was a girl. (1992: 17)

Our speech is being evaluated through the lens of gender before it is even speech! And this process continues on through adulthood, leading to girls and boys being evaluated differently for similar speech patterns in the classroom (e.g. Kelly 1988; Swann 2003) and men and women later being evaluated differently for similar behaviors in professional settings (e.g. Kendall 2008; Mullany 2008; Sung 2012), online forums (e.g. Herring 2003), and elsewhere. Ultimately, these expectations do affect behavior, which may account for some of the gender differences we see in the research. If you are taught by society as a little boy that you shouldn't use words like *lovely* or *cute*, because those are "girl words," then that will be likely to affect your language behavior.

In terms of what we see in the public discourse, a great deal of the language policing is aimed at women. An overarching theme is that women should be "polite," coupled with a counternarrative saying that women should be more assertive (in essence, less polite) to get what they want. This discourse creates a double bind, of course, especially as women inhabit traditionally masculine spaces with greater frequency (e.g. academia, c-suite executive jobs, etc.). Women now encounter the additional pressure to orient towards masculine norms of behavior, such as assertiveness and hierarchical dominance, while simultaneously maintaining a feminine (read: polite) demeanor. We predict, then, that the linguistic expectations related to femininity in our films may be highlighted more directly than those around masculinity, especially for the Disney Princess films. At the same time, we've made a conscious effort to avoid treating the analysis of language and gender as if it meant the analysis of language and women (or language and femininity) and to spotlight the often "unmarked" construction of masculinity. Both types of linguistic ideologies will be on our radar throughout the book.

## Mass Media and Cultural Discourses of Gender

A concept that will be critical to situating our work within the social constructionist framework is the idea of cultural discourses, a term that initially appeared in Foucault 1972, but that has been applied to the realm of language and gender research by Scott Kiesling. In his study of fraternity brothers, Kiesling defines cultural discourses as "widely shared 'background' assumptions, or 'truths,' about how the world works. Cultural discourses of masculinity thus refer to the ways that men are assumed by the majority of society to act, talk, and feel" (Kiesling 2005: 696).

One important concept that Kiesling brings up in his work is the *discourse of gender difference*, which he defines as "a discourse that sees men and women as naturally and categorically different in biology and behavior" (Kiesling 2005: 696). Gender difference is a linchpin of heteronormative gender ideology. Beneath every language stereotype of masculinity and femininity usually lurks the foundational idea that gender is a binary, immutable concept with boundaries between the two camps that cannot (and should not) be crossed. It was also, as we saw earlier, reified in the early models that were proposed to explain language and gender.

While a modern sociolinguistic perspective rejects this simple analysis, it's likely that the discourse of gender difference *does* reflect in some speech patterns – just not in the straightforward way that the two cultures model, for example, would suggest. Instead, we expect that if a community begins with widely shared assumptions that men and women *are* inherently different, and then judges the behaviors of real people against those assumptions, it will result in some actual differences in behavior to match stereotypes. Indeed, this is exactly what Kiesling saw in his work: that frat boys responded to the discourse of gender difference by orienting towards masculine-linked linguistic behaviors and carefully avoiding anything that could be coded as "girly."

Importantly, Kiesling notes in his study that cultural discourses are "reflected in, and created by ... performances, and in widely shared cultural performances such as *literature and film*" (2005: 696, italics ours). He supports this claim through observations of cultural reference points for homosocial desire in the fraternity, including films like *Stand By Me*, *Star Trek*, and *The Lord of the Rings*. He even references Disney's *The Lion King* in a footnote. His research does not extend into exploring the specific discourses of gender reproduced in such films, though, and other linguists have not addressed this particular aspect of the model, which is partly what motivated our work.

Animated films are of particular interest to us in this regard because, as discussed above, their fantastical nature frees them from the expectation of being representative of actual behavior. Instead, effective writing in this case seems to rely more on the effective representation (and therefore reproduction) of cultural *ideas* about language and gender. In exploring scripted film data, we can learn about the discourses and myths that are prevalent in society based on the speech behaviors of animated characters. We can explore how female and male characters' speech is written to get a sense of how the writers of our scripts *think* that men and women speak. We can unpack how the juxtaposition of these ideologically based speech styles bolsters an underlying discourse of gender difference, creating male and female cartoon characters as groups that are fundamentally and categorically different.

In addition, we can explore how language is tied to specific roles in each film, to see if there's any "moralizing" of these gendered discourses of language. Who speaks in certain ways, and who doesn't? How do good or bad people speak? Which language behaviors are tied to which identities? We can also rely on moments of language policing in the scripts to further reinforce our observations. When do characters comment on another character's language?

The fact that Disney and Pixar script writers are so often men is interesting, of course, in terms of the fact that they are putting words into the mouths of female characters without themselves being female. Still, our understanding of hegemonic gender discourses predicts that writers of any gender will draw on many of the same dominant ideologies. The drag queens in Barrett (1999) or Mann (2011) embrace the same language features in their construction of femininity that the nerd girls in Bucholtz (1999) avoid. These discourses about femininity or masculinity are the ones we compare ourselves against, the expectations we carry around, whether we ultimately choose to embrace or reject them in our performance.

### Intersections with Ethnicity

We want to take a moment on the topic of intersectionality here, before we move on. The cultural discourses of gender that are dominant tend (not surprisingly) to center white masculinity and femininity, and frame gender for people of color in a secondary and "othering" way. Linguists and other social scientists who study gender must take this dynamic into account (and be willing to decenter whiteness) if they are to have any hope of understanding how identity is constructed. Morgan (1999), in her critique of postmodern gender theorizing, notes:

African-American women's identity exists in relation to White women's identity, perhaps more so than to (Black) male identity. Black women are presented as problematic but with respect to both feminist issues and patriarchic ideals of White womanhood. (28)

If we think about representations of masculinity and femininity in the media specifically, we find that the same entrenched racial hierarchies dominate there as well. Discourses and models of how to be "a woman" or "a man" in the media are likely to be, in reality, models of how to be "a white woman/man," with other alternatives offered only rarely and in more limited distribution.

As we will return to at various points, these discourses are an essential part of how Disney "does" gender. In most cases, our observations about masculinity and femininity will correspond to ideologies that are inextricably intertwined with whiteness. We expect this to be true even where Disney or Pixar films attempt to show characters of color, although such instances may also reveal broader interesting patterns. As Byerly and Ross (2006) explain, in their discussion of women of color in the media:

the African Caribbean or exoticized female "other" provides a benchmark against which white femininity under patriarchy can be better understood and the normative nature of whiteness itself, as an ethnic category rendered visible and problematized. (30)

The Princess line in particular has embarked on a quest to represent main characters of color, with … mixed success. So looking at how Disney treats characters that they frame as people of color, particularly female characters, can help us understand how the ideologies of masculinity and femininity they are presenting are tied in with and perpetuate whiteness.

There is a further complication here in that it is not clear how many Disney or Pixar characters actually represent people of color, linguistically. Whatever shade the animators may have used to color them in, the voice actors are often white (as we saw for the *Aladdin* cast) and the scriptwriters and creative teams in general almost certainly are. As we discuss in Chapter 2, more recent productions have at least attempted to do better background research with respect to specific cultures (such as the Pacific Islander culture represented in *Moana*) and to be better at hiring people of color to voice the roles. Still, it's unclear whether that "research" extends to the elements of language use specifically, and it is also unclear how much say the actors of color get in how their characters talk (a question which is a bit out of scope for us).

Unfortunately, we don't have room here to give ethnicity the space and attention that it truly deserves and still cover the critical aspects of gender to which we are committed.[5] So where ethnicity emerges as particularly salient in the analysis of a variable or a particular character, we have included some discussion of how that affects the analysis. We have also tried to suggest promising areas for future research on ethnicity in these films. But we acknowledge that our coverage of this aspect of intersectionality will necessarily be incomplete.

### The Structure of This Book

*The Plan: Methods in Broad Brushstrokes*

So here we are, bringing our linguistic toolkit to bear on two of the behemoths of children's film, Disney and Pixar. The process itself is simple on the surface, but as we work through each variable, we will try to describe the challenges we uncovered and the quandaries we had to work through to make our analysis rigorous and true to our sociolinguistic framework.

Here is our overarching question:

> How do Disney and Pixar films represent the speech used by (and about) male and female characters, and how do the filmmakers' choices in this regard support or challenge particular ideologies about language and gender?

---

[5] In addition, due to our own positionality as white women, we are not the ideal researchers to take on this task. We are hopeful that e.g. Bloomquist's forthcoming work will address this gap.

As noted earlier, our study combines quantitative and qualitative methodologies in order to get the fullest possible picture of gendered language in Disney and Pixar. After measuring representation and speech amounts in general as a baseline, we turn to a series of specific speech acts, which we have selected based on their having been associated with gender-linked patterns of use in the linguistic literature. We collect each instance of these speech acts from across our datasets, and then determine if there are meaningful gender-based differences in use. In addition to the comparisons of frequency by gender, we also explore the form and function of the speech acts.

In order to do so, we made the conscious choice to code gender in our dataset as a binary element. Gender identity in real life is certainly not a binary; however Disney and Pixar clearly intend the vast majority of their characters to be read as one of the two binary genders. Throughout the book, we refer to our coding throughout the book in terms of "male characters" and "female characters." We acknowledge that "male" and "female" are not ideal adjectives given they tend to be used to describe sex rather than gender. But in the interest of using consistent terminology we opted for this language with the caveat that we are talking about the apparent gender of characters portrayed.

The specific details of each speech act we study will vary widely because they are based in part on previous research on real-life speech communities.[6] For example, much has been said in previous literature about the topic of compliments and how they vary by gender; we want to follow that thread and ask the same questions. But in the case of directives, it's the syntax of the sentence that has been shown to vary by gender, so that's what we analyze. In each case, we rely on the patterns of gender differences that previous scholars have already suggested, to see if we can find reflections of these patterns in the films.

Our quantitative question, though, is not how accurate these films are in portraying the behaviors of real-life speakers, although we admit to being frankly curious about whether the scripts will have any similarities with these studies or go off in their own direction. What we really want to know is how these speech acts are being used to give the viewer different ideas about what is expected of them, especially in relation to gender. Where studies of different communities find gendered speech patterns, we take these as *possibly* indicating something about the behaviors of male- or female-identifying speakers, but *definitely* indicating something about the ideologies associated with these speakers: Who has the right to tell others what to do, and how? When is it

---

[6] A caveat about studies of language and gender, though. Methods and sample sizes differ wildly, and different studies vary in the amount of attention they give to intersectionality and other factors that may be playing a role in language behavior. Older studies also often ignore the existence of genders outside the binary and cisnormative paradigm, rendering their findings necessarily incomplete.

permissible to insult someone else? What do compliments tell us about what society interprets as valuable?

In each chapter, we build off our quantitative results with in-depth qualitative analysis. In this part of the analysis, we focus on the broader context of the utterance, including the conversational context, paralinguistic features of speech, and reactions of characters besides the speaker. We also try to take the context of each utterance seriously, considering character appearance and animation, as well as at the plot, framing, cinematography and so forth. Just as the characters on screen are "communicating" to one another and to us, production teams also communicate to the audience in the language of film, encouraging us to interpret lines as comic, tragic, heroic, or pathetic. These factors end up being just as important as the speech act itself in understanding the ideology being represented on screen.

Now we turn to the most traditional piece of any introduction: the chapter summaries. So if you opened up the book and skimmed the first part looking for these, here you go:

- *Chapter 1*: This one.
- *Chapter 2*: *Gender, Disney, and Pixar in Historical Context.* This chapter will provide a historical account of the two animation studios (now merged into one) and their relationships to popular gender politics. We'll focus in particular on the dialogue about feminism in the media and how it relates to children's media, particularly the Princess movies.
- *Chapter 3*: *Representation, Speech Amounts, and Talkativeness.* We present an overview of the presence of male and female characters and speech, in each film and across the entire set of films, and discuss issues of representation, conversational dominance, and talkativeness. We look at (a) the distribution of male and female characters in these films and (b) which group talks more (if there is a difference).[7] We also explore the kinds of discourse we see in these films *about* quantity of speech and its relationship to gender. This chapter also serves as a baseline for the quantitative analysis of specific speech acts.
- *Chapter 4*: *Compliments.* Here we begin the sociolinguistic variation part of our project, that is, the quantitative analysis of specific speech acts (with additional nuance added through qualitative analysis). In this chapter we look at who gives and receives compliments, comparing against the stereotype that complimenting is associated with femininity. We also analyze how compliment topic correlates with gender, and qualitatively explore how compliment topic is related to social evaluations of the "ideal" qualities associated with being a woman or a man.
- *Chapter 5*: *Directives.* We present a quantitative analysis of directives and the variation in their linguistic forms as related to gender and power. We focus on who gives and receives directives generally, and more specifically

---

[7] ... but spoiler alert: there is.

on the role of linguistic mitigation strategies and how they correlate with the gender of the speaker and addressee.

- *Chapter 6: Insults.* In this chapter we turn our attention to the performance of impoliteness, through the lens of insults and other mocking language. Impoliteness has been documented as a tool to help speakers perform masculinity and to promote homosocial bonding between men. On top of documenting who gives and receives insults, we zero in on the perceived intent of insulting, to explore whether the social role of insults varies according to gender in the world of Disney and Pixar.
- *Chapter 7: Apologies.* As a counterpart to our study of impoliteness and possible tears in the social fabric in Chapter 6, we now turn to a strategy for repairing those tears: apologies. There is a clear perception that women apologize more, or apologize unnecessarily, so we look at whether or not that is reflected in Disney and Pixar. If not, are there other ways in which apologies are linked to gender? We look in particular at ways of minimizing apologies, as well as the kinds of things different characters apologize for, to track possible gendered differences.
- *Chapter 8: Queerness.* Here we devote a considerable space (because we feel it is so crucial) to a discussion of queerness in Disney. Despite the overwhelming propagation of a heteronormative ideal in these films, queerness does exist, at a variety of levels. We look at some of the different ways that queerness is constructed, particularly exploring the question: Is there a linguistic style associated with queer characters and their performances? Then we discuss the effects of these portrayals, and the ways in which they construct queerness as deviant but also contain a subversive and potentially empowering counternarrative to the traditional story of the heterosexual prince and princess.
- *Chapter 9: Conclusion.* In our concluding chapter, we collect the various findings from throughout the book together into a few larger themes, and offer some final observations on the linguistic construction of gender ideology in Disney and Pixar. We also consider patterns of change over time: What have the studios begun to do differently, and can we say whether or not this represents a type of progress? We conclude with our personal hopes for the future of children's animated films, the types of changes we hope will take place, and the ways in which we would like to see these films push the boundaries of what currently exists.

### Limitations: What Is Outside the Scope

> There are a few provisos, a couple of quid pro quos …
>
> Genie, *Aladdin* 1992

We feel it is worth mentioning a few possibilities that people have repeatedly asked us about but that are not part of what we are hoping to accomplish with this book.

*We don't cover many aspects of representation other than gender that are also important.* This includes such factors as age (where are all the stories about the prince and princess at middle age or retirement?), social class, disability, or body type (oh, we came so close to including this but weren't able to quite get it in). Occasionally these factors will appear in the discussion, but always in a secondary role to gender.

*We won't pretend to be "neutral."* It's not our goal at the outset of this book to trash Disney as a company, or to judge the artistic or political merit of particular films. However, we also cannot (and don't want to) claim that our analysis is neutral or objective. First of all, we're pretty sure that's not possible: even more "objective" measures, like counting speech amounts or measuring syntax variation in directives, include subjective decisions. Even though we think these measures are providing an important numerical viewpoint on these movies, we still encourage you to read our methods closely and critically.

Additionally, we take the stance that all language is on some level political. How the mass media choose to represent linguistic reality has inherent political ramifications. We will refer consistently back to the political and historical context of the movies we study to understand how the language portrayed reflects the dominant gender ideologies at the time of each film's release. For this reason, we've taken the time to lay out a fairly detailed history of the gender politics of Disney and Pixar in Chapter 2.

We lastly are also women who live in this society that Disney has dominated for so many decades. The second author was actually of the "Disney generation," raised in the midst of the Disney Renaissance. Although we've tried to resist excessive editorializing, we recognize that to us (and likely to many readers) these movies are deeply personal texts. In that light, "neutrality" is simply out of the question.

*We will ruin your childhood.* Well, maybe that's dramatic. But it's likely that after reading this book, any fictional media you consume, from beach novels to the latest Star Wars film, will look different to you. You will be more aware of who is on the screen and who is not, for example. We want to explicitly acknowledge that these films are integral to many readers' histories, and as such, reading our findings may invoke a personal response, as well as an intellectual one. Some of the results and analysis in our book are indeed highly critical of Disney Animation Studios, and may "ruin" a good portion of the Disney or Pixar experience that you treasured as part of your childhood. So, heads up – last chance to get off of the ride before it enters the tunnel.

# 2 Gender, Disney, and Pixar in Historical Context

"Come on!" I continued, my voice rising. "It's 2006, not 1950. This is Berkeley, Calif. Does every little girl really have to be a princess?"

My daughter, who was reaching for a Cinderella sticker, looked back and forth between us. "Why are you so mad, Mama?" she asked. "What's wrong with princesses?"

Peggy Orenstein (2006)

## Introduction

We believe as sociolinguists that studying language without knowing its social context just doesn't work very well. Our field frowns upon imagining language in a vacuum, or spoken by some "ideal speaker." We want to know things like: Who said it? Who were they with? What parts of their identity were important at that moment? Only after we know those things do we have enough background to properly analyze any variation we see.

A movie is much the same way. While a film obviously doesn't use language socially in the exact same way that a person does, it still employs language as a social tool. Beyond the movie itself, the people who create and consume the work are also themselves historically and politically specific. As Queen (2015: 21) puts it:

We can consider the scripted media to be fundamentally interesting precisely because of the ways in which *they are of the culture of which they are a part*, even as they play a role in shaping that culture. The primary difference between the scripted media and other sources of information about sociocultural life is that what appears in the media derives from imagination and thus represents a highly edited version of social and cultural life. Thus, the scripted media offer a fairly contained, and edited, microcosm of the places from which their players come. (Queen 2015: 21, emphasis ours)

We agree that scripted media can provide a fascinating look into the culture in which they were created, which is in large part why we've done this project. But movies are so much a product of their historical context that to attempt to analyze their linguistic construction of gender without first situating the texts politically would produce a woefully incomplete analysis. And this feels especially true of Disney and Pixar movies. Because, oh, what a political life they have led! Disney and Pixar aren't just producing any old texts; their movies are some of the most marketed, most consumed, and most discussed pieces of media in our modern world. To examine these particular texts without properly considering when, how, and why they were made would be a disservice to the rich social lives these films have lived.

In this chapter, our primary aim is simply to orient readers to our dataset: we'll introduce the details of which movies we're analyzing, why we chose them, as well as the particular ways we've decided to divide our movies into subsets and why. We also want to situate these movies in the larger story of gender representation on screen in America, with a focus on the impact that feminism in particular has made on how audiences expect masculine and feminine characters to be portrayed. As we discuss each set of films, we'll give a brief overview of the larger political zeitgeist as it pertained to gender in the media at the time of their creation.

Although the movies we analyze in subsequent chapters are produced in equal parts by Disney and Pixar, the bulk of this chapter is going to be spent on the history of the Disney Princesses. We spend extra time on the topic because, in our view, Disney's Princesses are a distinctive bunch in the world of children's media. They're not just movies that have women in them; rather, at their core, they are *about femininity*. Each Princess movie is focused on creating a "role model" heroine – so focused, in fact, that it can feel like Disney's goal isn't to create a great story so much as it is to create a great woman whom they can later market to young girls. The Princesses' deliberate centering of gender representation and performance is unparalleled in any other children's media franchise, and as such bears extra discussion. In fact, this symbolic conflation of "princess" and "ideal" (or "ideally marketable") women is what inspired us (along with many other scholars, we're sure) to begin our analysis of children's media with this set of films in particular (while setting aside other Disney blockbusters such as *The Lion King* or *Wreck-It Ralph*). While the fascination with depicting an ideal femininity is consistently at the heart of Princess movies, what exactly "ideal femininity" means has shifted dramatically over the years due to the growing influence of feminism in popular culture. The historical scope here is pretty grand: Disney Animation has been producing princesses for 85 years at the time of publication, compared to Pixar's mere 27 years. We want to make sure to properly contextualize each era of Disney animation in feminist history, so we can better understand the ways Disney uses language to respond to audiences' demands at any given moment.

Pixar Animation doesn't necessarily have the same hyper-fixation on gender that Disney does, but that doesn't mean that there isn't political context (and political ramifications) to their choices surrounding gender representation.

We'll spend the latter part of this chapter discussing what sets Pixar Animation apart from Disney culturally, and how we expect those differences to emerge in our subsequent analyses.

## The Evolution of the Disney Princess

### *The Cult of the Princess*

A definition of terms before we go further: when we say we're analyzing Disney Princess movies, what we mean is that we're looking at every movie that Disney as a company counts as part of their "Disney Princess" brand.

We follow previous literature in splitting the Princess brand films up into three distinct "eras" of movies (Do Rozario 2004; England et al. 2011; Stover 2013; Towbin et al. 2004). The three eras are presented below.

- **The Classic Era (1937–1959)**
  *Snow White (1937)*
  *Cinderella (1950)*
  *Sleeping Beauty (1959)*
- **The Renaissance Era (1989–1997)**
  *The Little Mermaid (1989)*
  *Beauty and the Beast (1991)*
  *Aladdin (1992)*
  *Pocahontas (1995)*
  *Mulan (1997)*
- **The New Age Era (2009–2019)**
  *The Princess and the Frog (2009)*
  *Tangled (2010)*
  *Brave (2012)*
  *Frozen (2013)*
  *Moana (2016)*
  *Frozen II (2019)*

These movies are all touted together as "Princess movies," and often discussed as a single topic. But for all that, the products of the three eras really are quite different. This is certainly true stylistically: there's a huge difference between the crooning jazz songs and sentimental tone of the Classic Era movies and the bombastic musical spectacle of the Renaissance. This may seem like an intuitive fact for people familiar with these films (especially those who, like the second author, grew up in the Renaissance Era and, even as a child, had an alarming amount of Disney song lyrics memorized). These eras are also set apart from one another in their attitude towards gender politics, which we will discuss more in depth below.

But despite their differences these films all have a central thing in common: the concept of "Princess," Disneyfied. Of course, the Princess as a storytelling archetype was not invented by Walt Disney. Long before *Snow White*, it was already laden with significant ideological baggage about how to be a woman. In America, the princess figure was being used throughout the 1800s and early 1900s as a stand-in for the "ideal girl." Princesses in older stories were often explicit tools for modeling ideal feminine traits, such as domesticity, sweetness, kindness, and the like; Cinderella and Pocahontas were two particularly popular stories at the turn of the century, the former demonstrating patience, kindness, and resilience, and the latter modeling the renouncement of "barbarous" girlhood (Forman-Brunell & Eaton 2009). It was such an established trope that by the early twentieth century authors were already deconstructing and remixing the princess trope in popular literature like *A Little Princess* (Burnett 1905).

However, while Walt Disney didn't invent the princess, he did raise her to a new level of importance in American culture. When *Snow White and the Seven Dwarfs* debuted in 1937, it was not only Walt Disney's first full-length movie, but the first-ever animated film with a feature-length run time. Adjusted for inflation, it's still one of the top ten highest earning movies in cinema history; it also earned Disney an honorary Oscar for "a significant screen innovation which has charmed millions and pioneered a great new entertainment field."[1]

Disney's name remained closely tied with princesses for the rest of his career, and later creatives built on his foundation to create a full-blown fairy-tale empire. It was princesses who revitalized Disney animation when it was near bankruptcy, not once, but twice (with *The Little Mermaid* in 1989 and *The Princess and the Frog* in 2009). And then there's the merchandising: the Disney Princess product line makes $4 billion per year according to 2014 figures, an amount that's second only to Mickey Mouse himself (Backman 2014). As Elizabeth Bell put it, "With the Logo 'Walt Disney Pictures,' Disney wrote his name and ownership on the folk stories of women, creating indelible images of the feminine" (1995: 108).

### *The Classic Era: Walt's Girls*

The Classic Era of Disney is what often comes to mind first when thinking about the Disney Princess: the tiaras, the gowns, the sparkles, the singing to birds, and all the rest of it. While iconic, these films also have a reputation for being extremely problematic in their representation of gender roles, and to that end they've been heavily criticized by modern audiences and scholars alike.

---

[1] Fun fact: the Oscar statue he was awarded was custom-made to be one full-sized golden statue surrounded by seven miniature statuettes, which is pretty adorable.

It's important to note that at the time these movies came out, feminism hadn't yet had any reckoning with the world of mass media. In fact, moral panic over Hollywood's culture was pushing gender politics on screen in the opposite direction. All three films were made during the era of the Hays Code, a production code enforced in Hollywood 1934–1968. Its raison d'être was that "no picture shall be produced which will lower the moral standards of those who see it" (Motion Picture Association of America 1930). The "moral standards" in question were rather conservative, particularly in regard to gender; the effect was that female characters at the time were less empowered, less brave, less sexual, and more likely to be a tragic victim than in older movies made before the code's enforcement (Dicker 2016).

On top of these standards, mass media in the 1940s and 1950s often had an openly propagandistic agenda to depict women as domestic and servile. This trend was a response to World War II, during which women had joined the workforce during the war to make up for the lack of working men in the country. After soldiers returned, postwar media switched to extremely regressive models of femininity in an explicit effort to convince women to return to the home. As Andi Zeisler writes:

The media forces that had hurried women into the factories were now herding them back into the home to make room for men – for whom, it was understood, the workforce was their rightful place. Women were no longer wooed with images of themselves as competent welders or military nurses; instead the postwar era of advertising ushered in a new set of representations of women as either dutiful wives and mothers or childlike sex kittens. (Zeisler 2008: 28)

The consistent depiction of women in this time period was, in sum, a product of conservative backlash against women. No thought was given to how to depict women as empowered; if anything, the opposite was true.

Even in this already repressive environment, Disney fostered a reputation as a conservative, "upstanding moral organization" (Griffin 2000). As early as the 1930s, Hollywood had nicknamed the studio as "Mickey's Monastery" thanks to their sentimental, 'wholesome' portrayal of romance and sexuality (Griffin 2000). It perhaps goes without saying that at this point in history, Disney's team of writers and animators were all men; women were only employed for the grunt work of inking and coloring animation. The princesses that resulted from these teams were the very picture of femininity as defined by the time period. One review called Snow White "the classical ingenue" (Nugent 1938). Cinderella was similarly praised for her femininity; one review delighted in the fact she had "a voluptuous face and form – not to mention an eager disposition" (Crowther 1950). Historical interviews reveal the lengths to which the animation and story teams worked to make Snow White and her cohort convincingly and traditionally feminine, "not a neuter to which a few crude symbols of femininity had been attached, as with Minnie Mouse's skirt and eyelashes, but a character that was female at her core" (Barrier 2003: 194).

It's clear in hindsight that the princesses themselves have remarkable similarities of character. In Disney's earnest and uncritical attempts to make a woman "female at her core," his team ended up making three characters who embody an extremely conservative version of hegemonic white femininity. While these traits aren't inherently bad (there is certainly value in resilience, flexibility, beauty, domestic know-how, and other feminized traits modeled by the Classic Era princesses), the formulaic portrayal of these traits sends a rigid message of acceptable femininity to viewers. Traditional or sentimental ideologies also manifested in much of what we consider key elements of the Disney Princess formula today: the innocent woman pitted against an older female villain, the twirling reveal of a beautiful gown, the sentimental love songs, the soft voice and affinity for animals, and so forth. Many of these elements repeated almost formulaically in these three movies, and in doing so, entrenched the aesthetic we associate with Princesses today.[2]

Much ink has been spilled about these older Princesses and their representation of femininity on screen. Their iconic nature and conservative ideals have made them low-hanging fruit for mainstream feminist media, especially in the 1990s and 2000s (a topic covered at length in subsequent sections). The primary criticism has been the passivity and submissiveness apparent in the behavior of the three Classic Era princesses. As author Peggy Orenstein says to her princess-obsessed daughter in her influential essay *What's wrong with Cinderella*, "It's just, honey, Cinderella doesn't really do anything" (Orenstein 2006). Other pop culture critics have noted that the early princesses are valued for their beauty over other character traits and that they're overly reliant on their male love interests, among a laundry list of other criticisms.

Scholars, too, have pointed out regressive or conservative values at play in these early films. Bell (1995) describes this trio as "ingenues" and notes that physically, they look and move like young classical dancers, which codes them as beautiful, feminine, and "politically innocent." Behaviorally, England et al. (2011) showed that princesses in these early years were more likely than other princesses to only engage in stereotypically feminine actions and emotions (such as being affectionate, fearful, nurturing, tentative, and submissive). Wiersma (2000) also observes that early Disney movies (princesses among them) show women disproportionately attending to domestic and maternal tasks, like cleaning and cooking. In sum, the Classic Era princesses feel

---

[2] Even critics at the time picked up on the sameness of the first three Princess movies. When *Sleeping Beauty* was released in 1959, one New York Times reviewer said that it was "more than a little reminiscent of his first and most memorable features, *Snow White*. Evidently, Mr. Disney is sentimental in his remembrance of things past" (Crowther 1959).

extremely "of their time": a product of a company (and a creative team) committed to a normative, unquestioned presentation of traditional gender roles.

### Renaissance: Girl Power and Protest Proofing

Fast-Forward 30 Years. *The Little Mermaid*, Disney's fourth Princess film, was released in 1989 and marked the beginning of a series of blockbusters that are now known as the Disney Renaissance. In the 30 years between Aurora and Ariel, the landscape of gender politics in the media shifted drastically, thanks in large part to the second-wave feminist movement. In the 1970s feminists began to sound alarms about the way women were portrayed in TV and movies, and mass media evolved in the public consciousness into a political battleground for gender representation. By the time the 1990s rolled around, making movies and advertisements that at least acknowledged feminist ideas, even shallowly, helped sell things to the increasingly large population of women who identified with feminist views (Zeisler 2008).

The pressure to make feminist role models further increased in the 1990s. In the early part of the decade, a sudden swell of concern emerged in the national consciousness for the psychological well-being of young girls growing up in a patriarchal society (Zaslow 2009). The issue was first popularized in Mary Pipher's best-seller *Reviving Ophelia* (1994). In it, Pipher summarized the growing body of research on the poor mental state of girls in America: "In early adolescence, studies show that girls' IQ scores drop and their math and science scores plummet. They lose their resilience and optimism and become less curious and inclined to take risks. They lose their assertive, energetic and 'tomboyish' personalities and become more deferential, self-critical and depressed" (Pipher 1994: 2).

The news of girlhood-in-crisis spawned a years-long wave of articles and self-help books about how to raise more confident girls.[3] Relevantly for us, many of these titles pointed a finger at mass media for keeping antiquated versions of femininity in circulation, thus damaging the modern girls' self-image.[4] In response, a trend developed in the mass media of trying to

---

[3] Zaslow (2009) has compiled an extensive list of these titles. To give you a brief sense, they include: *Growing a Girl: Seven Strategies for Raising a Strong Spirited Daughter* (1996), *Any Girl Can Rule the World* (1998), *Deal with It! A Whole New Approach to Your Body, Brain, and Life as a gURL* (1999), *200 Ways to Raise a Girl's Self Esteem: An Indispensable Guide for Parents, Teachers, and Other Concerned Caregivers* (1999), and literally dozens more.

[4] In fact, it was at this time that the first major critical works about Disney first began appearing: books such as *From Mouse to Mermaid* (Bell et al. 1995) and *The Mouse that Roared* (Giroux 1999) were the first of a flood of Disney criticism that continues to ... well ... right now, in this chapter.

model what the public imagined to be "empowered girlhood." By the late 1990s, the slogan "Girl Power!" had become somewhat of a rallying cry for mainstream feminism, propelled by the countercultural Riot Grrrl movement and later by popular celebrities like the Spice Girls. TV shows featuring badass, take-no-shit women had a heyday in this era: shows like *Buffy the Vampire Slayer* (1997–2003), *Xena, Warrior Princess* (1995–2001), or kid's cartoons like *The Powerpuff Girls* (1998–2005) and *Sailor Moon* (1992–1997) were common fare.

Disney had certainly caught on to the cultural hunger for more feminist figures by the time they began to produce *The Little Mermaid*. There's a stark difference between the way Walt Disney and his team talked about their heroines – "wholesome," "feminine to the core," the "ideal American girl" – and the way the creative teams in the 1990s talked about their creations. The discourse of the latter belied a concerted effort to make the princesses as "empowered" and "real" as possible. Ariel's supervising animator, for example, said of Ariel that "she's not a sugar-coated princess. Whenever we had a choice, we wanted real rather than what is pretty" (Jarvey 1989). Linda Woolverton, who wrote *Beauty and the Beast*, said in an interview: "Belle is a feminist. I'm not critical of Snow White, Cinderella … they reflected the values of their time. But it wasn't in me to write a throwback. I wanted a woman of the 90s, someone who wanted to do something other than wait for her prince to come" (Dutka 1992).

Importantly, Linda Woolverton was also the first woman to have a major role in the creation of a Disney Princess movie. In that same interview, she hints at the fact that Disney hired her specifically to help the political image of the film. She says: "There was no mandate from on-high to counteract the finger-pointing … but I think the studio felt confident that, as a woman, I wouldn't write a sexist character" (Dutka 1992).

The finger-pointing here refers to some negative feedback Disney received after releasing *The Little Mermaid*. Although many praised it as a political triumph compared to the Classic Era, feminist critics were quick to point out its shortcomings as well as the all-male creative team. The *LA Times* reported after *Mermaid*'s release:

At a USC screening of "The Little Mermaid" the other night, a young woman asked the co-authors and co-directors, in a tone that could be characterized as civilly indignant, whether a woman had been consulted in the creation of the script. Was what she called the "Some-Day-My-Prince-Will-Come" Syndrome (in which the answer to any mermaid's prayer is simply to find a good man) their work solely or a coeducational enterprise? (Champlin 1989)

And indeed, it does seem like Woolverton contributed some painstaking efforts towards creating a more progressive figure. She describes how she had written a draft of the script that had Belle pushing pins onto a map of places she wanted to visit, which was unexpectedly changed by male co-writers into Belle baking a cake. The team eventually arrived at the book-reading we actually see on screen, which seemed to the studio to strike the right balance of femininity and . . . empoweredness. Later Renaissance movies also had female co-writers and story contributors,[5] which we take to be some kind of progress for Disney, even if it's only so they could sell the story of being "better" to their audiences. This only went so far, though, since Linda Woolverton was the one solo female writer in this Era, and Disney employed no female directors despite their dedication to making "empowered" female characters.

Interestingly, one of the defining characteristics of the Renaissance prin-cesses is how much the texts themselves call attention to their new, shiny, feminist talking points. Their consistent move is to do so by placing the princess in a patriarchal structure that is usually cartoonishly oppressive in some way, and having them struggle against it to gain freedom. Interestingly, the exaggerated patriarchies of the 1990s films are in themselves a callback to the sentimental sexism of the Classic Era, which made Disney famous in the first place. Stover (2013) explains:

Disney utilizes [postfeminist] ideology to buoy the narrative conflict, creating a world where heroines are trapped and breakout signifies a happily-ever-after. Jasmine expli-citly states this feeling, and [the other Renaissance princesses] all express a desire to escape from their surroundings. In tune with post-feminism strategies, Disney often appropriated the rhetoric of feminism with quips like when Jasmine states that "I am not a prize to be won," or when Belle sings "I want so much more than they've got planned." This sense of powerful spirit coupled with a longing for change positions these new Disney princesses as a representation of the prefeminist woman, constrained by society through marriage pressure, royal status, or even having fins instead of legs. The situations of these princesses are, in effect, a criticism of the very situations with which Disney began its princess empire. (Stover 2013: 4)

Stover points out that the plots of the Renaissance princess movies are, in some ways, direct criticisms of the ideologies that influenced the first three films, further underlining Disney's desire to sell their new brand as suitably progres-sive for the audiences of the 1990s.

The resulting set of films does, in some ways, seem to succeed at rejecting the ideologies of their predecessors. As Stover comments, "If Snow White, Sleeping Beauty, and Cinderella exemplified the traditional Disney female as docile, beautiful objects waiting for their prince to come, then Belle, Jasmine, Pocahontas, Meg, Mulan, and Tiana are exactly the opposite: focused,

---

[5] Susannah Grant co-wrote *Pocahontas*; Rita Hsiao and Eugenia Bostwick-Singer helped write *Mulan*.

ambitious, and in the case of Pocahontas and Mulan, literally heroic as they perform the traditional prince role and save the day" (2013: 3). Content analysis by England et al. (2011) shows that the proportion of stereotypically feminine behaviors demonstrated by Renaissance princesses is much lower than the ones from the Classic Era, and the proportion of masculine-coded behaviors – like being assertive, athletic, brave, or independent – is much higher.

Audiences at the time of the films' releases also seemed to respond positively to this perceived shift away from the Classic Era's gender ideology. For example, Roger Ebert's review of *The Little Mermaid* reads: "Ariel is a fully realized female character who thinks and acts independently, even rebelliously, instead of hanging around passively while the fates decide her destiny" (Ebert 1989). Linda Larkin, the voice of Jasmine, commented on her audiences' reaction at one point as well: "When I see the way little girls respond to Jasmine, I know what's exciting about her to them. She's not a victim. She's not sheltered. She's got spirit and she has power. And I think it's really great to be the voice to this character that is strong" (Boothe 1989).

However, these films are far from perfect feminist triumphs. Again, the modern viewer with 20–30 years of perspective on these movies can probably easily see plenty of issues. The princesses, for example, may exclaim that they are worth more than their appearance, but at the same time are drawn as both more mature and more sexually alluring than their earlier counterparts.[6] There are also troubled relationship politics that worry scholars and audiences alike, for example that Ariel gives up her life and livelihood for the sake of a man (Stover 2013), or that Belle may or may not have Stockholm Syndrome (Grady 2017).

Many of these concerns are particularly evident in the Renaissance movies that take place in non-Western cultures. Scholars have pointed out that setting woman-versus-patriarchy plots in historical, non-white spaces allows a white, Western audience to feel smug about a feminist-sounding message without having to engage in their own participation in oppressive structures, at the expense of a fair portrayal of non-Western histories (e.g. Yin 2011). In addition, the portrayal of the female characters in these films as tough and physically skilled can reinforce stereotypes that other and exoticize women of color, as can the tendency to make them sexually alluring that we noted above.

---

[6] *A Diamond in the Rough: The Making of Aladdin* describes how Aladdin actually had to be redesigned because they had accidentally made Jasmine so hot that her being with Aladdin was no longer believable. John Musker related the feedback his team got from motion picture head Jeffrey Katzenberg: "Jeffrey was like, 'Guys, you got Julia Roberts and Michael J. Fox. They don't fit together. You need Tom Cruise and Julia Roberts. They fit together. You need more Tom Cruise'" (Boothe 1992).

Géliga Vargas (1999) discusses the history of scripting roles for Latinas, for example, as both tough and hypersexualized. Even though we are dealing with children's movies here, we do find women of color being hypersexualized in Disney to the extent that such is possible. Jasmine (*Aladdin*), for example, was the first princess to combine physicality and overt sexuality. She pole vaults alongside Aladdin over the rooftops, but then uses feigned sexual advances to seduce and distract the villain, Jafar. With Pocahontas, these elements are taken to extremes: her physical actions when she meets John Smith include an unsettling animal-like crouching, as well as paddling a canoe and diving off a cliff; she does all of this while clad in the skimpiest outfit of all the princesses. So while these portrayals of characters intended to be women of color do break with the passivity of e.g. Snow White, they do so while reinforcing other harmful stereotypes.

On top of that, Disney played pretty fast and loose with the cultural portrayals themselves, despite the research they purport to have done.[7] *Pocahontas* was the most egregious example of this, as Disney aged up the heroine considerably and rewrote the history of Pocahontas to ignore the more violent and racist elements of the story (Tunzelmann 2008). *Mulan* and *Aladdin* both have their own demons, too, from *Aladdin*'s racist lyrics to *Mulan*'s use of oriental tropes to make ancient China seem more regressive than it actually was (King et al. 2010; Yin 2011). And on top of all of *that*, it's difficult to ignore the selective white-washing of the characters themselves. Lippi-Green (1997) shows the problematic tendency of Disney to cast heroines of color with actors who are white[8] and/or who speak in Mainstream US English, whereas villains and background characters are typecast with non-standard English varieties.

Beside these issues (or perhaps beneath them) lies a more fundamental problem in the Princess formula of the 1990s. The studio made changes that were visible on the surface, but has never dealt with the fact that the Princess archetype exists to idealize one single version of femininity. Essentially, the newer Princess films still show an ideal woman. It's just that the ideal woman is a sporty hottie now, instead of a demure ballerina. She says cool things! She can do physical exercise! She's basically a badass! Unfortunately, without much significant deviation from this model, the new Girl Power princess amounts to a "replacement for one set of stereotypes for another" rather than genuine progress (Ross 2010, cited in Stover 2013). Additionally, a good number of Classic Era behaviors and choices (like giving everything up for

---

[7] Granted, the research wasn't necessarily for the purpose of authenticity or respect, but to avoid negative publicity. One news article from 1995 called the research process on Pocahontas "protest-proofing" (Bruni 1995).

[8] Linda Larkin, quoted earlier about what a powerful experience it was to voice Jasmine, is a white woman from Los Angeles.

love at first sight) persisted. So did much of the aesthetic qualities of earlier movies: affinities with animals, beautiful ball gowns, unrealistic body types, and soaring love songs are all still present. All told, there's enough to keep the new Girl Power princess still recognizable (and marketable) as "Princess," despite some new empowered window dressing.

### The New Age: Postfeminist Princess

Finally, we come to the era of Princess movies that we are currently living in. The New Age of movies started in 2009 with *The Princess and the Frog*, and continues up to more or less the time of publication. In fact, one of the things we did to kick off the writing of this book was to sit down with a bottle of wine and watch the newly released *Frozen II*. (It was OK.)

The quiet period between the Renaissance and the New Age was much shorter than the 30-year span that separated *Sleeping Beauty* and *The Little Mermaid*. Nevertheless, the shifts in societal discourse were substantial, accelerated by the explosion of internet culture in the 2000s. Blogging and social media created an array of new spaces for feminist discussion that had previously been limited to physical meet-ups, zines, and the like. This culture lead to the rapid evolution of online feminist criticism, and its dissemination to a newly wide audience. It's also led to a new level of accountability (or rather, nervousness) for mass media creators, whose work is now subject to the social/political/entertainment engine that is social media.

Disney Princesses have also expanded their presence since the 1990s, due to the creation of the official Disney Princess brand in 1999, which gathered all the princesses of the Classic and Renaissance Eras together and slapped them on tiaras, bedsheets, backpacks, T-shirts, and every other object under the sun, all in trademark pinks, purples, and powder blues. In Disney's own words, the Disney Princess has expanded beyond a simple merchandise line to become a "powerful lifestyle brand that touches every aspect of girls' lives" (Foster et al. 2005). Peggy Orenstein (2006) writes that "princess culture" had become so pervasive in the mid-2000s that she couldn't seem to go anywhere with her toddler without running into princesses, up to and including her dentist asking her whether she'd like to "sit in my special princess throne so I can sparkle your teeth" (Orenstein 2006). Princesses have grown into a more powerful pop-cultural force than ever before, and so the pressure for them to be feminine role models has also become more urgent.

The interesting twist is that there's no longer a single, mainstream target of ideal feminism for Disney to hit. Third-wave feminism was also evolving during this time period, and has become part of the mass online conversations. We don't have time to go into the history of feminism, per se, but we'll highlight a couple of important evolutions.

First, third-wave activists have worked to decenter white feminism as the only form of feminism. There's a push for more intersectional understandings of femininity and for more room in mainstream discourse for discussions about how race, queerness, trans and nonbinary identities, class, disability, and other identities shape the experience of gender-based oppression. We can't speak to how successful this push has been, because as two white, cis, straight women, it's a little out of our lane. But we hope that newer Disney movies may respond to this by taking, for example, the portrayal of non-white cultures (especially their princesses) more seriously than when they wrote that *Aladdin* lyric about how Middle Eastern people will "cut off your ear if they don't like your face." Interestingly, *Moana* received both positive and negative reviews of its portrayals of Pacific Island culture, but the reviews of Moana herself, as a female lead, were very positive. Herman, in a review for the Smithsonian Magazine, for example, has a number of specific critiques about cultural concerns in *Moana*, but he takes the unambiguous position that "[t]he Moana character is strong and her voice (portrayed by Auliʻi Cravalho) is clear and powerful" (Herman 2016).

Some of the third wave also rejects the second-wave notion that "empowerment" means disavowing traditionally feminine traits. Feminists of the 2000s and 2010s have attempted to reclaim the trappings of traditional femininity and sexuality, such as makeup, formal feminine clothing, and high heels. This, however, isn't an unchallenged idea; contemporary feminist thinkers also question whether this is true empowerment, or whether it's just repackaged self-objectification for the male gaze. Modern advertisers also have a distinct interest in blurring these lines, since it allows them to capitalize on the third-wave embrace of femininity to push traditional and even regressive feminine behaviors back onto women under the guise of "celebrating" feminine stereotypes (Lazar 2009). Online culture has fostered an environment where feminist communities proliferate and form their own subcommunities online, producing discourses of feminism that have become both more accessible and more variant than ever before. When it comes to Disney, the political expectations audiences have of new releases become more numerous, more complicated, and *louder*.

The immediacy and intensity of audience response can be seen in the discourse surrounding *The Princess and the Frog* (2009). While earlier Princess films had some controversy during marketing and release, the response to *Frog* cycled through several full-blown scandals before the movie was even released. Activists pushed back on many new details that were leaked about the film, which were often met with some course correction from the studio, even as they were finishing the film. For example, Princess Tiana's name was originally going to be Maddy, but was changed due to online criticism that her name (and her planned role in the film) would be too close to the racist and sexist "mammy" archetype (Breaux 2010). Disney altered course in response to this feedback, demonstrating their interest in being respectful enough to at least be "protest-proof."[9] This instance also shows a new variety of viewpoints in mainstream feminist discourse.

In response to this more fractured atmosphere, the New Age princesses are a less cohesive bunch than the princesses of the two previous eras. To their credit, they seem to have increased the diversity of gender role representation far beyond the Renaissance princesses. Disney is beginning to play with plot structure more, for example. Instead of all being romances, some movies skip the romances in favor of hero's journey adventure stories (*Moana*) or heart-warming mother–daughter dramas (*Brave*). *Frozen* stands out particularly in this way by not only subverting plot expectations from earlier movies, but actively mocking them (see the hero Kristoff asking Anna incredulously, "You were going to marry a man you just met *that day*?," something that Cinderella, Aurora, and Snow White all in fact did.) More quantitative analyses of Disney also seem to show some kind of progress: Hine et al. 2018 found that the princesses since 2009 showed less traditionally feminine traits than all older princesses, and "suggest that Disney is indeed presenting more diverse ... balanced characters to viewers" (Hine et al. 2018: 1).

Still, Disney works to remind its audience that no matter how diverse these movies seem, either from each other or from earlier eras, they're very much still Princess movies. Sometimes they like to do this in a kind of tongue-in-cheek way. In *The Princess and the Frog*, for example, Tiana's friend Charlotte is comically obsessed with the idea of princesses, something that is juxtaposed with the more down-to-earth Tiana. Charlotte also wears a dress clearly inspired by Cinderella's classic ball gown. In *Moana*, Moana argues with her co-star Maui that she is "not a princess, I'm the daughter of a chief," to which Maui responds "if you wear a dress and have an animal sidekick, you're a princess." These meta-discursive texts are charming to watch because it feels like Disney is in on the joke about how absurd the whole princess culture thing is. But even as it winks and nods at its own ethos, these texts also help to cement the princesses even further as a single entity of which these modern entries are very much a part.

### Language in the Royal Kingdom

The common element tying almost all criticism on the Disney Princess movies together is the Princess herself. Our eyes have been fixed on the appearance

---

[9] We barely want to give Disney this much credit. It seems like true respect would have started with handing the creation of this movie over to people who are from the cultures being represented. But alas, *The Princess and the Frog* and later *Moana* were both written and directed by teams of white men.

and behavior of the central characters of this set of films, and for good reason. As an archetype, the Princess looms large in our culture, especially in the modern ages thanks to Disney's impeccable marketing and their creative team's efforts to evolve the traditional princess to be palatable to modern audiences. One thing that we hope to do with the analysis of the rest of the book is add a fresh perspective to the already long conversation around how the Princesses model femininity. But personally, we see the fixation on the choices and behavior of the princesses (to the exclusion of other characters in the film) to be a response that reifies the Princess's place as a feminine role model. Furthermore, although this extra scrutiny of this archetype comes from wanting the best for young girls, we also want to consider the possibility that criticizing *only* the main female character is in and of itself a reflection of the high expectations and gender policing that plague femininity in other contexts.[10] In any case, we hope that our approaches, which consider patterns across multiple characters and films instead of single characters, can add some thinking around these popular film franchises as a whole.

In particular, depiction of masculinity in Disney is a drastically understudied subject, despite the fact that princes (especially beginning in the Renaissance Era) are arguably at least as much a main character as the princess. So, whatever we can provide in terms of describing how masculinity is depicted, and how it is constructed in relation to femininity, will certainly be helpful in filling out a fuller picture of gender in Disney.

There's also the issue of progress: can we use language to show, in any way, that the Disney Princess movies have gotten "better," quantitatively speaking? This is a question we're asked a lot, and one we want to push back on a bit, as "progress" is heavily subjective and laden with moral implications. We don't want to tell you which ones are "good" or "bad."

However, we are interested in asking a related question, which is how the language in Disney constructs a portrayal of gender roles in ways specific to the Era they were created in. We will explore how the more traditional/ regressive gender politics of the Classic Era are reflected in speech – particularly, how the female characters reflect feminine-coded stances and speech stereotypes, such as polite language, complimenting strategies, and avoidance of conflict and impoliteness. Concerning the Renaissance movies, we will explore the ways in which these stereotypes are updated, subverted, or just upheld in the face of the Girl Power ideology permeating the films. And concerning the New Age, we consider the ramifications of the heightened attention and criticism of the time period and how those may impact the

---

[10] It's always "Belle has Stockholm Syndrome," and never "Beast is a whiny man baby who had a whole castle of servants and multiple decades of time and still couldn't figure out basic human decency," you know?

construction of femininity on screen. Lastly, we hope to quantitatively compare these three Eras, and in doing so piece together an understanding of how Disney's linguistic constructions of gender have changed through the decades.

## Pixar and the Boys' Club

Pixar is the other gear in Disney's massive family-friendly engine. Pixar entered the public consciousness in 1995 with the release of the first-ever feature-length computer-animated film *Toy Story*. *Toy Story*, like *Snow White*, revolutionized the industry and had a lasting impact that is hard to overstate. Director John Lasseter, like Walt Disney before him, earned an honorary award at the Oscars for his contribution to cinema. *Toy Story* kicked off Pixar's hot streak of critically acclaimed films throughout the late 1990s and early 2000s, and their studio remains immensely popular through to this day. This book examines Pixar's full filmography from 1995–2017. This includes a total of 18 films, as listed below:[11]

> *Toy Story (1995)*
> *A Bug's Life (1998)*
> *Toy Story 2 (1999)*
> *Monsters, Inc. (2001)*
> *Finding Nemo (2003)*
> *The Incredibles (2004)*
> *Cars (2006)*
> *Ratatouille (2007)*
> *Up (2009)*
> *Toy Story 3 (2010)*
> *Cars 2 (2011)*
> *Brave (2012)*[12]
> *Monsters University (2013)*
> *Inside Out (2015)*
> *The Good Dinosaur (2015)*
> *Finding Dory (2016)*
> *Cars 3 (2017)*
> *Coco (2017)*

Princess movies are conveniently separated into historical eras, but there are no comparable divisions for the Pixar films. Pixar Studio release dates run continuously from 1995 to the present with basically no breathing room in

---

[11] *WALL-E* (2008) is the only exception. More details on this decision in Chapter 3.

[12] *Brave* is listed both here and in the Disney canon. Again, more details on this decision in Chapter 3.

between. But if we were to place them chronologically alongside the Princesses, they would overlap in equal parts with the Renaissance and the New Age films, as well as breach the time in between. For context, *Toy Story* debuted in the same year as *Pocahontas*; Pixar's ninth film, *Up*, debuted the same year as *The Princess and the Frog*.

In addition to Pixar being historically synchronous with later Princess movies, they are, as a point of order, technically in the same company as Disney Animation. Pixar and Disney have worked closely together since Pixar's inception, and Disney formally acquired Pixar in 2006. Since the merger, top talent has also mingled somewhat. John Lasseter and Ed Catumull (both from Pixar studios) were installed as Creative Officer and President, respectively, of Disney Animation when the two studios merged, and it was actually John Lasseter who led the creative effort on *The Princess and the Frog* and revitalized Princess movie-making in the land of Disney. Given these various synchronicities it's tempting to stop writing right now, and just say "look at what we wrote in the Princess sections; that, again, but for these movies."

*Mais non*. We cannot do that. Firstly, although Pixar and Disney Animation are both owned by Disney, we cannot reasonably lump them creatively together. Pixar was insistent during their acquisition that the two studios keep their own separate brand identities and creative processes. Despite similar leadership, each studio creates their movies entirely on their own, with little to no input or staffing help from the other. The resulting style difference is probably obvious to even the casual viewer: *Toy Story 3* and *Tangled* were made in the same year, and we're guessing nobody would mix up which one came from Pixar and which from Disney.

But more importantly for us, Pixar and Disney are two separate entities politically, and they have very different relationships to mainstream discourses of gender. We've taken the stance that the Disney Princess brand is unique in how symbolically feminine it is, and how overtly it attempts to produce "role models." That relationship has made it a lightning rod of sorts for feminist critique (present company included). Pixar doesn't have the same relationship to feminine representation.

Quite the contrary, actually: the vast majority of Pixar's movies are about men. In fact, we chose to study Pixar not only because its popularity rivals Disney, but because, given their male-heavy franchises, they were honestly the closest we could get to a set of children's movies that feature lessons about masculinity. But the comparison to Disney Princess is fundamentally asym-metrical. Pixar's brand is heavy on male characters, sure, but it doesn't position itself to be movies that are *about men* or *about masculinity*. On the contrary, Pixar's reputation is for making "human stories" that are universally relatable. So while Disney and Pixar may occupy similar moments in history, they don't have the same orientation to the feminist conversations *du jour*.

## The Nonissue of Pixar's Gender Representation

Writing about Pixar's relationship with gender in the public sphere is actually kind of difficult. That's because there barely *is* one, or at least, that's what you'd think based on the way most of their films were received by the public. For the first 10–15 years of Pixar's existence, there was little to no discussion of their gender representation at all. Partially, we can attribute this to the "technical marvel" angle of Pixar's history. *Toy Story* was the first-ever full-length CGI film, which was revolutionary at the time; so a lot of the stories about the creation and subsequent release of the early Pixar movies were focused on the mythos of Lasseter and his dream, not totally unlike the nation's earlier obsession with Walt Disney. Secondly, Pixar movies (deservedly) stood out among other family-friendly movies for their emotionally complex stories and witty dialogue, which won them positive press, great box office numbers, and no small amount of awards. Professional reviews generally focused on these artistic qualities, rather than any political commentary.

We suspect, though, that the real reason the studio has also been the focus of so little political commentary is that most of their stories are about men. Popular culture has been focused on the crisis of girlhood and the issue of feminine representation for decades now, but critical examination of male role models has been much slower to catch on in popular discourse (Wooden & Gillam 2014). Pixar's first 12 films – the first 17 years of their filmmaking – were created by male directors, written by (mostly) male writers, and featured exclusively male protagonists.[13] We honestly think the manliness of it all allowed them to mostly slip under the radar of feminist criticism. In fact, making movies starring men probably facilitated their brand reputation at the time: their stories were lauded as exploring relatable, universal struggles, a narrative that was likely enabled by telling stories only through the default male point of view.

Pixar's movies also floated above the fray of academic critique for many years. In fact, they are *still* understudied considering the studio's prestige and reach, especially compared to the veritable mountain of literature that's been written about Disney Animation. The relatively small handful of Pixar studies that do exist paint a comparatively rosier picture of gender representation, especially when it comes to masculinity. Scholars have pointed out that Pixar's

---

[13] Only three women contributed to writing the first 12 Pixar movies. Rita Hsiao co-wrote *Toy Story 2*, Jill Culton worked on the story for *Monsters, Inc.*, and Kiel Murray helped write *Cars*.

male characters are emotionally driven (Finklea 2016) and even somewhat maternal (Brydon 2009), two traditionally feminine traits. Decker's (2010) content analysis of Pixar films found that there were no significant differences between the male and female characters' bodies, social roles, amount of authority, or personality traits.

Perhaps most notably, Gillam and Wooden (2008) pointed out that Pixar's male characters tend to be much more sensitive and community-oriented than other male heroes in children's media. They wrote:

Unlike many of the princesses, who remain relatively static even through their own adventures, these male leads are actual protagonists; their characters develop and change over the course of the film, rendering the plot. Ultimately these various developing characters ... experience a common narrative trajectory, culminating in ... a kinder, gentler understanding of what it means to be a man. (Gillam & Wooden 2008: 3)

This particular scholarly team ended up walking back that claim in a subsequent book, which we will return to shortly (Wooden & Gillam 2014). However, their initial analysis reflected the general acceptance, or at least lack of strong critique, with which the Pixar protagonists were met, especially compared to criticism of Disney films.

### Feminine Representation and the "Boys' Club"

Pixar's female characters have also not met with much political commentary compared to the Princesses. Again, though, these movies weren't *about* the female characters. They were about men, and so the female characters don't claim any symbolic role-modely power,[14] either in the texts or in the advertising surrounding them, and weren't critiqued as such. Even academics who were hypercritical of Disney Animation don't have much to say of these characters. Stover (2013), for example, throws out casual praise for Pixar while smack dab in the middle of skewering gender politics at Disney Animation:

Disney's entertainment partner Pixar has proven that it is possible to make profound, quality narratives for children, and still produce iconic, marketable images. It is time for Disney to invest in female-driven narratives that have staying-power with consumers, to create female protagonists with the cultural endurance and profitability that lie in the character and personality of Pixar's male heroes. (Stover 2013: 8)

In fact, it seems as if the first time gender politics became salient for Pixar at all was in the second half of the 2000s, as the online public began to notice and

---

[14] Throughout this book, we will be inventing words like "role-modely" and "evility" as needed. We are authorized to do this, because we are professional linguists. Use caution with this technique at home.

comment on the studios' increasingly long streak of making movies starring exclusively male protagonists. Pieces like "Pixar's Gender Problem" (Hopkins 2008), "Pixar: No Chicks Allowed" (Kottke 2009) and "Is Pixar a 'boys only' club?" (Hanscom 2006) began to crop up. But where Disney Animation films tend to get impassioned criticism, this slate of think pieces and blog posts were less critical and more along the lines of a polite request. A popular NPR op-ed at the time literally opened with "I'm not complaining; I'm asking. I'm asking because I think so highly of you. Please make a movie about a girl who is not a princess" (Holmes 2009).

Indeed, *Brave* (2012) – Pixar's first movie starring a female protagonist and only Princess movie – is the exception that proves the rule of Pixar's gender nonissue. Because Pixar had held off for so long making a movie starring female characters, *Brave*'s Merida had the tense responsibility of being a thesis statement of sorts on what Pixar thought female protagonists could be. On top of that, the fact that *Brave* was going to be a princess movie immediately gave Pixar just a taste of the chaotic gender storm that swirls around the Disney Princess brand constantly. In this movie alone among Pixar's films, the main character was in the cross-hairs of critique. And the fact that she was a princess among Pixar's otherwise "deeply human" characters was a failure to many. As one writer put it:

This wouldn't feel so vaguely unsatisfying if Brave were just one of many Pixar movies that featured a strong female lead. It's the absence of others that turns the spotlight on Brave. And having a princess protagonist isn't inherently bad. It's just that she is so chapter one of what girls can be – and so many other Pixar movies skipped most known chapters and moved on to whole new volumes. (Pols 2012)

Concerns that *Brave* would potentially be sexist were amped up when, mid-production, Pixar fired director Brenda Chapman – the first (and to this day, only) female director at the studio – and replaced her with Mark Andrews. The disappointment in the film fed further into the growing awareness of the problems with Pixar's company culture, which now has a reputation for being a hostile work environment for female employees (Desta 2017). The narrative arose that if Chapman hadn't been replaced, then *Brave* might have stood up to the Pixar giants that came before it, and might have even been a "human" Pixar story despite its princess premise. As it was, it received mediocre reviews, considered lukewarm both artistically and politically. We think it's telling that, although Pixar's culture had apparently been hostile for quite some time, attention didn't turn to it until we had a female character – a princess – to scrutinize.

In some ways, *Brave* seemed like a wake-up call for Pixar. In the following years, Pixar released two more films with female leads (*Inside Out* in 2015 and *Finding Dory* in 2016). They also seemed to be putting a more intentional foot forward with the representation of ethnically diverse characters, something that had been lacking in their previous years. *Coco*, for example, was the "the first film with a nine-figure budget to feature an all-Latino principal cast" (Coyle 2017). Following Disney's example, Pixar spent a lot of resources on research and consultation to ensure the film was authentic and respectful (Lang 2016).

However, it turns out that the scrutiny that rose so sharply during *Brave's* production was less a permanent rise in temperature for Pixar and more like a flash in the pan. *Inside Out* and *Finding Dory* were positively reviewed, but neither drew the focus on critiquing gender representation that was present with *Brave*. *Inside Out* starred three different female characters, but most reviews were devoid of discourse around whether or not Joy, Sadness, and Riley are strong role models. The closest thing anyone made to a political commentary in the mainstream focused on the relative accuracy of the depiction of the psychology of emotions, and how the film might be a good teaching tool for young children learning about emotion (Keltner & Ekman 2015). *Finding Dory's* critiques centered more on the depiction of disability than of gender (Robinson 2016; Scott 2016). No additional attention has been brought to the fact that Pixar has not hired a single female director since *Brave*, either. Although its reputation is not quite so politically golden as it once was, Pixar still seems to elude much negative attention from critics.

### Critique Beyond the Bird's-Eye View

The interesting thing about the criticism that Pixar has received about gender (*Brave* excluded) is that the problem was almost always framed in aggregate, not as a critique of individual films. Individual characters are fine, if not great, in the public eye. Scholarly work, too, has generally praised representation of gender in Pixar through the lens of individual character behavior (e.g. Brydon 2009; Decker 2010; Finklea 2016). The gender problem for most audiences is only in the bird's-eye view. As blogger Matt DeButts put it: "It is only when Pixar's films are viewed in aggregate, and the lack of female protagonists becomes systemic, that my scruples begin to arise. Or to put it in the rarefied speech of Generation Y: it's a thing because you made it a thing" (DeButts 2012).

Even in cases where femininity is scrutinized in Pixar, depictions of male characters seem to be above (or, depending on the opinion of the scholar, below) serious consideration. Wooden and Gillam (2014) are one of the only major exceptions to this rule. Their analysis of Pixar male characters was initially optimistic (Gillam & Wooden 2008); however, their subsequent book, *Pixar's Boy Stories* (2014), points out patterns in Pixar's depictions of masculinity that are hyper-traditional and harmful to male and female viewers alike. They comment in this work on the double standard applied to gender analysis of Pixar films:

Though nearly every review of *Brave* – dozens of them – refers to its protagonist's gender, for example, and many explicitly consider her interpretation of femininity in pedagogical relation to young female viewers, virtually no one mentions that Lightning McQueen, Buzz Lightyear, and James P. Sullivan are male, and virtually no one has discussed whether these representations of maleness might too have ramifications for boy viewers learning how to define themselves as men . . . Indeed, *Brave*'s depiction of men as buffoonish thugs, amid its supposedly bold stride forward toward gender equality in children's film, reveals one contemporary attitude toward masculinity that merits some serious attention. (Wooden & Gillam 2014: xii)

We're hopeful that as linguists we can contribute a more in-depth critical analysis of Pixar's gender representation. Of course (a quick spoiler here), we can (and will) add credence to the "boys' club" concept. Men truly are everywhere in Pixar – we'll present our receipts in Chapter 3. But beyond that, we aim to linguistically interrogate how Pixar ideologically constructs masculinity and femininity through language with more detail than just "too many men."

Because there is so little scholarship on Pixar and masculinity, and so few external pressures for Pixar to present masculinity in any particular way, we are very curious about how masculine language will appear in these films. How do movies that center male characters and male homosocial relationships construct masculine language behavior? Do male characters in largely same-sex environments exaggerate their masculinity through language? Or is part of the appeal of these films that the characters are presented as complex individuals with nuanced language behaviors that defy easy categorization?

Similarly, we are intrigued by the paucity of female characters in Pixar and the implications that may have for language. Will the "boys' club" of writers and directors produce female characters being written poorly and/or stereotypically? Or will the female characters be so varied that they don't show any patterns of gendered language? Also, the general apathy towards Pixar's female characters by scholars and critics makes us raise our eyebrows. We hear that people mostly like them. But we also see that they aren't paying as much attention as they do with Disney. Are the ladies as good as they seem? If so, how is this reflected in their language? Or are there damaging linguistic stereotypes hidden just below the surface?

## Conclusion

Through the course of this chapter, we have hoped to show that Disney and Pixar, though under the same umbrella company, hold very different public relationships with the politics of the content they produce. Disney Animation, the ostensible originator and maintainer of the modern Princess symbol, is an enduring lightning rod for gender critique. Disney has cultivated and maintained the Princess as a feminine icon for over 80 years now, and in doing so, has engaged with mainstream feminist concepts as they've evolved over the decades. While their "progress" hasn't always been straightforward, Princess films have at least managed to respond to the political zeitgeist of their creation enough to stay relevant to an increasingly critical media landscape. On the other hand, Pixar, whose prominence in the box office and the awards circuit is just as prominent, doesn't have much of a political footprint. Pixar's audiences, popular and academic alike, have by and large not examined the gender politics of their movies beyond noting the underrepresentation of female characters, and Pixar in turn doesn't push their movies as "feminist" or "progressive" innovations.

We will return throughout the book to the various ways that the different political orientation of the two studios (and the different time eras within Disney) may end up having significant explanatory power in our analyses. As we explore how language is used as a tool in gender construction from various angles, we will document how each feature of speech may reflect some of the information presented in this chapter, often in interesting and unexpected ways. We begin these linguistic explorations in the following chapter with perhaps the most basic linguistic question we can ask: How much do characters actually talk? By considering this question in light of historical context, we can begin to understand just how much (or how little) Disney and Pixar have changed to fit the times.

# 3    Representation, Speech Amounts, and Talkativeness

> The men up there don't like a lot of blabber
> They think a girl who gossips is a bore
> Yet on land it's much preferred for ladies not to say a word
> And after all dear, what is idle prattle for?
>
> Ursula, *The Little Mermaid*

## Introduction and Background

One powerfully enduring myth about women is that they talk a *lot*. Chatty, gossipy, nagging, scolding, giggly – there are many ways to say it, but the fundamental message is the same. As linguists, our favorite example of this myth is the set of empirical "data" that circulate now and again that claim men speak an average of 7,000 words per day, and women speak an average of 20,000. This statistic is, as far as scholars can tell, completely made up, and nobody actually knows where it came from (Liberman 2013). But it's shared anyway, along with a number of other stories, sayings, jokes and stereotypes about chatty women (Eckert & McConnell-Ginet 2013). Empirically, we've found that these stereotypes do indeed influence how real people interpret women's speech. Multiple scholars have found that people believed women to be more polite, gentle, friendly, emotional, trivial, and talkative compared to men (Edelsky 1981; Kramarae 1981; Siegler & Siegler 1976; Spender 1980).

However, it's largely accepted in the academic community that the myth of female talkativeness is just that: a myth. In fact, research tends to point to men being the more talkative ones, not women. Leaper and Ayres (2007) surveyed 70 independent studies of talkativeness and found that, accounting for variation in method and context, results were significantly more likely to conclude that men are more talkative than women rather than the other way around. James and Drakich (1993) similarly looked at 53 studies of mixed-gender interaction and found that in 43 percent, men were more likely to talk more regardless of context. In the majority of cases, speech amounts were found to be influenced by other contextual factors (e.g. institutional status, expertise, relationship style, and conversational topic), rather than tied solely to gender. Only *two* of the surveyed studies found that women spoke more regardless of context. In sum, although men may not speak more in every situation, it's masculinity, not femininity, that's more likely to be empirically linked with talkativeness.

And yet, the myth endures. Granted, there is a growing public consciousness about the masculine tendency towards conversational dominance: the last few years have seen news articles like "The Universal Phenomenon of Men Interrupting Women" and viral YouTube supercuts of female pop stars and politicians being spoken over by their male colleagues. But on the other hand, Popp et al. (2003) found that stereotypes of women as emotional, indirect, trivial, and talkative are very much alive and well. Humorous plays on the stereotype of the talkative woman can also still be found in prime-time entertainment, with women nagging male characters, spiraling into hysteria and verbal excess, or simply being a constantly talkative presence in the background (Macdonald 1995). Language and gender scholars have reasoned that the enduring perception of women as talkative hinges on a deep-seated historical double standard on how much men and women *should* talk – that historically, the ideal woman was silent, and "when silence is the desired state for women ... then any talk in which a woman engages can be too much." (Spender 1980). Even though we are increasingly aware of male conversational dominance, part of the social consciousness still resists the concept of women occupying equal conversational space. And unfortunately, this has a real-world impact on girls and women. We undervalue and/or punish feminine participation in public spaces, from the classroom (Eckert & McConnell-Ginet 2013; Kelly 1988; Spender 1980; Swann 2003) to online forums (Herring 2003) all the way to the US legislature (Kathlene 1994; Rosenthal 1998).

Media plays an important role in setting expectations for how and when women participate in conversation. Failing to see women represented in the public sphere on screen helps perpetuate the expectation that women aren't to be seen or heard in public settings in real life. This has the obvious immediate effect of making women and girls less likely to have aspirations for certain industries that they don't see themselves represented in (as the saying goes, "if you can't see it, you can't be it") (Cheryan et al. 2015). But there are also linguistic implications to the lack of representation: as Eckert and McConnell-Ginet (2013) note, it could actually damage women's ability to participate conversationally when they *do* find themselves in public settings; feeling like the "odd one out" in a public space makes it all the harder to speak up. As they put it,

The effect of one's verbal activity depends, among other things, on one's apparent legitimacy to engage in that activity. The words of a person who doesn't appear to be a professor are less likely to be taken as authoritative than the same words coming from someone who does look like a professor. And, of course, being a professor in the first place depends on one's looking (and sounding) sufficiently like one to get the job. (Eckert & McConnell-Ginet 2013: 91)

Unfortunately, women are currently underrepresented in all manner of media. Women make up 29 percent of lead roles in top-grossing films in the last decade (Smith et al. 2019), 39 percent of characters on prime-time TV, and are even covered on local news at only half the rate of men (Desmone & Danilewicz 2010). And in terms of talkativeness, a 2016 review of 2,000 movie scripts found that just 9 percent of the analyzed films had a female speech majority, as opposed to 76 percent of films that had a male speech majority (Anderson & Daniels 2016).

To be fair, female representation is (slowly and unevenly) improving. In 2019, a full 43 percent of top-grossing films were led by women (Smith et al. 2019). We'd guess that part of this improvement has been the direct result of pressure on the film industry by a public that is increasingly aware of the potential impact representation can have in shaping our expectations of the real world. The impact of this attention can be seen in children's media in particular: a review of children's media by the Geena Davis Institute on Gender in Media found that 45 percent of examined episodes of kid's TV in 2019 had female leads, up from the 40 percent it was a decade ago, and that women actually spoke the majority of words (58 percent) in the analyzed scripts (Heldman et al. 2021).

We now want to turn our analytical attention to the question of representation in Disney movies in particular. Because Disney and Pixar have such an outsized presence in the landscape of children's media, we believe a review of their filmography will be a helpful addition to the conversations already being had about gender representation on the silver screen and in real life. However, as linguists, we want to offer more than just a count of bodies on screen; we want a more in-depth look at the ideologies of talkativeness, conversational dominance, and silence that Disney and Pixar construct.

## Methodology: Overview of Script Analysis

### Our Datasets

This chapter and all subsequent chapters (except Chapter 8) will analyze 31 feature-length animated films from Disney and Pixar. A full list of films analyzed can be found in Tables 3.1 and 3.2. We divide our data into two separate sets for most analyses, detailed below:

> *The Princess Movies*: 14 movies from Disney Animation Studios. In most cases we defer to Disney on who counts as an official

Table 3.1. *Disney Princess films included in analysis*

| Era | Movie title | Year |
|---|---|---|
| Classic Era, 1937–1959 | *Snow White* | 1937 |
| | *Cinderella* | 1950 |
| | *Sleeping Beauty* | 1959 |
| Renaissance Era, 1989–1999 | *The Little Mermaid* | 1989 |
| | *Beauty and the Beast* | 1991 |
| | *Aladdin* | 1992 |
| | *Pocahontas* | 1995 |
| | *Mulan* | 1998 |
| New Age Era, 2009–present | *The Princess and the Frog* | 2009 |
| | *Tangled* | 2010 |
| | *Brave (Pixar)* | 2012 |
| | *Frozen* | 2013 |
| | *Moana* | 2016 |
| | *Frozen II* | 2019 |

Table 3.2. *Pixar films included in analysis*

| Movie title | Year |
|---|---|
| *Toy Story* | 1995 |
| *A Bug's Life* | 1998 |
| *Toy Story 2* | 1999 |
| *Monsters, Inc.* | 2001 |
| *Finding Nemo* | 2003 |
| *The Incredibles* | 2004 |
| *Cars* | 2006 |
| *Ratatouille* | 2007 |
| *Up* | 2009 |
| *Toy Story 3* | 2010 |
| *Cars 2* | 2011 |
| *Brave* | 2012 |
| *Monsters University* | 2013 |
| *Inside Out* | 2015 |
| *The Good Dinosaur* | 2015 |
| *Finding Dory* | 2016 |
| *Cars 3* | 2017 |
| *Coco* | 2017 |

princess. Twelve of the 14 movies were selected for their inclusion in the Disney Princess brand, as discussed in Chapter 2. Only the first film in each Princess film franchise was included in the dataset; sequels were excluded because of their "straight to VHS" quality (except *Frozen II*).[1] The Princess films have been split into three distinct 'eras' of movies, following suit with previous methods (Do Rozario 2004; England et al. 2011; Stover 2013; Towbin et al. 2004).

*The Pixar Movies:* 18 films from Pixar Animation Studios. We have included every major Pixar release from 1995 to 2017 except *WALL-E* (2008), which was excluded due to the ambiguity of the "speech" of the robots who make up most of the cast.[2] We opted to include the franchise sequels in the Pixar dataset, because Pixar tends to publicize its sequels as major releases and see box office reception equaling or exceeding the original release.

A quick point of order: *Brave* (2012) appears in both tables. That's because it exists in an interesting limbo between the two studios, having been created by Pixar Studios but also being included in the Disney Princess brand. To accommodate this, we include *Brave* in our separate aggregate analyses of both datasets. On the rare occasion that both datasets are considered together, *Brave* is only counted once. The cross-listing of *Brave* means that there are 14 Disney Princess films and 18 Pixar films, but a grand total of 31 scripts in our dataset.

Prior to any analysis, scripts for all 31 movies were collected and checked against each film by researchers to ensure linguistic accuracy. At this stage, we also excluded all of Disney's musical lyrics for the purpose of quantitative analysis throughout the book; they're serving a different enough purpose in the script that we didn't want to quantitatively conflate them with scripted speech. However, we recognize Disney songs as centerpieces of their movies and worthy of examination, and take them into account in qualitative analysis whenever relevant.

After script collection and coding, perceived gender was assigned to each speaking character. We made a conscious choice to examine gender in a binary light for most of our linguistic analyses because, although gender is a complicated, nonbinary phenomenon in real life, Disney tends to clearly code its characters along a strict binary as either men or women. We assigned each character a gender category based on pronouns used to refer to them. In the

---

[1] For example, *Toy Story* earned $350 million worldwide. *Toy Story 2* passed it at $497.4 million worldwide; *Toy Story 3* made more than the first two combined. Compare with *Aladdin and the King of Thieves*, the second highest grossing Disney Princess sequel, which didn't premiere in theaters and made an estimated $130–180 million in video sales – less than half of *Aladdin*'s $287 million. We say *Frozen II* is the exception because it actually surpassed *Frozen* as the highest grossing animated film of all time at $1.5 billion dollars.

[2] There's only so much arguing about whether a given "beep-boop" noise should be counted as gender representation that we could do before we decided it would be better to set it aside for this analysis. We look forward to any scholarship that decides to take on this particular challenge.

absence of pronouns, we used various gender indicators such as attire, body shape, and vocal pitch to determine intended gender. A third category was reserved for characters who spoke little enough to have no gender-defining characteristics.[3]

The one exception to our coding rules is Mulan from *Mulan* (1998), who is referred to as a man by most characters around her for the bulk of the film. When she speaks, we code her and her speech as female, since the audience is aware that she is a female character and we believe she should count as female representation. However, when she is the *recipient* of speech acts, we coded her gender based on how she was being perceived by the speaker. For example, if Shang gives her a compliment while she's acting as her male alter ego Ping, we count that as a male-to-male compliment.

## Methodology: Representation and Speech Amounts

In each chapter where we analyze the films to look for a specific linguistic variable or pattern, we list the questions that will be our focus. This chapter will address the following questions.

---

**Key Questions**

- In terms of representation, how many characters of each binary gender (male or female) are **present** in each film?
- How much do male and female characters **speak** in each film?
- In male–female character pairs, how much does each character speak (in other words, is one binary gender portrayed as **conversationally dominant** over the other)?
- How is **talkativeness qualitatively framed** in the films? Are characters of a particular gender framed as either too talkative or not talkative enough?

---

By addressing these questions, we can provide an overview of representation, speech amounts, and discourse around talkativeness in the Disney and Pixar films. These results will be interesting in their own right, but will also help to set up a baseline for the rest of our study. By knowing how much characters of a particular gender talk, we can estimate whether they are using other features more or less than expected. We can also determine whether or

---

[3] This category totaled 19 Disney characters and 85 Pixar characters. These included children, animal characters with high-pitched voices or who "spoke" animal noises (e.g. worms, mice, owls, and in one case an anthropomorphic pizza), crowd members whose voices weren't distinct enough from the rest of the crowd to discern implied gender based on pitch, and lines voiced in unison from multiple crowd members of different genders. Combined, this category accounted for 2.3 percent of Pixar speech and 0.2 percent of Disney speech.

not the ideologies around who "talks a lot" actually match the quantitative reality of relative speech amounts in the films.

To answer the main research questions in this chapter, we use the four following analyses:

*Aggregate character count.* All characters (named or unnamed) who speak at least one word of dialogue were tallied for each film. Totals were compared between genders. Characters who have singing parts but no spoken dialogue were not counted.[4]

*Aggregate word count.* Word counts for each character were tallied using a custom Python script and aggregated by gender for comparison across films. We ran a binomial statistical test on the aggregate speech proportions of each film, testing whether the amounts that male and female characters talk match what we would predict based on the proportion of male and female characters (assuming all characters spoke at similar rates).

*Analysis of mixed-gender dyadic conversations.* To examine the question of conversational dominance within the context of individual conversations, we extracted the subset of scenes from each movie wherein two leads of mixed genders were having a one-on-one conversation. In the majority of Princess movies, the extracted scenes featured the princess and her romantic counterpart.[5] In the Pixar movies, scenes were extracted from films that had two leads of different genders, regardless of the nature of their relationship. Pixar movies that did not have a female co-lead were excluded from this analysis. Once all scenes were extracted, the total speech count for the male and female lead of each movie was calculated and compared. We once again ran a set of binomial tests, this time to determine whether the proportion of speech from each gender was significantly different from an equal 50–50 split.

*Qualitative exploration of talkativeness and silence.* We searched all films for instances where the subjects of character talkativeness or silence were called to the audience's attention. Examples of such instances included, but were not limited to: characters telling others to talk softer, less, or not at all, humor based on a character talking too much or talking in an inappropriate context, and humor based

---

[4] Our methods here are heavily inspired by Lippi-Green (2011). See her work for a detailed breakdown of Disney characters by a variety of metrics out of our current scope, principally ethnicity and dialect use.

[5] Our two exceptions were *Moana*, where the extracted conversations featured Moana and her platonic co-lead Maui, and *Brave*, where we opted to use conversations between the king and queen since Princess Merida has no male counterpart.

on a character talking too little, disengaging from conversation, or failing to speak when it is appropriate for them to do so. With gender as our analytical lens, we looked for patterns in the ways characters are the focus of humor or drama because of the amount they speak.

## Character and Speech Representation

### Characters and Speech in Disney Princess Films

The results of our character analysis show a massive discrepancy in representation of male and female characters in the Disney Princess movies. We might have expected female characters to be the primary presence in these films, since all Princess movies except one (*Aladdin*) feature a main female character, and they are generally considered to be "girl movies." But in actuality, male characters outnumber female characters in every single film in this dataset. Gender representation comes close to parity in only three films (*Cinderella*, *Sleeping Beauty*, and *Moana*).

Surprisingly, the movies that overrepresented male characters the most weren't the earliest films (often slammed for their regressive gender politics), but rather the movies of the 1990s and the early 2010s. This discrepancy can be pinned on a couple of things. First, Disney's storytelling style had evolved

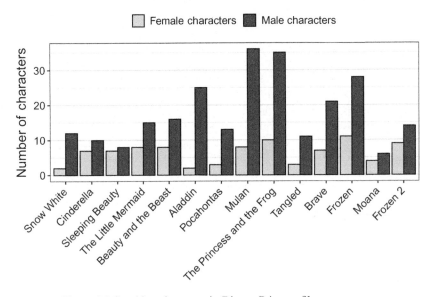

Figure 3.1 Speaking characters in Disney Princess films

significantly between the Classic and Renaissance Eras. The oldest movies purposely evoke traditional dramatic tellings of fairy tales; movies of that style had small casts, minimal (and by our standards, formal and stilted) dialogue, and very few superfluous speaking roles. But in the 1990s, Disney Animation reinvented Princess movies as modern Broadway musicals, even hiring Broadway writers Alan Menken and Howard Ashman to write their music and help with story structure (Do Rozario 2004). Big musicals have big casts, and so the amount of minor speaking roles written into each movie increased dramatically. Our analysis shows that these new small parts were overwhelmingly male, unless there was some gendered element of the role that required the character to be a woman.[6] We can, in fact, exhaustively list the professions (we use the word liberally) of minor female characters of the 1990s Princess films:

> Maid *(The Little Mermaid, Beauty and the Beast)*
> Sister *(The Little Mermaid)*
> Scared mother *(Beauty and the Beast)*
> "Bimbette" *(Beauty and the Beast)*
> Housewife/professional laundress *(Aladdin)*
> Mother *(Mulan)*
> Grandmother *(Mulan)*
> Matchmaker *(Mulan)*
> Ancestor *(Mulan)*

And that's it. With the exception of Mulan's ancestors, each role has a decidedly domestic bent; all other speaking roles were cast as men.[7]

Another contributing trend to gender discrepancy in the Renaissance was a shift in plot structure, specifically in regards to the movies' villains. In the Classic Era, all three villains are female. As Do Rozario (2004) comments, they are all three mature, power-hungry women who are pitted against the feminine innocence of the princess. These tropes are undeniably sexist; but for what it's worth, they did make for a majority female world. Classic movies also have substantial supporting roles for women in the form of stepsisters and fairy godmothers.

The Girl Power Princess movies of the Renaissance are cut from a different cloth. Though the plots vary, at the core of all the Renaissance movies is a princess struggling against restrictive social roles to empower herself.

---

[6] As an interesting anecdote on the theme of connecting Disney to the human world, a student at a presentation on this topic suggested that the reason male characters dominate in Disney is for "historical accuracy," since men would have been doing a lot of those jobs at the time. We asked him if he could help fill us in on the "historical context" for *The Little Mermaid*. He claimed he was not very familiar with that movie and could not help. We personally feel that Disney stepped off the historical accuracy train with talking teapots and dragon sidekicks, but we digress . . .

[7] Lippi-Green (2012) gives a similar analysis for her dataset, showing that this effect goes beyond just the 1990s films.

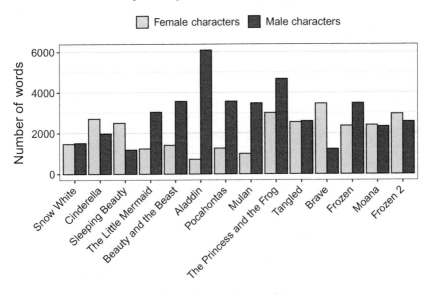

Figure 3.2 Words spoken in Disney Princess films
Every word count proportion shown in Figure 3.2 is significantly different than predicted based on proportion of male and female characters ($p < 0.05$)

As discussed in Chapter 2, Girl Power was the theme *du jour* in the 1990s, since media companies were trying hard to sell "empowered" role models for concerned mothers to show their young girls. But to make their empowerment plots have tension, Disney constructed each Renaissance storyworld to have its own form of amped-up patriarchy intent on keeping its princess down. These movies have male villains and overbearing father figures, instead of female villains and helpers, to fulfill the role of personifying the patriarchy. The oppression/empowerment theme likely also motivated the cast of minor characters being so overwhelmingly male: it helps sell the woman-versus-the-world story if your princess is literally the only woman in the world.

The New Age films carry on the empowerment plot tradition, though not so rigidly. *The Princess and the Frog*, *Moana*, and *Frozen* all contain fathers or other patriarchal figures telling the princess her "proper place" in the world. *Tangled*, *Brave*, and the *Frozen* franchise feature conflict between female characters, but still have a Western patriarchal world as background. Their continued reliance on patriarchy as an antagonistic element means that the story worlds continue to be disproportionately masculine.

The results of our analysis of words spoken (seen in Figure 3.2) are more varied than what we get from just counting characters. In five out of the 14 Princess films (*Cinderella*, *Sleeping Beauty*, *Brave*, *Moana*, *Frozen II*), female characters speak the majority of the time. Additionally, results from binomial tests reveal that in all cases except *The Little Mermaid* and *Beauty and the Beast*, female speech accounts for more than the predicted amount based on how many female characters are in the movie, meaning that the female characters who are present in the films are doing more than their "fair share" of talking. This makes sense: though the princess may be one of the only female characters, she is still the star of the show. In fact, each princess by herself tends to speak an average of 25 percent of all the dialogue in a given Disney Princess film.

That being said, we do want to call attention again to the difference that the timing of the film's production makes in the representation of female speech. Female speech is the most consistently high not in modern movies, but in the Classic Era, thanks to the aforementioned foregrounding of female villains and side characters. The Renaissance films, on the other hand, stand out as strikingly male-dominated. The male villains, the extra minor speaking parts, and the advent of the male comic sidekick character – e.g. Genie (*Aladdin*), Lumière and Cogsworth (*Beauty and the Beast*), Mushu (*Mulan*) – all contribute to a huge discrepancy in speech amounts between male and female characters. In *Aladdin*, the ratio of male to female speech approaches 8:1. This era also contains the only two films (*The Little Mermaid* and *Beauty and the Beast*) wherein women speak significantly *less* than would be expected based on their character count.

The New Age films do not follow such a clear trend. Newer Princess scripts spend more screen time developing the relationship between the central two characters than previous eras – that is, the princess and the prince, the princess and her sister, or in some cases, the princess and demigod. Or bear-mom. Consequently, the speech ratio increasingly weighs the presence of the princess, and the side characters lose proportional screen time. In fact, princesses alone account for 31 percent (*Frozen*) to 45 percent (*Brave*) of all words spoken in the New Age movies.

Additionally, *Brave*, *Frozen*, and *Tangled* all could be said to have female antagonists, a concept reintroduced by the New Age movies, which further increases the amount of female speech in those three films. We know there's a lot of nuance lost when we group the three female characters from these films together under the umbrella "antagonist." Mother Gothel from *Tangled* is a classic Disney villain, and one who refreshes antiquated stereotypes that we haven't seen since the days of Cinderella. Elsa and Queen Elinor are also antagonists in that they have different goals from the main characters and ultimately drive the plot's conflict forward. However, they do so not because they are the classic, shallow archetype of an older female villain, but rather because they are relatively complex characters who grow through character flaws. Although it's true that all three drive up "female representation" in the bluntest sense, this fact is in its own way a case study in why qualitative analysis is just as important as aggregate quantitative measure.

### Characters and Speech in Pixar

Figure 3.3 confirms what many movie-goers and film critics have already impressionistically observed: there are a *lot* of men in Pixar movies. The most obvious factor here is that Pixar movies overwhelmingly star male characters, which is a stark departure from Princess movies (which are almost definition-ally required to have a female lead). There are only three films in the Pixar canon with female protagonists: *Brave, Inside Out,* and *Finding Dory.* The other central factor is that Pixar tends toward the same issue as large-cast Disney films: masculinity is the assumed standard choice for minor roles, unless there is a specific reason for the role to be cast as female. The imbalance is exacerbated by the sheer number of minor parts in Pixar movies compared to Disney Animation. The more minor speaking roles that are added for the sake of gags or world-building, the faster the male character counts rise.

Some later films, like *Coco, Inside Out,* and *Finding Dory* seem to be more conscientious about splitting extra roles between genders, and as such, their character counts approach equity. This is potentially a direct response to the public criticism leveled at Pixar after the release of *Brave* in 2011 (as discussed in Chapter 2). Indeed, there seems to be almost a methodical approach to

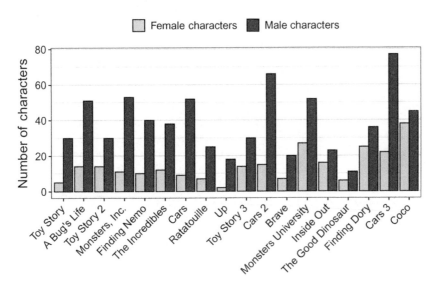

Figure 3.3 Speaking characters in Pixar films

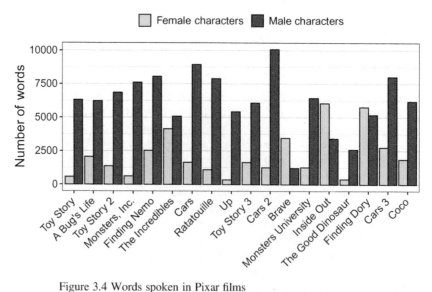

Figure 3.4 Words spoken in Pixar films
Every word count proportion shown in Figure 3.4 is significantly different than predicted based on proportion of male and female characters (p < 0.5)

gender representation in some later films: in *Coco*, for example, unnamed "Musician #1" is male, "Musician #2" is female, "Musician #3" male again, and so forth. However, even taking these efforts into account, Pixar has still never had a film with a majority female cast.

Speech comparisons in Pixar movies also strongly favor male characters. As with the Princess movies, we can expect this partially as a natural effect of the male-heavy cast: all those three-line bit parts eventually add up. However, Pixar's movies (much like the New Age Princess movies) are dialogue-heavy and focus screen time on the development of the central characters and their relationship.[8] Consequently, the three films with female protagonists are also the three that have a female speech majority. In movies with a minority female speech, those that had female co-leads alongside the male protagonist, (e.g. *The Incredibles* and *Finding Nemo*) came somewhat close to gender parity, while movies with no female co-lead (e.g. *Toy Story*, *Up*) tended to have higher proportions of male speech.

The results of binomial tests do not show a clear pattern as they do in Princess movies. The three movies with female leads all have significantly

---

[8]  Actually, it's more like the New Age movies are like Pixar. Disney Animation's style notably shifted after Pixar head John Lasseter took control of the studio, and presumably began making movies more closely aligned with Pixar's filmmaking style.

more female speech than predicted. But outside of that, where Princess films have their "girl-versus-world" story template, which results in low female character representation but proportionally higher speech amounts, Pixar plot structures are both more complex and more varied and so women's representation becomes less predictable. However, the Pixar movies where female characters' speech is significantly more than their character count predicted do seem to share a spiritual link with some of the Princess movies, in that they tend to have one Strong Woman™ in a relative sea of somewhat misogynistic men. These characters aren't often princesses, but they do often have a position of power equal to or above the male protagonist, are self-confident and assertive, and often even share some of the overt girl-power messaging common in the Princess movies. For example, Mrs. Incredible is introduced in *The Incredibles* by stating in an interview, "Girls, come on. Leave the saving of the world to the men? I don't think so. I don't think so." The clearest example of this is Colette, the only female cook in *Ratatouille*, who is tasked with mentoring the male protagonist, Linguini. As Linguini introduces himself to Colette she cuts him off with the following monologue:

### Excerpt 3A "I'm the Toughest Cook in this Kitchen" (Ratatouille, 2007)

COLETTE:   I just want you to know exactly who you are dealing with. How many women do you see in this kitchen? Only me. Why do you think that is? Because Haute Cuisine is an antiquated hierarchy built upon rules written by stupid old men, rules designed to make it impossible for women to enter this world. But still I am here. How did this happen? Because I'm the toughest cook in this kitchen. I've worked too hard for too long to get here, and I'm not going to jeopardize it for some garbage boy who got lucky. Got it?

Here, much like in many Princess movies, one of Colette's primary motivations is to assert herself as a powerful woman in a male space. Undertones of this motivation are in other films as well, particularly Mrs. Incredible (*The Incredibles*), Sally (*Cars*), and the occasional actual Pixar princess (Atta, *A Bug's Life*; Merida, *Brave*).

Setting Girl Power aside, Pixar women are generally well received for being strong and complex characters. Movies where female characters speak significantly more than predicted all have a central female character co-starring alongside a male protagonist (e.g. Atta, *A Bug's Life*; Dory, *Finding Nemo*; Elastigirl, *Incredibles*; Sally, *Cars*; Cruz, *Cars 3*). However, not all strong Pixar ladies tip the scales: *Toy Story 2*, *Cars 2*, and *Ratatouille* (home to "toughest cook in this kitchen" Colette) all have strong female protagonists, and in all of them, female characters speak significantly less than predicted.

## Talkativeness and Conversational Dominance in Dyadic Conversation

The results of our first inquiry are interesting, but really only address the matter of *representation*; that is, how much each gender gets to be on screen. Analyzing speech in the aggregate seems to correlate more to how many characters of each gender there are, and how important they are to the plot, more than the actual speech behavior of any individual character. To that end, our second analysis is a little more pointed, and concerns *talkativeness*: when two equally important characters of different genders are on screen at the same time, who is portrayed as conversationally dominant?

### *Disney Does Rom-Com: Talk in Disney Leading Pairs*

Figure 3.5 shows the word counts of male and female lead characters totaled from dyadic conversations with each other. In this data, we see that not only do female characters speak less overall in Princess movies, but that princesses also speak less than their male co-lead in isolated conversation, with only two exceptions (*Sleeping Beauty* and *Mulan*). This shows us that although the

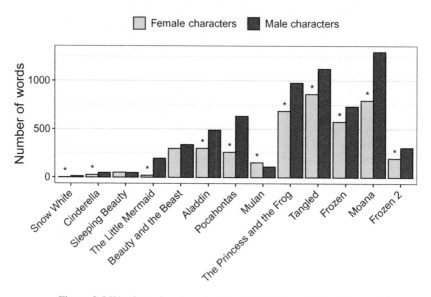

Figure 3.5 Words spoken by mixed-gender leading pairs in Princess films
* Denotes that word count proportion is significantly different than 50–50 (p < 0.05)

princess tends to have a larger screen presence in the narrative as a whole, this does not translate into holding the floor in individual conversation.

The Classic Era films all have strikingly low word counts in this analysis; each movie has only one conversation between leads to establish their romantic connection.[9] All three of these establishing conversations have the same arc: the princess runs away from the encounter, and the prince pleads with her to stay. The relative speech amounts between the two leads is not particularly telling vis-à-vis conversational dominance, because the princesses' word count depends almost entirely on how elaborate of an excuse she comes up with about why she has to leave.[10] Consider the two romantic conversations from *Cinderella* and *Sleeping Beauty*:

**Excerpt 3B "Goodbye!"** (*Cinderella*, 1950)

| | |
|---|---|
| CINDERELLA: | Oh my goodness! |
| PRINCE: | What's the matter? |
| CINDERELLA: | It's midnight. |
| PRINCE: | Yes. So it is but why— |
| CINDERELLA: | Goodbye! |
| PRINCE: | No, no wait. You can't go now. It's only— |
| CINDERELLA: | Oh I must. Please! Please I must! |
| PRINCE: | But why? |
| CINDERELLA: | Well, I-I— oh the prince. I haven't met the prince. |
| PRINCE: | The prince? But didn't you know— |
| CINDERELLA: | Goodbye. |
| PRINCE: | No wait. Come back. Oh please come back! I don't even know your name! <br> How will I find you? Wait! Please wait! |
| CINDERELLA: | Goodbye! |

**Excerpt 3C "Well, maybe someday"** (*Sleeping Beauty*, 1959)

| | |
|---|---|
| PHILLIP: | Who are you, what's your name? |
| AURORA: | Hmm? Oh, my name. Why, it's, it's... Oh no, no, I can't, I... Goodbye! |
| PHILLIP: | But when will I see you again? |

---

[9] Fun fact: the conversations are also limited because, as it turns out, early animators thought realistic-looking men were almost impossibly difficult to draw. So they slashed the prince scenes down to the barest minimum possible to keep the plot rolling. (Arends 1994). Hence, a single scene and a love song.

[10] On a troubling side note, we think it's worth mentioning that there are four other princess movies besides these (*Cinderella*, *The Little Mermaid*, *Pocahontas*, *The Princess and the Frog*) – making a total of six canon films, almost half the Princess collection – whose meet-cute scene involves a woman running in fear.

AURORA:     Oh never, never!
PHILLIP:    Never?
AURORA:     Well, maybe someday.
PHILLIP:    When, tomorrow?
AURORA:     Oh no, this evening.
PHILLIP:    Where?
AURORA:     At the cottage, in the glen.

Both conversations featured here are more negotiation than casual conversation. And in both cases, the prince drives the conversation with questions and requests towards the fleeing princess, while the princess's role in the conversation is entirely reactive to the prince's cues. Cinderella's answers are shorter, and the Prince's requests more complex, resulting in a male speech majority; Aurora, on the other hand, speaks more than the Prince, but that's because his questions require more complex answers. The question of who talks more is incidental due to the small sample size.

The Renaissance movies feature significantly more one-on-one conversation between princes and princesses. This makes the data more reliably interpretable. And indeed, as the amount of conversational time between leads increases overall, the pattern of male conversational dominance also becomes more visible. The only exception to the trend is *Mulan*, which decenters the romantic element of the plot in favor of the gender-swap comedy/war story it tells. Mulan's interactions with Shang aren't the emotional focal point of the film, and when they do happen, they are under the pretense of two male soldiers for the majority of the run time.

This trend may seem counterintuitive given the Renaissance era princesses' consistent characterization as ambitious, independent, and assertive. However, although the *content* of the princesses' speech is less passive than their Classic Era predecessors, the *structure* of conversation with princes still portrays male characters as conversationally dominant. This time it's the princesses who are asking questions; but these questions are not for urgent information gathering like the Classic Era princes. Instead, they are engaging in *conversational facilitation* (or as Pamela Fishman [1978] calls it, *conversational shitwork*), a stereotypically feminine practice of facilitating flow of conversation through backchanneling, follow-up questions, and the like. Close analysis of the meet-cute scenes of several of these films reveals princesses playing a reactive or facilitative role to the male lead, as in example 3D from *Pocahontas*.

**Excerpt 3D "London? Is that your village?" (*Pocahontas*, 1995)**

POCAHONTAS:   What was that?
JOHN SMITH:   My compass.
POCAHONTAS:   Compass?

JOHN SMITH:      It tells you how to find your way when you get lost. But it's all right, I'll get another one in London.
POCAHONTAS:      London? Is that your village?
JOHN SMITH:      Yes, it's a very big village.
POCAHONTAS:      What's it like?
JOHN SMITH:      Well, it's got streets filled with carriages and bridges over the rivers and buildings as tall as trees.
POCAHONTAS:      I'd like to see those things.
JOHN SMITH:      You will.
POCAHONTAS:      How?
JOHN SMITH:      We're going to build them here. We'll show your people how to use this land properly. How to make the most of it.
POCAHONTAS:      Make the most of it?
JOHN SMITH:      Yes, we'll build roads and decent houses and—
POCAHONTAS:      Our houses are fine.
JOHN SMITH:      You think that, only because you don't know any better. Wait a minute, don't take it that— Hey, hey, wait! Wait, wait! There's so much we can teach you. We've improved the lives of savages all over the world.
POCAHONTAS:      Savages?!
JOHN SMITH:      Uh, not that you're a savage.
POCAHONTAS:      Just my people.
JOHN SMITH:      No, listen, that's not what I meant. Let me explain—
POCAHONTAS:      Let go!
JOHN SMITH:      No, I'm not letting you leave. Look, don't do this. "Savage" is just a word. You know. A term for. . . people who are uncivilized.
POCAHONTAS:      Like me.

In this example, the majority of substantial dialogue is given by John Smith. He delivers the majority of the expository information, and also the majority of emotional information. Pocahontas, on the other hand, plays a facilitative role: most of her lines are either minimal responses, generally in direct reaction to the topic or question from the male lead, or questions encouraging John to talk further.

Notably, none of the movies in the Renaissance draw negative attention to this dynamic. This is particularly interesting because, to serve Disney's Girl Power brand of the 1990s, princesses in these films do call out their co-leads for behavior the film frames as problematic. Pocahontas does exactly this in Excerpt 3D by calling out John Smith on overtly racist statements. Jasmine, too, challenges Aladdin's assumptions in *Aladdin*: as he explains how dangerous Agrabah can be, she outperforms him on maneuvering through the streets before telling him she's a "fast learner." However, conversational dominance does not seem to be on the table as a behavior to be critiqued. In fact, almost the opposite seems to be true: these conversations and their correlates in other films are framed as a meeting of two different but equal minds, and the beginning of a romantic connection.

The amount of dyadic dialogue in the New Age films is substantially higher than in the Renaissance. But as the numbers rise, the discrepancy between male and female speech amounts remains. This is true even as the overall proportional amount of female speech in these films is usually equal to or greater than the amount of male speech, and the individual princesses on their own take up more screen time than either of the previous eras. It seems as if even though princesses are becoming more agential and take up a greater portion of the story, gendered speech expectations are still playing a role when engaging in one-on-one conversations.

### Girlfriends, Buddies, and Bosses: Pixar's Mixed-Gender Leads

Unlike Disney's leads, Pixar's leads do not have a clear pattern in terms of who dominates conversation. Only six films (*Toy Story 2*, *Finding Nemo*, *The Incredibles*, *Ratatouille*, *Cars 2*, *Cars 3*) have ratios of male to female speech that differ significantly from an even 50–50 split. Of those, three (*The Incredibles*, *Ratatouille*, *Cars 3*) show the female lead speaking significantly more than the male lead. No clear patterns emerge when considering potential social factors that could contribute to conversational dominance. For example, the nature of the relationship doesn't have a clear effect: romantic pairs (e.g. *A Bug's Life*, *The Incredibles*, *Cars*, *Ratatouille*, *Cars 2*, *Brave*)

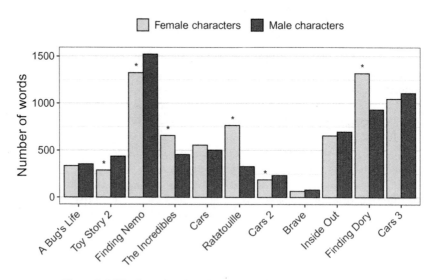

Figure 3.6 Words spoken by mixed-gender leading pairs in Pixar films
* Denotes that word count proportion is significantly different than 50–50 (p < 0.05)

have all three outcomes represented. Implied ethnicity/class differences (e.g. *Ratatouille*, *Cars 2*, *Brave*, *Cars 3*) also yield no clear pattern, nor does time of release.

The lack of a clear gender-based pattern speaks to Pixar's wide variation in both plot structure and characterization. Pixar's more complicated plot structures lead to characters interacting in a more diverse range of contexts, landing them in a variety of situations where social factors besides gender may affect how their dialogue is written. For example, in *Ratatouille*, the majority of Colette's and Linguini's dialogue takes place inside their place of employment, where Colette is ranked higher than Linguini. In example 3E, the power difference shows as she teaches Linguini how to properly cut vegetables.

**Excerpt 3E "You cannot be mommy" (*Ratatouille*, 2007)**

COLETTE:    What are you doing?
LINGUINI:   I'm cutting. Vegetables. I'm cutting the vegetables?
COLETTE:    No. You waste energy and time! You think cooking is a cute job, huh? Like mommy in the kitchen? Well mommy never had to face the dinner rush when the orders come flooding in and every dish is different and none are simple and all have different cooking times but must arrive on the customer's table at exactly the same time, hot and perfect. Every second counts – and you cannot be Mommy!

Colette's dominance in this exchange is obvious. Linguini only speaks when asked a direct question, and even when he answers, it's stuttering and unsure. Colette interrupts his only line firmly, and finishes the exchange with a long teaching monologue. She has institutional power and expertise, both of which give her the right to the floor over Linguini, gender notwithstanding.

Situations where female leads have the institutional right to the floor tend to come up more often in Pixar than in Disney: Atta is the leader of Flik's colony in *A Bug's Life*, Joy is the leader of Riley's brain in *Inside Out*, Cruz is Lightning McQueen's trainer in *Cars 3*, and so forth. Comparatively, most Disney princesses either have no power at the start of the film (e.g. *Sleeping Beauty*, *Cinderella*, *Beauty and the Beast*, *Mulan*, *Tangled*) or are away from the context where their power matters (*Snow White*, *The Little Mermaid*, *Pocahontas*, *Brave*, *Moana*).

## Qualitative Discussion: Framing Talkativeness and Silence

Our quantitative findings so far have revealed that male characters talk decidedly more than female characters in the aggregate in both Disney and Pixar, and that they also tend towards conversational dominance in one-on-one conversations in the Disney Princess films. For Pixar lead characters, gender doesn't appear to be a primary factor in who dominates conversation. But importantly, our data absolutely do not confirm the myth that women talk more than men, at least as portrayed in these films.

With that in mind, we now turn our attention to a qualitative analysis of "talkativeness," a salient concept in Disney and Pixar. There are quite a few characters throughout these films that could be described as talkative, chatty, fast-talking, and the like, and still others who are taciturn, shy, or disengaged. In the following sections, we qualitatively explore gender differences in how Disney and Pixar choose to frame different personalities vis-à-vis their talkativeness, and compare their characterizations with our own understanding of the films based on our quantitative data.

### Framing Men's Talk

Both Disney and Pixar have quite a few male characters that could easily be called talkative. However, we want to make a key distinction between "talkative" and "*too* talkative." Male characters tend to be framed as the former, not the latter. Disney and Pixar often encourage the viewer to interpret male talkativeness as a measure of wit and charm. Certain Renaissance and New Age Disney princes, like Aladdin (*Aladdin*), Naveen (*The Princess and the Frog*), and Flynn Rider (*Tangled*) illustrate the trope particularly well. Aladdin and Flynn Rider are both the most talkative characters in their respective films, and all three characters talk significantly more than their romantic co-lead (as illustrated above). They're each characterized in their film as being talkative in conversation with others, but this isn't really framed as a bad thing. For example, Prince Naveen is introduced in the following scene in *The Princess and the Frog*:

**Excerpt 3F "Dance with me, fat man" (*The Princess and the Frog*, 2009)**

| | |
|---|---|
| LAWRENCE: | Sire... I've been looking for you everywhere! |
| NAVEEN: | Ooh what a coincidence, Lawrence. I've been avoiding you everywhere! |
| LAWRENCE: | We are going to be late for the Masquerade. |
| NAVEEN: | Listen, Lawrence, listen. Ah ha ha! It's jazz, it's jazz music! It was born here. It's beautiful, no? |
| LAWRENCE: | No! |
| NAVEEN: | Oh, dance with me, fat man. Stay loose, Lawrence! |
| LAWRENCE: | We're supposed to be at La Bouff's estate by now. |
| NAVEEN: | Yes, yes, yes. But first... I buy everyone here a drink! |
| LAWRENCE: | With what? At this point you have two choices – woo and marry a rich young lady or... Get a job. |
| NAVEEN: | Ugh. All right, fine but first... We dance! |
| LAWRENCE: | Oh this is idiocy. |

NAVEEN:      For someone who can't see his feet, you're very light on them! *[Lawrence falls, lands on tuba.]* Ha ha! It's perfect. You finally got into the music! Do you get my joke? Because your head is, it is in the tuba!

LAWRENCE:    Get me out!

NAVEEN:      All right all right. Hold on.

In this exchange, Naveen interrupts, ignores, or talks over his assistant Lawrence's utterances at almost every conversational turn. He also continues to talk at Lawrence even when he has fallen and is physically unable to respond. Naveen's behavior in this scene is meant to introduce him to the audience as a carefree character who is extremely charismatic (albeit a bit conceited). The things he says are clever (like the quip *I've been avoiding you everywhere*). He always seems to be in control of what he says and when he says it, and he doesn't seem particularly concerned with the reaction his conversational dominance will elicit in Lawrence. Other fast-talking male characters share a similar amount of wit and control. Characters around these charismatic heroes often yield the floor to let them speak, and although they may take issue with *what* the male character says, they almost never take issue with *how long* it took for him to say it.

When negative attention is drawn to male speech patterns, it's not about their talkativeness – it's about their silence. The dynamic of the silent or stoic male character pitted against a more talkative character (usually female) is a trope we found several times over, particularly in Pixar films. For example, in a scene in *Inside Out*, the main character Riley sits at a dinner table with her mother and father. The central conceit of this film is that each character's "brain" is visualized as a set of internal emotions. As Riley's mother asks her about her day, Riley's father remains distant and disengaged; the punchline turns out to be that the father's emotions are watching a rerun of a hockey game instead of paying attention. When the mother finally catches his eye, his emotions panic and scramble to figure out the subject of the conversation.

*The Incredibles* is an even more exaggerated example of male disengagement. This movie has a similar dinner scene to *Inside Out* in that while the family is seated at the table, Mrs. Incredible asks the children about their days while Mr. Incredible reads the newspaper and ignores the social situation around him. Unlike the father in *Inside Out*, Mr. Incredible actively resists conversational participation even though Mrs. Incredible calls him out on his disengagement (*Do you have to read at the table?*). Eventually, the scene escalates and the two children begin fighting at the table, and still Mr. Incredible stays out of the conversation until Mrs. Incredible yells, *Bob! It's time to engage. Do something! Don't just stand there! I need you to intervene!* In both examples, the patriarch of the family is characterized as inappropriately taciturn, and the wife as the speaker responsible for conversational and emotional facilitation.

Male characters can also be shown as not only silent, but as poor communicators even when they're attempting to engage. This is used to comedic effect when male characters attempt to talk to their romantic interest: Shang in *Mulan*, for example, is obviously a competent leader and communicator throughout the film until he tries to tell Mulan he has romantic feelings for her, at which point he can only stutter out, *You... you fight good.* Buzz Lightyear, another cool and collected character in a leadership position, stutters through talking to his crush Jessie for the first time in *Toy Story 2* by saying *Uh, m—ma'am, I, uh— well, I just wanted to say you're a bright young woman with a beautiful yarnful of hair. Uh, a hairful of yarn. It's uh— whoo— uh— I must go.*

Male characters' lack of communicative competence also comes out in higher-stakes emotional situations. They are often depicted as shunning emotional communication, and though they may open up, it occurs only after intense goading from another character (who is, once again, often female). Traditionally masculine characters like Sully (*Monsters, Inc.*), Buzz (*Toy Story*), and Mr. Incredible (*The Incredibles*) all have dramatic moments in their respective franchises that are defined by their deliberately disengaging from an emotional conversation mid-conflict, leaving their conversational partners hanging. We find a particularly dramatic illustration of this dynamic in *Moana*, when Moana asks her co-star Maui (an otherwise confident and talkative demigod) about his tattoos:

**Excerpt 3G "Nunya business" (*Moana*, 2016)**

MOANA:    How do you get your tattoos?
MAUI:      They show up. When I earn them.
MOANA:    How'd you earn that one? What's that for?
MAUI:      That's man's discovery of Nunya.
MOANA:    What's Nunya?
MAUI:      Nunya business.
MOANA:    I'll just keep asking. What's it for?
MAUI:      You need to stop doing that. Back off.
MOANA:    Just tell me what it is.
MAUI:      I said back off.
MOANA:    Is it why your hook's not working?
MAUI:      [doesn't respond]
MOANA:    You don't want to talk, don't talk. You wanna throw me off the boat, throw me off. You wanna tell me I don't know what I'm doing, I know I don't. I have no idea why the ocean chose me. You're right. But my island is dying, so I am here. It's just me and you. And I want to help but I can't, if you don't let me.

In this exchange, the female character is once again characterized as the facilitator of conversation, and the male character as resistant to communication. Maui uses several strategies to stay disengaged: he makes jokes (*nunya business*), gives insufficient/minimal responses to her questions *(They show up)*, overtly tells Moana to stop talking *(back off)*, and eventually just shuts down entirely. Moana, meanwhile, doggedly tries to keep the conversation going by asking questions and ignoring these uncooperative strategies. When he finally shuts down, she responds by desperately trying to convince him to re-engage.

Instances like those in *Moana, The Incredibles,* and *Inside Out* once again hearken to the stereotypical concept of women as more interactionally facilitative than men. This idea is consistent with a gender difference approach, as seen in the two cultures model we mentioned in Chapter 1, associated particularly with Maltz and Borker (1982) and Tannen (1996). This model argues that men and women speak differently because they are socialized in different peer groups. Boys play with other boys, and girls play with other girls, and the childhood separation leads to two models of how language should be used, similar to the differences between people from two different countries. What results is a view of language wherein men's speech is supposedly hierarchical and full of arguing and verbal posturing (what Tannen calls *report talk*), while women's speech is supposedly more focused on cooperation and mutual engagement (what Tannen calls *rapport talk*).

The two cultures model has mostly been relegated to history by scholars in linguistics or gender studies, because it ignores intersectionality, reinforces a binary, and fails to explain how our daily interactions with people from the alleged "other culture" don't lead to a high degree of mutual understanding.[11] Some evidence suggests that women do tend to use facilitative, rapport-based conversational strategies at higher rates than men, including backchanneling (Eckert & McConnell-Ginet 2013), supportive laughter (Eckert & McConnell-Ginet 2013), and attention beginnings (Fishman 1978). And indeed, readers socialized as women may resonate with the experience of doing an undue amount of interactional labor to keep conversation going, which can be frustrating. It would be more accurate, though, to say that there are enduring ideological links between facilitative style and feminine performance, which women may or may not draw on depending on context.

However, the idea that men and women have fundamentally and immutably different relationships to conversation is powerfully enduring, and on display in all of the scenes listed above. In all three, the women in the scene are portrayed as ostensibly responsible for the continued flow of conversation, as

---

[11] Amusingly, it also suggests, if taken to its natural conclusion, that couples consisting of two men or two women should have minimal difficulties with communication.

well as the emotional well-being of all interlocutors, keyed into the emotional connection at the heart of the conversation in a way that lines up with Tannen's description of *rapport talk*. The male reticence or even resistance, on the other hand, paints men as naturally less talkative, interested in preserving independence and status (as Tannen argues).

These examples also suggest a natural opposition between the two approaches to conversation. The male characters continue to resist or struggle with communication even with explicit demands, explanations, and assistance from the female characters, implying that this is not merely a miscommunication but a deeply ingrained difference that can't be surmounted. *Inside Out* even goes so far as to tie the difference to literal biology, implying that men interact differently at the dinner table because their brains are wired to wander off. Although all our examples in this section frame the male character's silence as the negative element rather than the female facilitation, the stereotype is still naturalized through the repeated pattern of male silence.

### The Exceptionality of Jewish Identity

We mentioned in the introduction that for the sake of scope, we're mostly limiting our analysis to gender in isolation and putting ethnicity, class, and other identity markers on the back burner until they become qualitatively relevant. Well, here we are at qualitative relevance. We found in our analysis that although male talkativeness is mostly neutrally or positively framed, and that male characters are more often called out for their silence than their chattiness, there is one notable exception: the case of characters who are linguistically coded as Jewish. Although this isn't our field of expertise per se, we nevertheless wanted to take a moment to linger on this troubling pattern.[12]

We define characters linguistically coded as Jewish by adapting Lippi-Green's (2011) methods of analyzing linguistic minorities in Disney. We particularly looked for two criteria: first, since modern movies are often sold on the star power of their voice actors, we looked at whether the voice actor of the character in question was Jewish, and particularly if their Jewish identity was part of their "brand" as a celebrity. And second, we looked at the linguistic performance itself. "Jewish English" is a difficult concept to nail down; it's "not a uniform linguistic entity spoken by a uniform group of Jews. It is an

---

[12] If you want to read scholarship from those for whom this is their field of expertise, we encourage you to go read one of the several excellent pieces of scholarship written about race- and class-based linguistic patterns in children's media. Lippi-Green (2011) has a seminal work on the subject.

abstract umbrella term representing the English-based speech of Jews in America, and it encompasses a great deal of inter-speaker and intra-speaker variation" (Benor 2009, 2011). However, one common element of the Jewish English repertoire is the borrowing or retaining of features from New York English. New York English has also become a national stereotypical symbol for Jewish English, potentially because of the many culturally influential Jewish New Yorkers who have helped define Jewish American identity in the popular consciousness (Nosowitz 2016). Because of that, New York English has become somewhat of an easy shorthand for Jewish identity and is often used in conjunction with lexical and visual markers to construct Jewish characters on TV (Porsgaard 2019).

Looking at characters who fulfill these criteria, we find that Jewish-coded men make up the vast majority of male characters who are characterized as *too* talkative. Some of these characters, such as Mike Wazowski (*Monsters, Inc.*), Rex (*Toy Story*), and Marlin (*Finding Nemo*), are portrayed as nervous over-thinkers who worry aloud. Others, like Scuttle the Seagull (*The Little Mermaid*), Molt (*A Bug's Life*), and more subtly, Olaf (*Frozen & Frozen II*), are portrayed as unintelligent or situationally tone-deaf types, whose urge to speak overrides any notion of inappropriateness. And still more, like Iago (*Aladdin*) and Mr. Potato Head (*Toy Story* franchise), are portrayed as worriers gone aggressive: characters who angrily or anxiously interject at inappropriate times with their negativity.[13] Unlike the other fast-talking male characters, these characters rarely seem in control of how much they're talking or how it will affect the people around them. These caricatures may have a root in the discursive style of New York Jewish families identified by Deborah Tannen (1981), which is characterized by fast rates of speech and turn-taking. But we also sense the presence of several Jewish American stereotypes, including neurotic behavior, neediness, and pushiness (Tanny 2017).

Although we saw this mostly manifested in male characters, the language stereotype does still seem to apply to female characters as well. Mrs. Potato Head from the *Toy Story* franchise is one of the only Jewish-coded female characters in Disney and Pixar, and – surprise! – she's also framed as inappropriately talkative. Her stereotypical behavior seems rooted in the stereotype of the "Jewish Mother" (Mock 1999). She's self-sacrificing and overbearing; several jokes take place throughout the franchise of her talking over Mr. Potato Head, even though he is also framed as talkative and aggressive.

---

[13] The actors playing the discussed characters in the above paragraph are, in order: Billy Crystal, Wallace Shawn, Albert Brooks, Buddy Hackett, Richard Kind, Josh Gad, Gilbert Gotfried, and Don Rickles. All Jewish; all from New York. We smell a pattern.

She's also comically punished for her talkativeness. In one particularly striking scene in *Toy Story 3*, Mrs. Potato Head gets in an argument with the central villain of the film, saying, *who do you think you're talking to? I have over thirty accessories, and I deserve more respect!* Or at least, that's what she begins to say – in the middle of the word "respect," the villain literally plucks her mouth out of her toy body, mockingly saying *ah, that's better.* In reaction to this, Mr. Potato Head comes to her defense – by taking the mouth back and returning it to his wife. But while doing so he exclaims, *no one takes my wife's mouth except me!* The alternate toy universe of *Toy Story* renders this violent exchange cartoonish, but we find the imagery both alarming and rather on-the-nose.

Male Jewish-coded characters are also often silenced by their peers, sometimes quite violently. Jafar silences Iago multiple times in *Aladdin* by kicking him, throwing him, or grabbing his beak or throat. In one scene in *A Bug's Life*, Molt interrupts his older brother Hopper with a very ill-timed and embarrassing story; Hopper responds by pinning him against a wall and saying, *I swear, if I hadn't promised mother on her deathbed that I wouldn't kill you... I would kill you!... Shut up! I don't want to hear another word out of your mouth while we're on this island. Do you understand me?* Other characters get treatments that are less violent, but still communicate negative reactions from other characters. Olaf and Iago, for example, both monologue to no one in particular during their movies, while their peers stare deadpan into the distance, suggesting a festering annoyance or dissatisfaction with the chatty character. In short, Jewish-coded male characters talk *too much* for the characters around them. The framing seems to hold true of the one female character who fits a similar stereotype, suggesting that it's Jewish identity, and not necessarily gender, that's being stereotyped as overly talkative.

### Framing Women's Talk

So, what about the myth of female talkativeness? Interestingly, Disney and Pixar both provide some explicit metacommentary on this stereotype. Earlier, we discussed how the Princess movies (and some Pixar movies, to a lesser extent) use cartoonishly exaggerated patriarchy as a foil for their female protagonists. Well, it turns out that one of the sexist talking points that Disney villains rely on is specifically that women shouldn't talk as much, or even that silence is ideal for a woman. One of the most prominent and well-known examples is the epigraph for this chapter: in *The Little Mermaid*, Ursula sings to Ariel, *The men up there don't like a lot of blabber / They think a girl who gossips is a bore / Yes on land it's much preferred for ladies not to say a word / And after all dear, what is idle prattle for?* In *Aladdin*, Jafar tells

Jasmine *You're speechless, I see. A fine quality in a wife.*[14] In *Mulan*, there are multiple characters who state that the status quo would be for Mulan to be silent:

> To please your future in-laws you must demonstrate a sense of dignity and refinement. You must also be poised... And silent! | Matchmaker

> You would do well to teach your daughter to hold her tongue in a man's presence. | Chi Fu

> A girl who's got a brain, who always speaks her mind? NAH. | Mulan's friends in the army

These examples suggest that Disney equates women's silence with sexism and patriarchy. And by having villains (or at least unpleasant side characters like the matchmaker) parrot those lines, they're clearly trying to align the audience against the overt expression of such regressive views.

But we find that this message is undercut by the fact that negative stereotypes of women as overly talkative are very much alive and well in Disney and Pixar. Often, they'll be in the exact same movie as the explicit feminist talking points: while the main character is busy talking about how much she doesn't want to be silenced, in the very next scene there will be some casual joke about how women talk too much.

These casual comedic stereotypes frame female talkativeness as a function of emotionality, shallowness, and airheadedness. *Beauty and the Beast*, for example, features three female characters who are nameless but are collectively known as the "Bimbettes" in the official script. These characters appear following Gaston around, offering constant commentary along the lines of, *Look there he goes, isn't he dreamy? / Look there he goes, oh he's so cute!* In some scenes, the content of their talk isn't even intelligible, but rather just a sort of mess of giggles and tittering in response to Gaston's actions. A similar unintelligible chatter is seen in *Mulan*, when three of the main male characters dress up as women to sneak into the royal palace: their drag performance

---

[14] Disney just doubled down on this line in their new remake of *Aladdin* from 2019 by giving Jasmine an entire song to herself called "speechless." Here are just a few of the lyrics:

> Written in stone
> Every rule, every word
> Centuries-old and unbending
> "Stay in your place"
> "Better seen and not heard"
> Well, now that story is ending
> ...
> I won't be silenced
> You can't keep me quiet
> Won't tremble when you try it
> All I know is I won't go speechless

consists mostly of wearing women's clothes, whispering constantly to each other, and giggling while approaching the male guards. This is the same movie where in so many places, they insisted that women's silence is regressive and abhorrent. It feels like Disney can't decide whether women's speech is admirable or laughable.

There are talkative female characters in Disney and Pixar that are more developed but still have similar Bimbette qualities of being shallow, somewhat empty-headed, and excitable. Some minor characters, such as Karrie, Violet's hapless babysitter friend from *The Incredibles*, or Mike's girlfriend Celia in *Monsters, Inc.*, fall into this category. Both are young and stereotypically feminine; both externally process their feelings; neither seems to particularly understand what's going most of the time.

But the queen of the Bimbette characters is undoubtedly Lottie, Princess Tiana's friend from *The Princess and the Frog*, whose talkativeness is the central focus of several different scenes in the film. Lottie is a young, blonde, white, traditionally feminine character; like all the bimbettes before her, she's characterized as emotionally volatile and not very smart. In the following scene, Lottie and her father are preparing to tell Tiana some important news:

### Excerpt 3H "Tell her, oh tell her Big Daddy!" (*The Princess and the Frog*, 2009)

LOTTIE:     Did you get the news? Tell her, oh tell her Big Daddy!
LABOUFF:    Oh, yeah. Prince Naveen. . .
LOTTIE:     Prince Naveen of Maldonia is coming to New Orleans! Ah ha ha! Oh isn't he the bee's knees? Oh tell her what you did, Big Daddy. Tell her!
LABOUFF:    Well, I invited. . .
LOTTIE:     Big Daddy invited the prince to a masquerade ball tonight! Oh! Oh tell her what else you did Big Daddy. Go on.
LABOUFF:    And he's stayin'. . .
LOTTIE:     And he's stay— *[LaBouff stuffs food into Lottie's mouth.]*
LABOUFF:    And he's stayin' in our house as my personal guest.

In this exchange, humor is drawn from Lottie's apparent inability to know when to be silent and let her father take the turn she is requesting that he take. The body language of each character enhances the humor of this scene: Lottie bounces around, speaks loudly and quickly, and even shakes her father in her excitement to share news. LaBouff is comparatively silent and stoic throughout this scene. LaBouff's final triumph in taking the floor from Lottie comes not from her willing relinquishment, but from the fact that LaBouff stuffs food in her mouth to make it impossible for her to talk.

In newer Disney Princess movies, even the heroines are being painted as overly talkative. Princesses like Rapunzel (*Tangled*) and Anna (*Frozen*) are both framed in their films as chatty – at times, *too* chatty. Although they're heroines, their particular brand of talkativeness traces easily back to the earlier Bimbette-style characters. They're young and feminine; they talk because they're excited and excitable; they process their feelings externally; they're extremely positive, almost to the point of naivete; they don't always seem to sense when their speech goes overboard. The audience's attention is sometimes drawn to the relative chattiness of the lead woman in relation to her male counterpart for comedic effect, even if the male character is otherwise considered talkative. Take *Tangled*, for example. Although Flynn Rider is a charming, fast-talking character, there's still a long gag sequence in the movie that features him being stoically silent compared to Rapunzel's uncontrolled monologuing. Rapunzel has just left her tower for the first time, and the audience is treated to a short montage of her emotionally processing her decision. Each line features a new scene in the montage; in every new scene Flynn Rider can be seen standing quietly in the corner of the frame, looking bored or annoyed.

**Excerpt 3I "A little at war with yourself" (*Tangled*, 2011)**

| | |
|---|---|
| RAPUNZEL: | I can't believe I did this. I can't believe I did this. I can't believe I did this! |
| | Mother would be so furious. |
| RAPUNZEL: | That's okay! I mean, what she doesn't know won't kill her, right? |
| RAPUNZEL: | Oh my gosh, this would kill her. |
| RAPUNZEL: | This is so fun! |
| RAPUNZEL: | I am a horrible daughter. I'm going back. |
| RAPUNZEL: | I am never going back! Woo-hoo! |
| RAPUNZEL: | I am a despicable human being. |
| RAPUNZEL: | Woo-hoo! Best. Day. Ever! |
| FLYNN: | Hmm. You know, I can't help but notice you seem a little at war with yourself here. |
| RAPUNZEL: | What? |

Flynn's response is indicative of the responses to a lot of talkative female characters. Unlike Jewish-coded characters, most female talkativeness isn't met with violence, or even with explicit requests for silence. Indeed, those kinds of overt requests seem mostly reserved for villains. Instead of violence, female characters get eye-rolls. Quiet glares. Resigned tolerance. Or even less than that, a quiet invitation from the movies themselves to chuckle at just how much women can talk if you let them.

## Conclusion

In this chapter, we've used a variety of techniques to try to uncover the relationship between Disney and Pixar and linguistic ideologies of talkativeness and conversational dominance. We especially wanted to explore these studios' relationships to female representation – how well they manage to foreground female characters and voices, and how they reinforce or challenge the pervasive myth of the talkative woman.

In the Disney Princess films, we found that male characters and male speech are both *very* overrepresented. The preponderance of minor male characters throughout Disney makes for skewed storyworlds where masculinity is the default gender. A more fine-grained analysis revealed that princes are conversationally dominant over princesses in every movie except *Mulan* (where the princess pretends to be a man for most of the plot). Although Disney's branding talks a big game about progressive feminist values, it seems like the studio still consistently underrepresents female characters, and reinforces the expectation that women should speak less than men.

Pixar also overrepresents male characters, at times even more drastically than Disney does. Male speech is also overrepresented except in the few films with female protagonists. This is a solid confirmation of Pixar's reputation as a "boys' club," where masculinity is the default expectation for both major and minor characters. However, analysis of Pixar's male and female co-leads showed neither gender consistently talking over the other. This suggests to us that Pixar has an issue of attention: when Pixar focuses on writing women, the result is a more diverse set of talkative, well-rounded female characters with varying levels of power and assertion within their relationships. However, the presentation of femininity outside these one or two characters in each film tends to be much more problematic, or altogether missing in favor of a host of male background characters.

Qualitatively, we found that in both studios the impression of talkativeness is at odds with the data we collected. While male characters consistently take up more space, both in aggregate and in individual conversations, the framing and characterization of talkativeness suggests that it's *women* who are emotional, gossipy, and overly talkative. Male characters are, on the other hand, more likely to be framed as disengaged or poor communicators. Not only does this support the myth of women as comparatively talkative, but it also supports a related language myth that women are more in tune with the emotional function of language, and therefore naturally put more effort into facilitating the flow of conversation.

Actually, it's not right to say that these qualitative findings are "at odds" with our quantitative results. In fact, they support the exact same-gender ideology that circulates elsewhere in mainstream media: that women talk too much, even when they don't talk as much as men. By using the stereotypes of "chatty lady" and "stoic man," Disney and Pixar contradict the amount they themselves show women speaking; but they do cohesively reproduce regressive expectations about when and how women participate in conversation. This is a shame, especially in light of how much the texts of some of these movies parrot feminist talking points about how women shouldn't be silenced.

That being said, we caution against drawing broad conclusions from analysis of representation alone. Questions like "who talks more" are tempting to spotlight, because they feel straightforward and definitive to answer. It's the same reason popular culture has gone through periods of obsession with the Bechdel–Wallace Test.[15] The idea of answering whether a movie is sexist by determining whether it checks off basic criteria on a list is in some ways very appealing (and very easy to write fun listicle articles about). Appealing, yes. But not adequate. We love the way Jennifer O'Meara (2016) put it:

> It is not enough to ask how many female characters talk . . . without also considering the broader complexities of their speech: what do they discuss? When and where do they discuss it? How do they phrase it? How is it performed? . . . Addressing these questions can help to create a more pluralistic understanding of female dialogue, one which resists the tendency found in literature on Classical Hollywood cinema to reduce all female speech to a single set of norms. (O'Meara 2016)

Simple counts like speech amounts or the Bechdel–Wallace test provide an interesting introduction to conversations about representation and feminist ideology. However, if it's the end of the conversation rather than the beginning, it becomes not only unhelpful, but also damaging and obfuscating to the nuance required for feminist inquiry; it becomes more likely to "conceal rather than reveal" (O'Meara 2016).

So, that's what the rest of the book is for. For the following four chapters, we're going to explore specific language features and how they vary in frequency and style depending on gender. We consider this chapter an important jumping-off point for subsequent analyses, since it will allow us to accurately account for the skewed representation we discovered. By using multiple "angles" of quantitative and qualitative linguistic analysis, we hope to add nuance to these preliminary findings.

---

[15] More commonly known as the Bechdel Test. It originally appeared in the comic *Dykes to Watch Out For*, authored by cartoonist Allison Bechdel in 1985 based on an idea by the author's friend, Liz Wallace. The criteria, for those unfamiliar, is that a movie must have (1) at least two named female characters, who (2) talk to each other, (3) about something other than a man.

# 4    Compliments

She's the one! The lucky girl I'm going to marry.
The most beautiful girl in town.
And that makes her the best. And don't I
deserve the best?

Gaston, Beauty and the Beast

## Introduction

We chose to begin our deep dive into linguistic variables with this study of the use of compliments in Disney and Pixar films. A compliment, formally speaking, is a broad speech category that includes any utterance that "explicitly or implicitly attributes credit to someone other than the speaker for some 'good'" (Holmes 1986). We wanted to start here because it represents a lot of what drew our interest to studying language in the media in the first place. Compliments, in attributing 'goods' to others, naturally carry with them larger value judgments about what a society views as 'good.' So, using compliments as an analytical lens for kids' movies gives us a great view into what the filmmakers considered worthy of praise in their characters – and importantly, whether that varies by gender.

The Princess movies are of particular interest to us in this regard. As discussed in Chapter 2, the concept of "princess" brings with it complicated ideas about ideal femininity, but one of the concepts at its base is the importance of physical beauty. Walt's original princesses are not exactly famous for their degrees in organic chemistry or their knowledge of fine wines. So we were curious to know how their appearance in particular was framed in the story, something on which compliments could offer an important window.

In addition to communicating value, compliments are also speech acts that have social lives of their own. The primary purpose of a compliment is to establish or maintain social rapport. Compliments are, on their surface, a way to be "nice" to someone, and because niceness (or *politeness*, as we will discuss shortly) is often associated with femininity, we anticipate that our analysis may find compliment use to be ideologically related to gender in some way. In this chapter, we examine compliments through these various lenses: who compliments whom in Disney and Pixar, and how are the uses and implications of compliments shifting according to the gender of the giver and receiver? On top of that, what do the compliments given to male and female characters say about the norms of societal "goods," and what message about that are we passing on to children?

## Background

### Gender and Politeness

Before digging directly into compliments, we want to pause and define exactly what we mean linguistically when we talk about *politeness*. Politeness is actually a broad theoretical framework in linguistics first introduced by Brown and Levinson (1987). They describe politeness as all language aimed at attending to another person's *face*. When we talk about people's *face*, we're talking about their basic social desires. On one hand, there's *positive face* – the desire to be liked, appreciated, and maintain self-esteem. And on the other, there's *negative face*, which is the desire to be autonomous and independent. Polite language is the act of catering to these two basic kinds of face needs through expressing affection and affirmation (*positive politeness*) or by trying to avoid imposition and maximizing choice (*negative politeness*). Politeness also means trying to avoid or mitigate *face-threatening acts*, which are those linguistic acts that in some way encroach on or damage someone's sense of self-esteem or autonomy. Attending to others' face needs is a crucial element of interacting with others, and so politeness tends to extend into almost every part of linguistic performance in some way or another.

So, when we say that women are imagined to be more "polite" than men, we don't just mean that they allegedly say "please" more often. We mean that women have historically been saddled with a greater expectation of catering to the face needs of others than men have. Consequently, research in numerous communities finds evidence that women adopt polite behaviors at higher rates than men, and conversely may tend to avoid impolite behaviors, at least in certain contexts. We return to this concept throughout the next four chapters, since politeness differences manifest across speech acts in ways that will be relevant for gendered analysis.

Compliments are a textbook positive politeness strategy, since their primary force is to affirm another's self-esteem. As Holmes (2013) points out, "Compliments are usually intended to make others feel good (see Wierzbicka 1987: 201). The primary function is most obviously affective and social, rather than referential or informative . . . serving to increase or consolidate solidarity between the speaker and addressee" (Holmes 2013: 118). However, while this is their primary purpose, compliments can be used as a mitigating strategy for other social purposes: they can butter someone up for a request, cushion or hide criticism, or even veil mockery. The following chapter, therefore, is partially an inquiry into whether female characters are involved with positive politeness more than male characters. But we also inquire as to how characters use and interpret this politeness strategy, and whether politeness as a means to an end (or as veiled criticism) is also presented in a gendered way.

### What We Know about Compliments in Humans and Other Non-Mermaids

Early studies of compliments based on corpora from English-speaking countries reported consistently that women tend to be both the givers and receivers of compliments at a significantly higher rate than men (Herbert 1990; Holmes 1986, 1988; Manes 1983; Wolfson 1984). More recent studies (e.g. Parisi & Wogan 2006) also support this finding, but to varying degrees. Rees-Miller (2011), for example, raised methodological questions about the preponderance of female fieldworkers in many studies, which may have skewed the data in favor of compliments to and from women. Her study found that women and men actually compliment each other about the same amount if there is a direct task at hand. In unstructured social environments, though, her data confirmed the finding that compliments are exchanged more by women. These studies also found gender-based differences in the syntactical patterns typically used for compliments (Holmes 2013), the choice of personal/impersonal focus (Herbert 1990), and in compliment response behavior, such as acceptance or rejection (Herbert 1990; Pomerantz 1978).

Much of the previous research focuses on compliment topics. Wolfson (1984) found that compliments based on the addressee's appearance were the most common type of compliment in the corpus, and that the vast majority of them were directed towards women. Compliments on the addressee's abilities or skill were the second most common type and by far the most common towards men. Holmes (2013) similarly found that appearance and skills were the most frequent topics, and that women were more likely to receive compliments on appearance, whereas men were most likely to receive compliments on their skills. This finding has been replicated by more recent studies as well (Parisi & Wogan 2006; Rees-Miller 2011). Rees-Miller comments that "Men infrequently compliment on appearance in any setting, and men almost never address appearance compliments to other men. Men are far more likely to compliment an addressee on performance, whether the addressee is male or female" (2011: 2682). She notes that women, on the other hand, give performance-based compliments in situations with a central task or goal, but in less-structured environments tend to favor appearance-based compliments.

Researchers have suggested that women's higher frequency of complimenting – particularly with one another – may be rooted in a gendered difference in how compliments are interpreted. Holmes (1998) posits that women interpret compliments as "primarily positively affective speech acts ... expressing solidarity and positive politeness," whereas men "may give greater weight to their referential meaning, as evaluative judgments, or to potentially negative face-threatening features" (106). She found this to be especially true with appearance-based compliments: "to compliment another man on his hair, his clothes or his body is an *extremely* face-threatening thing to do, both for speaker and hearer. It has to be very carefully done in order not to send out the wrong signals" (Britain, personal communication, cited in Holmes 2011: 82). Kiesling (2005) suggests that the taboo on male-to-male compliments has to do with heterosexual men's aversion to appearing affectionate toward or desirous of other men, even platonically; this in turn is related to the fear of being perceived as queer, and therefore less masculine. In his studies, he found that college fraternity brothers avoid earnest compliments almost entirely, and instead used socially indirect methods of showing affection, such as insults.[1]

Evidence suggests that inter-gender compliments also carry their own connotations. Previous research has shown no clear pattern about who gives and receives cross-gender compliments more; Holmes (2013), and Parisi and Wogan (2006) suggest that men give more compliments to women than they receive, but Herbert (1990) and Rees-Miller (2011) show no substantial differences. But one thing that is consistent is that appearance-based compliments are very much more likely to be given from man to woman than the other way around. Rees-Miller (2011) posits that when men give appearance compliments to women, it usually signals romantic interest. Parisi and Wogan found in interviews with female participants that they practice active restraint from complimenting men, especially on their appearance, because they were "constrained by gendered rules of romance: that is, females sense they have to be careful not to look like they're 'coming on too strongly' with males" (2006: 23).

It's important to note that the majority of these studies look at a narrow community of speakers (usually college students), and we know very little about the gender identities or sexual orientation of the speakers, or about other relevant social factors. So we don't want to generalize too freely or confidently about gender-related compliment behaviors. At the same time, we think we

---

[1] To read way more about that, skip ahead to Chapter 6.

*can* infer something more general about gender ideology. It appears that compliments are an unmarked (perhaps even expected) social practice for women, whereas they're much more heavily marked for men, and that cross-gender compliments have strong romantic implications; these associations impact behavior of real-life speakers to varying degrees.

Compliments also give us unique information about gender politics because they articulate positive societal judgments. Manes (1983) (among others) argues that compliments, in aggregate, serve as normative reinforcements of approved behavior. Inasmuch as these norms are enforced differently according to gender, we can expect compliments to follow suit. The topic of the compliment is particularly critical in this sense, as repeated complimenting on one topic will ultimately communicate value, or even expectation, to a listener. With regard to the gender differences in receiving appearance and skill compliments, Eckert and McConnell-Ginet (2013) posit that such a split "construct[s] normative expectations that looks and likeability will matter a lot to women and that talents and active projects will matter more to men" thereby helping to "construct and regulate the gender order" (2013: 127). Tiggemann and Boundy (2008) found in a psychological study that the societal standard of giving women appearance compliments can do some real damage:

The appearance compliment, conceptualized as part of the social environment, resulted in improved mood for everybody, as common sense would dictate. More interesting, however, for those women with high trait self-objectification, the compliment was accompanied by an increase in state body shame ... Even a positive compliment about one's appearance, which made participants feel good in general, paradoxically led to increased body shame. This counterintuitive finding supports objectification theory's contention that anything that focuses attention on external appearance, even a compliment, as in the present case, can produce negative consequences. (2008: 404)

This is why we (among many other scholars) believe it is crucial to examine and critique compliment topics: though compliments may seem nice, building a narrative of feminine value based only on appearance is not.

There's some evidence to support the notion that patterns of commentary and compliments in the media correlate with dominant gender ideologies, especially when it comes to femininity and norms of appearance and beauty. Lauzen and Dozier (2002) found in their exploration of prime-time TV that female characters received appearance comments at twice the rate of male characters. The Disney Princesses have also been called out specifically; Towbin et al. (2004) found that in a majority of Disney movies, "a woman's value is determined by her appearance rather than her intellect" (30). These studies, though there aren't many of them, suggest that female characters are valued disproportionately for beauty, perpetuating harmful ideologies about women's bodies in real life. Outside of these few, however, not much previous research has been done on complimenting behaviors in scripted media. We use this chapter to examine these behaviors from a variety of angles, and see whether Disney's and Pixar's presentation of compliment behavior reinforces (or in any way challenges) dominant ideologies of language and gender.

## Methodology

The questions we hope to answer in this study include the following:

---

**Key Questions**

- Is there a gender-based difference in **who gives and who receives compliments** in the films? If so, how is it similar to or different from the patterns found in previous studies of gender and compliments?
- Are the **topics of compliments** in the films similar to those found in previous studies? Does topic correlate with the gender of the recipient and if so, how? What ideologies of gender are being reinforced (or possibly challenged) by the use of compliments?
- Are gendered patterns of complimenting **different between the Disney Princess films and the Pixar films**, which, as discussed in Chapter 2, present gender in very different ways?
- Do patterns of gender and complimenting in the films **change over time**, particularly in the Disney films, which span almost 80 years? If so, do these changes reflect social changes in ideas about gender and gender roles?

---

### Data Collection

For the purposes of our analysis, we used the definition of compliments provided here by Janet Holmes (1986):

A compliment is a speech act which explicitly or implicitly attributes credit to someone other than the speaker, usually the person addressed, for some 'good' (possession, characteristic, skill, etc.) which is positively valued by the speaker and the hearer. (1986: 446)

To track the topic of the compliments in our dataset, we used the taxonomy of compliment subjects created by Holmes (1998) and Wolfson (1984) and later applied in other compliment corpora (e.g. Parisi & Wogan 2006; Rees-Miller 2011). The categories that these scholars regularly apply are appearance, skill/abilities, possessions, and personality/friendliness, detailed and adapted for our own purposes in Table 4.1.

Coders initially collected compliments from the scripts along with the gender of the speaker, the gender of the recipient, and the type of compliment according to the categories above. The scripts were then checked by a second coder and any compliments that were missed on the first pass were added. The

Table 4.1. *Taxonomy of compliment types*

| Category | Definition | Example |
|---|---|---|
| Appearance | Addressee's physical characteristics, hair, clothing, etc.; other sensory inherent attributes of addressee, such as smell | "She's mighty Pretty. She's Beautiful!" (Dwarfs, *Snow White*) |
| Skill | Addressee's skills, abilities, strength, intelligence; positive responses to addressee's performance of a task | "You... You fight good." (Shang, *Mulan*) |
| Possessions | Object in addressee's ownership, addressee's riches/treasure, family members of addressee | "This is quite a remarkable device." (Sultan, *Aladdin*) |
| Personality | Addressee's intangible personal qualities or moral values; declaration of closeness to addressee | "He's really kind and gentle... He's my friend." (Belle, *Beauty and the Beast*) |
| General/Other | General goodness of addressee, or compliments not fitting in other categories | "Some people are worth melting for." (Olaf, *Frozen*) |

primary researchers then examined the dataset together and discussed cases of ambiguous elocutionary force, rewatching the original scene in the film if needed. We erred on the side of exclusion in the case that consensus couldn't be reached, although in general there was good agreement between us, and relatively few cases were so complicated that they merited much discussion.[2] This process yielded a total number of 1,282 compliments.

As always happens in linguistic research, we ended up needing to fine-tune which types of tokens would be excluded and included. For example, we chose to exclude compliments given in the voice-over or narration (*She was the fairest in the kingdom*) or purely sarcastic remarks (*Oh yeah you're an excellent judge of character, right*). We did, though, include insincere compliments designed to manipulate without the knowledge of the recipient. We also excluded self-compliments, which fall outside of Holmes' definition.

One methodological issue that we found particularly challenging was the imbalance in the amount of speech for male and female characters, as discussed at length in Chapter 3. It wouldn't be particularly interesting to find out that male characters give the majority of compliments overall, since male characters speak so much more than female characters to begin with. We control for this by using binomial tests to compare the ratio of compliments given or received against the ratio of male to female speech. In a world in which gender did not influence complimenting behavior, we might expect each

---

[2] In an exception to this rule, we once argued for 10 minutes about how to code the example where Kristoff from *Frozen* (2013) gives himself a compliment while pretending to be the voice of his reindeer, Sven. This example was ultimately excluded.

gender to give and receive compliments at about the rate that they actually talk in the films; that is, if male characters speak 59 percent of the time in Disney movies, then we would expect them to give and receive about 59 percent of the compliments. The binomial test tells us whether that's the case or whether the proportion of compliments differs significantly from that expected rate.

It's important to note that using words spoken as a benchmark for how many compliments characters should give isn't an ideal measure, since it does flatten other factors, like personality, importance to the plot, and so forth. Comparing words spoken against compliments received has its own problems as well, since a character doesn't have to be speaking or even be on screen in order to be complimented. Still, the discrepancy of representation we found in Chapter 3 was big enough that we needed a way to take it into account, and this system offered a straightforward way to do so without introducing other variables. So we're going to begin there and triangulate by using other measures, such as intra-gender comparisons and qualitative observation, to fill out the picture.

We also look specifically at the breakdown of our five compliment types within each permutation of givers and receivers. We focus the bulk of our analysis specifically on the difference between appearance-based and skill-based compliments. In previous studies, compliments about skills and appearance comprise the large majority of compliments exchanged (Parisi & Wogan 2006; Wolfson 1984; Holmes 2013). They're also the biggest site of reported differences between men and women. Also, because compliments are recognized as an indicator of social value, conversations about appearance compliments (specifically, how often they are given to women) are especially relevant to pop-culture conversations about feminism and media.

## Compliment Givers and Receivers

### Who Gives and Receives Compliments?

Our first question – who gives and receives more compliments? – is relatively straightforward to answer. Table 4.2 shows the breakdown of compliments given and received by male and female characters, with the collective speech amounts for each gender as a comparison. Percentages are bolded if the binomial test reported that the reported number for that gender differs significantly from the proportion of words spoken by that gender ($p < 0.05$).

In general, the results of our binomial tests show that the proportion of compliments that each gender gives doesn't deviate significantly from the proportion we predicted based on the amount each gender speaks. In the Classic Era, male characters speak 41 percent of words and give 36 percent of the compliments; the 5 percent difference does not reach significance. In the Renaissance Era, the proportions are not significantly different, and in fact are

Table 4.2. *Compliments given and received by character gender*

| | Male characters | | | Female characters | | |
|---|---|---|---|---|---|---|
| | Words spoken | Compliments given | Compliments received | Words spoken | Compliments given | Compliments received |
| Classic | 41% (4,684) | 36% (21) | 40% (23) | 59% (6,710) | 64% (37) | 60% (35) |
| Renaissance | 78% (19,756) | 79% (148) | 65%* (121) | 22% (5,643) | 21% (39) | 34%* (63) |
| New Age | 50% (16,899) | 60%* (109) | 38%* (68) | 50% (16,762) | 39%* (71) | 57% (103) |
| Pixar | 74% (111,662) | 74% (648) | 73% (637) | 26% (38,950) | 26% (227) | 23% (203) |

* Proportion is significantly different than predicted based on proportion of words spoken ($p < 0.05$)

almost identical: male characters speak 78 percent of the words and give 79 percent of the compliments. The New Age Era is the only one where there *is* a significant difference between speech and compliment proportions, with male characters speaking 50 percent of the words and uttering 60 percent of the compliments. And in the Pixar films, the proportions are once again not significantly different, with the proportions of male character-given speech and compliments both being exactly 74 percent. The results for female characters closely mirror those of the male characters (e.g. in the Classic Era, female characters' compliment proportion is 5 percent higher than their speech proportion, offsetting the male characters' compliment proportion being 5 percent lower). Taken together, the data show evidence that the frequency of *giving* compliments isn't a behavior that varies based on gender of the speaker, except in the New Age films, where male characters are slightly *more* complimentary than their female character counterparts.

It's tempting to say that this result (male characters giving compliments as much as or slightly more than female characters) means these films are radically different from the nonanimated communities that have been studied, given that the majority of studies on US speakers have shown that women are more likely to give compliments than men (e.g. Holmes 2013; Parisi & Wogan 2006). But we actually don't think that's the case. If you'll recall, Rees-Miller (2011) found that men and women actually gave about the same number of compliments when they were involved in a direct task. To the extent that our characters do spend a lot of time engaged in tasks that advance the plot, then, the lack of a difference by gender is less surprising. Another factor to consider is that those studies that found a clear gender difference in who gave compliments (e.g. Holmes 2013) noted that women gave lots of compliments in particular *to each other*. We'll return to the question of same-gender versus cross-gender dyads in a moment, because it's a thorny one. But for now, suffice it to say that one rarely finds two female characters on screen talking to each other in any of these movies, so the most favorable context for them to give compliments is almost nonexistent.

Receiving compliments is a somewhat different story. In the Classic Era of Disney, male and female characters receive compliments at a rate that isn't significantly distinguishable from the predicted rate based on speech amounts: male characters speak 41 percent of the words, and receive 40 percent of the compliments. In the Renaissance and New Age, however, male characters receive significantly fewer compliments than we predicted based on the proportion of words spoken. In the Renaissance, they speak 80 percent of words, but only receive 65 percent of compliments; in the New Age, they speak 50 percent of the time but only receive 38 percent of the compliments. And in Pixar, there are once again no significant differences. Once again, female characters' proportions mirror those of the male characters. Female characters

Table 4.3. *Compliments and gender of participants in Disney and Pixar*

|  | Disney | Pixar |
| --- | --- | --- |
| Male-to-male | 30% (125) | 57% (480) |
| Male-to-female | 35% (142) | 18% (147) |
| Female-to-male | 21% (86) | 19% (156) |
| Female-to-female | 14% (59) | 7% (56) |
| Total | 412 | 839 |

\* This chart excludes compliments given or received by characters with no gender signifiers, as well as compliments given to people of multiple genders simultaneously.

receive compliments at a significantly different rate in the Renaissance (21 percent speech vs. 34 percent compliments received). The difference isn't significant in the New Age, but it does approach significance ($p = 0.07$). In aggregate, the results suggest that in the Renaissance and New Age Eras, female characters are disproportionately likely to receive compliments, and vice versa for male characters.

We were honestly surprised by this result. We expected that most of the compliments throughout the films might easily go to (and from) the female characters. We especially thought we might see that be the case since those movies are famous for the ways the Princesses are valued for their beauty above anything else. We'll look at some qualitative examples of compliments to both male and female characters to see if there are differences other than frequency that may be interesting in the sections below.

These quantitative results are very broad, so we want to dig into them at a narrower level of analysis. In particular, the studies we cited framed female-to-female compliments as an unmarked, natural type of occurrence, while male-to-male compliments were less frequent, due at least in part to some sort of heternormative taboo against open affection between men. Table 4.3 shows the breakdown of how compliments are distributed in Disney and Pixar according to the gender of the giver and recipient. We will spend the next few sections discussing and qualitatively analyzing the same-gender compliments found in each set of films.

### Way to Go, Buddy! Male-to-Male Compliments

Male-to-male compliments make up 30 percent of all compliments in the princess movies, and a whopping 54 percent in Pixar. These numbers surprised us in terms of just how many compliments happened between male characters, even given their much higher representation. For comparison, Parisi and Wogan (2006) found that just 10 percent of compliments were between men;

for Holmes (2011), it was 9 percent. Again, the popular imagining of compliments tends to be that they're a thing that women do, so it is surprising to see male characters compliment each other at all in popular media, let alone this much. The writers could have elected not to have the male characters give any compliments at all, since compliments are a social act rather than a functional one, and their presence isn't strictly necessary in any given conversation.

However, we found it less surprising when we compared our data with Rees-Miller's (2011) study, which showed that in goal-oriented settings, male-to-male compliments comprised 45 percent of total compliments given, even more than female-to-female compliments (36 percent). She notes that compliments in goal-oriented situations, even among men, are expected signs of group solidarity – like athletes telling each other *good play* in a game, these are often positive judgments that help accomplish goals and increase group bonding. This perspective is relevant because the plots of these movies are driven by goals, from stopping an eternal winter, to returning the heart of Te Fiti, to training for a race, to building a bird to defeat evil grasshoppers. Qualitatively, we found many compliments between male characters are therefore in contexts where they were working towards a specific goal:

> Way to go, buddy! | Mater to McQueen, *Cars*
> Good work, Lightyear. | Lotso to Buzz, *Toy Story 3*
> Such a smart boy! Yes! Great idea, yes! | Hector to Miguel, *Coco*
> Perfect timing Abu! | Aladdin to Abu, *Aladdin*
> Well done Smith! | Ben to John Smith, *Pocahontas*

It won't escape most readers that all these compliments are based on skill, performance, or intelligence – it didn't escape us either. We'll say more about that in the next section.

But not all male-to-male compliments are given in the context of immediate goals, and even the ones that are goal-oriented still establish connection and community with others. Given that men in modern society are often mocked for showing open admiration or desire for connection with other men (Kiesling 2005), we appreciate that male characters in children's movies are modeling being openly positive towards one another.

We want to talk about Pixar in particular for a moment, since male characters in Pixar movies are even more likely than male characters in Disney movies to compliment each other. Again, we grant that the proportion of male characters in Pixar movies is especially high; even so, this amount of complimenting feels surprising, and at times, progressive. Our findings align with what Gillam and Wooden (2008) call Pixar's "New Man" archetype, who often leans into traits that traditional masculinity doesn't; notable among these traits is open dependence on, and desire for, social connections and community.

We think this does bear out linguistically. There are many male characters in Pixar who praise each other openly, sometimes making themselves very vulnerable in the process. This is a pattern starting all the way back in Pixar's first movie, *Toy Story*. Buzz and Woody, the two main characters, antagonize each other for most of the movie despite being forced to work together. But in the emotional climax of the film, Woody finally opens up and admits his insecurities, and in doing so, earnestly compliments Buzz:

**Excerpt 4A "You are a COOL toy" (*Toy Story*, 1995)**

BUZZ:     You were right all along. I'm not a Space Ranger. I'm just a toy. A stupid little insignificant toy.

WOODY:   Whoa, hey— wait a minute. Being a toy is a lot better than being a Space Ranger.

BUZZ:     Yeah, right.

WOODY:   No, it is. Look, over in that house is a kid who thinks you are the greatest, and it's not because you're a Space Ranger, pal, it's because you're a TOY! You are HIS toy.

BUZZ:     But why would Andy want me?

WOODY:   Why would Andy want you?! Look at you! You're a Buzz Lightyear. **Any other toy would give up his moving parts just to be you. You've got wings, you glow in the dark, you talk, your helmet does that— that, that whoosh thing— you are a COOL toy. As a matter of fact you're too cool.** I mean— I mean what chance does a toy like me have against a Buzz Lightyear action figure? All I can do is... [pulls drawstring] Why would Andy ever want to play with me, when he's got you? I'm the one that should be strapped to that rocket.

In this exchange, Woody makes Buzz feel better by affirming his general status (*Being a toy is a lot better than being a space ranger*). At Buzz's continued insecurity, Woody elaborates on what exactly makes Buzz great, complimenting him multiple times in a row on his possessions (*You've got wings, your helmet does that whoosh thing*), his skills (*you glow in the dark, you talk*), and emphatically overall (*you are a COOL toy*). Although up to this point Woody has at times praised Buzz for a good idea or a well-timed action, this is the first time he expresses open admiration for Buzz as a person ... er, toy. It is worth noting that it takes the whole film to build to this single moment of vulnerability and open admiration, and it's still framed as a "big deal" that Woody was able to make this admission. However, it's still head-and-shoulders above many depictions of male buddy pairs in modern cinema for whom mutual vulnerability isn't even on the table. In this way, we're glad to see that Pixar has Woody and Buzz, as well as a range of other male characters who openly give compliments to support each other and express vulnerability both inside and outside of goal-oriented situations.

Pixar also features a lot of father–son or surrogate father–son relationships that are constructed through the use of compliments. Bob and Dash in *The Incredibles*, Doc and McQueen in *Cars*, Fergus and his boys in *Brave*, Carl and Russell in *Up*, and Hector and Miguel in *Coco* are all examples of relatively healthy father–son(ish) relationships, and all of them are characterized in some ways with praise from father to son. In *Finding Nemo*, Nemo has not one but two praising father figures – one literal (Marlin) and one more figurative (Gill). Both give him encouragement throughout the film:

> Nicely done! (Gill)
> That's great, kid! (Gill)
> That took guts, kid. (Gill)
> You're right. I know you can. (Marlin)
> You're doing great, son! (Marlin)

Parents and friends are two kinds of dynamic that contribute significantly to Pixar having so many male-to-male compliments. We're personally heartened to see compliment behavior in male-to-male social and familial relationships depicted on the silver screen.

### *You Look Beautifuller: Female-to-Female Compliments*

Female-to-female compliments are the least common kind of compliment in both Disney and Pixar films. This would be interesting if it meant that female characters genuinely don't compliment each other much, given our expectations based on previous research. But that's not the case – the biggest factor here is just that there are hardly ever two female characters substantially interacting with one another on screen, so the air time barely exists for the dynamic to come to light. When we list the movies with the highest rates of female-to-female compliments in Pixar, the top three movies (in fact, the only three movies with rates above 10 percent) are *Inside Out* (48 percent), *Brave* (30 percent), and *Finding Dory* (22 percent). Wise readers may recognize these as the only three Pixar movies with female protagonists. The top rates for Disney are *Sleeping Beauty* (47 percent), *Cinderella* (38 percent), *Brave* again (30 percent), *Tangled* (28 percent), and *Frozen* (22 percent). Here the determining factor seems to be having female family members: *Brave* and *Tangled* both feature mother–daughter pairs, *Sleeping Beauty* has a trio of maternal fairies, *Cinderella* has the stepmother and stepsisters, and *Frozen* features sisters. So while a lot of the princesses are mostly alone, the ones who have other female characters around end up giving and receiving more compliments.

Multiple examples confirm that when female characters are occupying the screen together, they often end up doing what audience ˙might consider the stereotypical "girl thing": complimenting each other not as an evaluation on a recent goal or performance (as with male characters), but as a routine positive politeness strategy or rapport builder. In *Frozen*, for example, there's a scene where Princess Anna goes to strike up a conversation with her estranged sister Elsa:

**Excerpt 4B "You look beautifuller" (*Frozen*, 2013)**

ELSA:      ...Hi.
ANNA:      Hi, hi me...? Oh. Um. Hi.
ELSA:      ...**You look beautiful.**
ANNA:      Thank you. **You look beautifuller.** I mean, not fuller.
           You don't look fuller, but more— more beautiful.
ELSA:      Thank you.

In this scene, the audience understands that the two haven't spoken in years, and we watch them awkwardly establish a rapport. Elsa's move to open with a compliment on Anna's appearance, which Anna then reciprocates, reflects and reproduces popular assumptions about how compliments operate in feminine friendships.

Interestingly, we find the female villains using compliments as well, for their own shady purposes. Often it could be argued that they are using gendered expectations about how women compliment each other, especially on appearance, to hide manipulative strategies. In *Cinderella*, Cinderella's evil stepmother wants to keep her from going to the ball. Although she has the authority to just tell Cinderella to stay home, she decides instead to use a back-handed compliment on Cinderella's ball gown to get her daughters to tear her down instead:

**Excerpt 4C "These beads give it just the right touch" (*Cinderella*, 1950)**

CINDERELLA:    Wait! Please wait for me. Isn't it lovely? Do you like it? Do you think it will do?
DRIZELLA:      Cinderella!
ANASTASIA:     Mother, she can't!
DRIZELLA:      You wouldn't!
ANASTASIA:     No!
STEPMOTHER:    Girls, please! After all, we did make a bargain, didn't we Cinderella? And I never go back on my word. Hmm. **How very clever. These beads, they give it just the right touch, don't you think so Drizella?**
DRIZELLA:      No I don't! I think she's— uh! Why you little thief! They're my beads! Give them here!

Mother Gothel, from the much later film *Tangled*, has a lot in common with Cinderella's stepmother. And she often uses similar complimentary tactics to hide her manipulation or distract Rapunzel. At multiple times in the movie, she criticizes Rapunzel as a way to get her to stay in line, and immediately covers it with compliments to maintain some semblance of rapport:

Okay okay, Rapunzel, please, stop with the mumbling. You know how I feel about the mumbling–blah-blah-blah-blah, it's very annoying, I'm just teasing, you're adorable, I love you so much, darling.

We're not saying that it's only female characters who use compliments to manipulate or disguise their motives. But we do think that compliments are deployed in the writing of these female characters to create a specifically feminine manipulation style, further linking giving and receiving compliments as a common or even socially expected behavior within female homosocial settings. Additionally, we find it fascinating that villains draw on this feminine style specifically as a performance to hide ulterior motives; this is a topic we will return to at length in Chapter 8.

## Compliment Topic

### *What Do Male and Female Characters Get Complimented About?*

As discussed earlier, compliments can serve as a way of highlighting and enforcing social norms. In this context it is the receiver of the compliment who is most significant, since it is their "goods" that are being evaluated, so for this part of our analysis, we focus only on how the topic of the compliment varies according to the receiver's gender. In particular, as mentioned earlier, we will be focusing on appearance and skill compliments, since they were the two most frequent topics in all the previous studies we looked at, and they have the greatest implications for how we societally value people of different genders.

Our results show that for both Disney and Pixar, the topics of compliments differ significantly according to the gender of the recipient. In Disney, female characters receive compliments based on appearance (31 percent) and skills

Table 4.4. *Compliment topic and gender of receiver in Disney Princess films*

| Compliment type | Female receiver | Male receiver |
| --- | --- | --- |
| Appearance | 31% (63) | 18% (39) |
| Skills | 29% (58) | 43% (91) |
| Personality | 14% (29) | 15% (31) |
| Possessions | 6% (13) | 4% (8) |
| General/Other | 19% (38) | 20% (43) |
| Total | 201 | 212 |

* $\chi^2 = 14.24$, $p < 0.01$

Table 4.5. *Compliment topic and gender of receiver in Pixar films*

| Compliment type | Female receiver | Male receiver |
|---|---|---|
| Appearance | 16% (32) | 8% (49) |
| Skills | 41% (84) | 52% (332) |
| Personality | 7% (14) | 13% (81) |
| Possessions | 9% (18) | 5% (34) |
| General/Other | 27% (55) | 22% (141) |
| Total | 203 | 637 |

\* $\chi^2 = 23.31$, p $< 0.01$

(29 percent) in close to equal proportion. On the other hand, male characters receive more than double the amount of compliments on their skills (43 percent) than on their appearance (18 percent). The differences in Pixar are more subtle, but still very much present. Characters of either gender are much more likely to receive compliments on their skills than on their appearance; however, this difference is more pronounced for the male characters (52 percent skill to 8 percent appearance) than it is for the female characters (41 percent skill to 16 percent appearance). For the other topics, there isn't much difference by gender, with male and female characters differing only by a few percentage points in almost all cases. For both Disney and Pixar, the percentage of compliments on appearance for female characters is about twice what it is for male characters.

In the next section we look at the individual films, rather than the datasets as a whole, to see if this pattern changes over time; in other words, are these proportions consistent across the movies or are they the averages of a pattern with more deviations? And if so, is there a historical trend corresponding to changes in the social landscape and ideas about gender roles?

### The Fairest of Them All: Compliments to Women

Figure 4.1 shows a surprisingly linear relationship in Disney films between the date of release and the topics of compliments given to female characters. In *Snow White*, 75 percent of compliments that female characters receive are about appearance, and a big fat 0 percent are on their skills or intelligence. This proportion shifts steadily over time: appearance compliments become increasingly rare, and skill compliments increasingly common. *Moana*, one of the most recent Princess movies, is the inverse of *Snow White*, in that there isn't a single appearance-based compliment for Moana or any other female character in the entire movie. Figure 4.1 confirms the impression that many viewers have of the Princess movies: that the modern princesses are valued for different traits than their early predecessors.

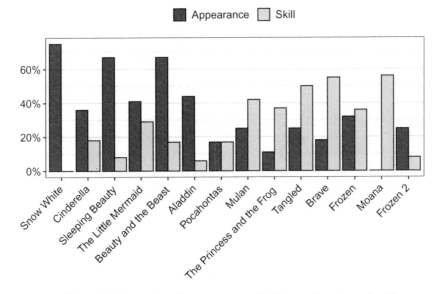

Figure 4.1 Proportions of appearance and skill compliments received by female characters in Disney Princess films

A qualitative comparison reveals just how much the princesses' "value" has changed over the years. In the iconic first lines of *Snow White*, Snow White's character is introduced exclusively through a description of her physical appearance:

**Excerpt 4D "Who is the fairest one of all?" (*Snow White*, 1937)**

QUEEN:   Magic mirror on the wall, who is the fairest one of all?
MIRROR:  **Famed is thy beauty, Majesty.** But hold, **a lovely maid I see. Rags cannot hide her gentle grace.** Alas, she is more fair than thee.
QUEEN:   Alas for her! Reveal her name.
MIRROR:  Lips red as the rose. Hair black as ebony. Skin white as snow.
QUEEN:   Snow White!

*Sleeping Beauty*, the third Princess movie, similarly introduces Princess Aurora's character with a blessing for her beauty, and her appearance continues to be a defining trait throughout the film:

**Excerpt 4E "The gift of beauty" (*Sleeping Beauty*, 1959)**

FLORA:   Each of us the child may bless with a single gift. No more, no less. Little princess, my gift shall be the gift of beauty. **One gift, beauty rare, Full of sunshine in her hair, Lips that shame the red red rose, She'll walk with springtime wherever she goes.**

Both *Sleeping Beauty* and *Snow White* communicate that the first thing we need to know about their titular characters is that they're beautiful (or, will be, since one of them is still a baby). These initial compliments on beauty indicate the way that the whole movie is going to go, since in both cases, the heroine's beauty serves as a driving factor for the plot. *Cinderella*'s narrator tells us explicitly that the stepmother was *bitterly jealous of Cinderella's charm and beauty*. The Evil Queen in *Snow White* orders her huntsman to murder the princess, not because she stands to inherit money or power, but solely because Snow White is more beautiful than she is. So in the context of the film, the Classic princesses' beauty is not only the *first* thing we often are told about them, but also arguably the *most important* thing too.

One might think that the princess in the 1990s would be valued more for skills than beauty, given that these are the princesses of the Girl Power generation. But Ariel, Pocahontas, Belle, and Jasmine are still complimented more on their appearance than on anything else. Upon examination, we found that this is mostly because these stories have more romantic scenes between the princess and her prince, and in this romantic context, compliments on appearance seem to still be the name of the game. Granted, there is acknowledgment that they have other traits as well, which frankly is an improvement over the Classic Era; still, their physical beauty plays a major factor in their suitors' attraction to them, and is also frequently commented on by others. For example, Eric from *The Little Mermaid* initially is attracted to Ariel because, as he puts it, *she had the most beautiful voice*; though this is technically a skill, it's being framed here as part of a kind of seductive and ethereal feminine beauty.[3] In the scene below, she changes into human clothes for the first time and joins her hosts (including Prince Eric) for dinner:

**Excerpt 4F "You look— wonderful"** (*The Little Mermaid*, 1989)

GRIMSBY:   Oh, Eric, **isn't she a vision?**
ERIC:      **You look— wonderful.**
GRIMSBY:   Come come come, you must be famished. Let me help you my dear. There we go— ah— quite comfy? Uh. It's— **It's not often that we have such a lovely dinner guest**, eh Eric?

Notably, this dialogue peters off because Eric is just … staring.[4] Directly at Ariel. without saying anything. To be fair, Eric goes on to find other things to value in Ariel (her bravery, her sense of adventure, etc.), but at this moment she's just a silent, beautiful dinner guest; her beauty is her primary value to Eric at this point, and continues to be a substantial point of value throughout the film.

---

[3] This is exactly how Prince Phillip falls in love with Aurora in *Sleeping Beauty*, by the way, so we guess it's a thing.
[4] The male gaze is feeling uncomfortably literal there, Disney.

It isn't until *Mulan* in 1997 that the balance shifts and female characters begin to be complimented more often on their skills than their appearance. *Mulan* is an interesting place for this shift to occur, because Mulan is actually masquerading in the army as a man named Ping for the bulk of the film. We should reiterate, though, that we coded compliments to "Ping" as compliments to a male character, since we're to assume that the characters around "Ping" believe they're complimenting a man. So for example, when Mulan's friend, Ling, says *Let's hear it for Ping, the bravest of us all!* We interpret this as part of the male-to-male bonding strategies discussed earlier in this chapter. But even when characters know that it's Mulan they're complimenting, it's often on her skill, bravery, and intelligence, rather than appearance. Romance is also notably downplayed in this film compared to all previous princess movies. Shang, her love interest, only finds out she's a woman in the final act of the film. But that being said, the one compliment he gives her is *um... you... you fight good.* We love a supportive gentleman.

Finally, in the New Age movies, the number of compliments that female characters receive on skills increases considerably, and appearance-based compliments fall to 25 percent or less of all the compliments received. A substantive shift takes place in establishing princesses' character as well. For New Age princesses, when they are introduced with complimentary descriptions, these are usually skill-based. *The Princess and the Frog's* opening sequences shows the main character Tiana cooking with her family in her childhood home and receiving compliments from her parents:

**Excerpt 4G "Our little girl's got a gift"** (*The Princess and the Frog*, **2009**)

| | |
|---|---|
| DAD: | Mmm, **gumbo smells good, Tiana!** |
| TIANA: | I think it's done, Daddy. |
| DAD: | Hmmm... |
| TIANA: | What? |
| DAD: | Well, sweetheart... **This is the best gumbo I've ever tasted!** Heh heh, come here. Eudora, **our little girl's got a gift.** |
| EUDORA: | mmhmm I coulda told you that. |
| DAD: | A gift this special just gotta be shared. |

Here, Tiana is established as someone who has a cooking skill that is valuable to those around her. Just like the Classic princesses, this early fact we learn about her also proves to be one of the most important things we know. Tiana's skill and passion for cooking are what drives the plot forward, generating a good deal of the conflict in the movie.[5]

---

[5] It is worth noting, however, that the skill in question (cooking) is still a heavily feminized skill, and it is initially introduced in a domestic setting. In this way, Tiana's character is a great illustration of how Disney updates its Princess archetype to be more empowered for a modern audience, while still keeping enough traditional femininity to be read as "princessy."

*Moana*'s opening lines are similar as we learn about her and the conflict between her and her family. Her father compliments her by saying, *Let's go back to the village. You are the next great chief of our people.* If you've seen *Moana*, you know this doesn't match up with what she thinks of herself – but nevertheless it's important that her perceived value is at least about leadership and power, not about beauty. It's indicative of a trend in modern movies to introduce and frame the leading women as skilled, intelligent, and/or powerful, rather than concentrating solely on their appearance.

This de-emphasis on appearance is qualitatively amplified in the romances of the New Age films: throughout all five New Age movies, princes only give three appearance-based compliments to the princesses. Moreover, none of them are the straightforward "you look beautiful" compliments that you'd see in earlier movies. In *The Princess and the Frog*, for instance, Tiana accuses Naveen of backing out of a promise, to which he angrily replies *I made that promise to a beautiful princess, not a cranky waiter!* This is ... technically a compliment, we suppose. We counted it. But it's a far cry from prince Phillip telling his pet horse that a girl he met had a voice *too beautiful to be real.*

Instead, romantic leads in later movies tend more toward compliments on qualities like intelligence, bravery, and that ineffable Disney quality of "having dreams." In *The Princess and the Frog*, prince Naveen confesses his love to Tiana by saying: *Tiana, I love... the way you light up, when you talk about your dream. A dream that, it is so beautiful I... I promise... I will do whatever it takes to make it come true.* In *Frozen II*, Kristoff proposes to Princess Anna twice, first referring to her as *feisty* and *fearless* and later as *the most extraordinary person I've ever known.* In this one respect, at least, we see Disney reshaping how the princesses are framed to some degree over time, with a decrease in emphasis on appearance.

Female Pixar characters receive an overall much lower proportion of appearance compliments than Disney female characters do. Appearance compliments comprise only 16 percent of all compliments to female characters throughout Pixar movies, compared to 31 percent in Disney; and conversely, skill compliments comprise a higher proportion, at 41 percent compared to 29 percent in Disney. Pixar movies do not have the consistent downward trend in appearance compliments that Disney movies do. However, it is interesting to note that there *is* something of a downward shift right around the time of *Cars 2* and *Brave*. Movies before these tended to have slightly higher amounts of appearance-based compliments and 50 percent or less compliments based on skill. Afterwards, skill-based compliments consistently (and substantially) outnumber appearance-based compliments, and are much closer to comprising the majority of all compliments given in each film. This may be indicative of the sudden spike of critical cultural attention Pixar received around the release of *Brave*, as discussed in Chapter 2.

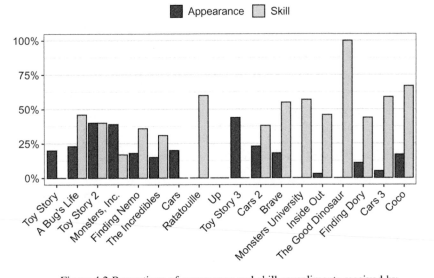

Figure 4.2 Proportions of appearance and skill compliments received by female characters in Pixar films

Given that the first Pixar movie debuted in 1995, the cultural zeitgeist was well beyond the *Snow-White*-ish idea that women should be (explicitly) defined by how hot they are. So appearance-based compliments like those discussed in the previous section, where third-party characters randomly make comments on female characters' appearance, don't happen much. Pixar doesn't rely on appearance compliments in romantic relationships, either: in romantic pairs such as Linguini and Colette (*Ratatouille*), Flik and Atta (*A Bug's Life*), and Mr. and Mrs. Incredible (*The Incredibles*), the female characters are more likely to receive skill compliments than appearance compliments from their love interests. Compliments take the tone of things like:

> Princess, you're doing a great job. (Flik)
> I love your advice. (Linguini)

In these scenarios, Pixar does a pretty good job of not only creating complex female characters, but also demonstrating that their love interests value them for their multiple skills and traits.

That being said, appearance compliments are still used in other films or couples to indicate romantic affection towards female characters. We see an example of this pattern in the relationship between Jessie and Buzz Lightyear in *Toy Story 2* and *3*. Buzz's attraction to Jessie is expressed almost entirely through appearance compliments:

Uh, m— ma'am, I, uh— well, I just wanted to say you're a bright young
   woman with a beautiful yarnful of hair. Uh, a hairful of yarn.
I'm immune to your... bewitching good looks.
Mi florecita del desierto! [My desert flower!]

We see another strong example in Mike Wazowski's relationship with his
girlfriend, Celia, in *Monsters, Inc.* We only see them interact a few times in the
film; their biggest scene together is an anniversary date, the dialogue of which
is shown in Excerpt 4H in its entirety:

**Excerpt 4H "The first time I laid eye on you" (*Monsters, Inc.*, 2001)**

CELIA:   What are you looking at?
MIKE:    I was just thinking about the first time I laid eye on you... **how pretty you
         looked.**
CELIA:   Stop it!
MIKE:    Your hair was shorter then.
CELIA:   Mm-hmm. I'm thinking about getting it cut.
MIKE:    No, no, **I like it this length. I like everything about you.**
CELIA:   Awww.
MIKE:    Just the other day someone asked me who I thought the **most beautiful
         monster was in all of Monstropolis. You know what I said?**
CELIA:   What did you say?
MIKE:    I said... *[Sulley appears in the window.]* Sulley?
CELIA:   Sulley?

In this scene, the intent of the filmmakers seems to be to set up the romance of
the date Mike and Celia are on, so as to heighten the humor and chaos that
ensues when Sulley interrupts. And the shorthand for romance utilized is a
string of compliments from a male to a female character, with a focus on
appearance. So we can say that Pixar has an interestingly uneven track record
here: although some female characters are valued by their romantic interests
for a variety of traits, others get primarily appearance compliments as a quick
way to show that they're in a romantic relationship.

### *My Handsome Prince: Compliments to Male Characters in Disney and Pixar*

The data show that male characters have a very different relationship to
appearance- and skill-based compliments than female characters do, across
both of our datasets. In both studios, male characters tend to receive exponen-
tially more compliments based on skill than on appearance, with a handful of
exceptions. In Pixar, this imbalance is both extreme and consistent. In Disney,
these numbers are slightly more variant, but the changes definitely do not
replicate the neat historical patterns revealed by the data on female receivers.

We think that this stands to reason given the difference in the levels of criticism that portrayals of masculinity and femininity have historically received. Earlier, we suggested that the changes in compliment topics to female characters reflected at least partially a change in how Disney is trying to portray the value of women on screen. If that's true, then we posit that this data suggests a *lack* of consideration or meaningful evolution in the way that men's value has been portrayed over the years. As discussed in Chapter 2, masculine role models have mostly been left aside in conversations about gender portrayal, so there's no push for Disney to do anything different. Much less is there any pressure on Pixar, since there has barely been any critical discussion of gender stereotypes in their films at all.

Qualitatively, we find that skill-based compliments to male characters are easily given and received. Earlier in the chapter we remarked that the preponderance of male-to-male compliments, especially in Pixar and newer Disney movies, may be part of a pattern of showing characters are supportive of one another. The vast majority of the "support" that male characters find from their friends is through these skill compliments. Male characters praise each other often for an achievement or accomplishment. In *Cars*, for example, Lightning McQueen paves a new road for the town of Radiator Springs. When he finishes, he gets all kinds of praise for the quality of his workmanship: *You make such a nice new road* (Luigi), *That punk actually did a good job* (Doc), and *I bet even the roads on the moon ain't this smooth* (Mater). In fact, the "that was great" kind of compliment to men, on anything from bright ideas to a cool stunt, from great cooking to good driving, is commonplace in the world of Pixar.

Appearance-based compliments, on the other hand, are *not* easily given between male characters. Instead, when male characters receive a compliment on their looks it's generally from a love interest. This is especially true of the romantic relationships between prince and princess in the Disney films, contributing to the greater variation in Disney as compared to Pixar. The stand-out era appears to be the Classic Era of Disney, where male characters actually receive more compliments on appearance than skill. It's important to note here that the bars on the graph represent percentages of the compliments by topic within that movie, not the actual numbers. Keep in mind that the princes have very little screen time at all in those first three movies, and the male characters are so infrequently complimented that the sum total of the first three columns in Figure 4.3 (*Snow White*, *Cinderella*, and *Sleeping Beauty* combined) is just nine compliments. So when Cinderella tells her mouse friends that Prince Charming was so handsome, that's a full half of what's depicted in Figure 4.3 for *Cinderella*

Overall, appearance compliments to male characters from their love interests are present across all subsets of our data. Ariel calls Prince Eric *very handsome*

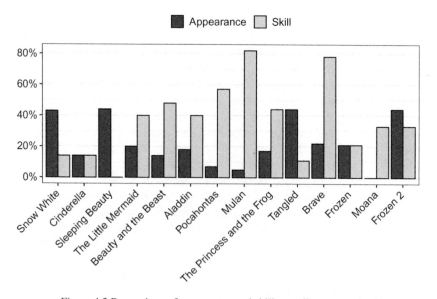

Figure 4.3 Proportions of appearance and skill compliments received by male characters in Disney Princess films

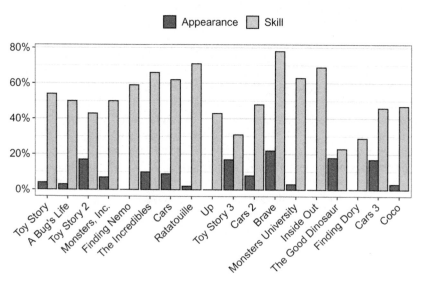

Figure 4.4 Proportions of appearance and skill compliments received by male characters in Pixar films

and *beautiful*; Jasmine calls Aladdin *my handsome prince*; in *Frozen*, when Anna is interested in Hans, she stammers out *I'm awkward, you're gorgeous*. This pattern holds steady through the most recent releases, an interesting juxtaposition against the way that Disney princes compliment the princesses on their appearance less and less over time. Similarly, in the Pixar movies, many appearance compliments to male characters are romantic or sexual in nature. Bo Peeps' compliments to Woody throughout the *Toy Story* franchise are appearance-based: she tells him, *You're cute when you care*, and says that his repaired arm makes him *look tough*. In *The Incredibles*, appearance-based compliments are given to Mr. Incredible by the villain's secretary Mirage (*Nice suit, you look rather dashing*) to insinuate potential sexual chemistry and to fuel Mrs. Incredible's jealousy. Importantly, all these compliments are easily spoken by the female giver, and well received by the male recipient.

But when male characters compliment each other on their appearance, it's a very different story. These instances are already few and far between, and when they occur, they're rarely sincere. There are a number of instances where male characters compliment each other's appearance to mock or belittle them in some way. They may, for example, give these "compliments" to each other to imply that they're conceited or vain. In *Brave*, Merida and her father King Fergus are making fun of one of Merida's potential suitors, and King Fergus sarcastically comments that he *has such lovely flowing locks!* In *Coco*, the main character Miguel tells his new friend Hector that Ernesto De La Cruz is the greatest musician of all time; Hector rebuffs this by saying, *Greatest eyebrows of all time maybe. But his music, eh, not so much.* In this line he not only tells Miguel that Ernesto is a poor musician, but takes a swipe at him by complimenting his eyebrows, implying that he is vain and cares more about his appearance than his music.

It's telling that (perceived) vanity or attention to appearance is a target of ridicule in male characters, since a focus on appearance has traditionally been a feminized trait. In more extreme cases, we found that appearance compliments can be used to mock a male character just for being too feminine or womanly. The most obvious and egregious example of this is in *Snow White*, which has an entire sequence in which six of the dwarfs take Grumpy, the seventh dwarf, and physically force him to bathe. They then proceed to dress him up with perfumes and flowers, feminizing him and making him the subject of group mockery. While doing so, they "compliment" him multiple times over: *He sure is cute! Ain't he sweet? Smells like a petunia!* These compliments are overtly meant to embarrass him for being clean and having feminine decorations on.

The few male characters who give earnest appearance-based compliments to other male characters are usually framed as effeminate in some way. Francesco, the Italian race car from *Cars 2*, is designed to be sleeker and slimmer than the main characters. He's also an "open wheel" car, which is implied in the *Cars* universe to be somehow more promiscuous than McQueen's design. Upon meeting McQueen, his first line to him is *You are very good-looking. Not as good as I thought, but you're good.* Later, he comments positively on his own open wheels, saying *Women respect a car that has nothing to hide.* McQueen responds to both of these with just a nervous chuckle, clearly not knowing what to say. Perhaps an even more telling example is from Genie in *Aladdin*, who, in order to comment on Aladdin's wardrobe, literally transforms into a 1990s stereotype of a gay fashion designer.

In sum, we find that appearance compliments are not only rarer for male recipients than for female recipients, but they are also significantly more troubled. Appearance compliments between men are almost never given without an alternative motive, often of mockery; when they are sincere, the giver is often framed as unmasculine. Female-to-male appearance compliments are framed as acceptable, but almost exclusively romantic. But skill compliments on the other hand, can be from anyone, at almost any time.

### Compliments to Children

There's a final compliment context that we want to bring up, however briefly: compliments to children. Appearance-based compliments to young girls on screen were common (from both male and female adult characters). However, perhaps predictably at this point, this pattern doesn't occur with boy character recipients. There's a particularly illustrative exchange in *The Incredibles* where we get to see how Mr. Incredible affirms both of his children after the climactic battle of the film:

**Excerpt 4I "You're wearing your hair back" (*The Incredibles*, 2004)**

BOB:     Hey, you're wearing your hair back?
VIOLET:  Huh? Oh, yeah, I— I just... yeah.
BOB:     **It looks good.**
VIOLET:  Thanks, Dad.
DASH:    **That was so cool when you threw that car!**
BOB:     **Not as cool as you running on water!**

Both Violet and Dash (the two children) participated equally in a fight for their lives moments before this scene occurs. And yet, Bob reaches out to Violet not with a commendation of her performance, but a compliment on her hair.[6]

---

[6] We do recognize that Violet's hair in this movie does symbolize her own character growth from insecurity to self-love, and Bob's compliment here could be read as an affirmation of her newfound confidence. But to that we say, why is it that so many female characters' transformations are visualized through a change in hairstyle or clothes? This trope resurfaces particularly often in the Princess movies, including *Cinderella*, *The Little Mermaid*, *Tangled*, and *Frozen*.

On the other hand, Dash interrupts the conversation with a compliment to his dad on the fight, which Bob enthusiastically returns, and doesn't include Violet in. We wanted to highlight this scene because we believe it points directly to the linguistic double standard discussed throughout this chapter. Female characters are rewarded for their appearance, and complimenting them in that fashion is shorthand for affection; whereas for male characters, young and old alike, the expected topic of a compliment is skill.

## Conclusion

As we had hoped, compliments turned out to be very revealing in terms of exploring ideologies about gender in Disney and Pixar, for both gendered behaviors and the qualities that society values in the ideal man or woman. In these films, compliment giving is not presented as particularly gendered. Compliment receiving, however, does skew towards female recipients. Qualitatively, we found that female characters on screen together are portrayed as using compliments as a routine politeness strategy, and that female villains use the guise of this practice to hide more nefarious purposes. All in all, it seems as if Disney and Pixar at least partially reinforce the ideological relationship between femininity and complimenting behavior.

The role of compliments in constructing masculinity is more complicated. First of all, complimenting other male characters, which was found to carry a strong taboo among heterosexual men in the research, seems to be fairly prevalent in our data. Some of this may be attributable to the task-oriented nature of the plots in most of these films. But we also found plenty of examples of male characters complimenting each other as part of buddy-type bonding, particularly in Pixar, supporting the "New Man" trope that was posited by some media scholars (Gillam and Wooden 2008; Jeffords 1995). At the same time, it continues to be rare for male characters to compliment each other on appearance in a neutral way. When it is done, it often is intended to be mocking at some level, or to suggest that the character is less masculine. The only exception to the rule is in cross-gender romantic settings; appearance compliments, whether given from male to female characters or vice versa, are not only acceptable in romantic situations, but are in fact used as a shorthand for romance (especially in Pixar movies). The relegation of appearance-based compliments to shorthand for romance provides ideological backing for the documented real-life reluctance to give cross-gender compliments (Parisi & Wogan 2006), and may also further cement the homophobic taboo against them in male homosocial settings.

We will return periodically to this question of whether the films are "making progress" and whether that is something we can measure linguistically. For this discourse variable we find that there is a clear change over time for Disney, and a parallel if more subtle change for Pixar: for both, in the more recent films, female characters are increasingly likely to be complimented on their skills rather than their appearance. For male characters, complimenting female characters on their appearance, especially in the case of a romantic relationship, becomes less frequent over time as well. We were glad to see this trend, and the chronological patterning suggests that it stems at least in part from conscious decisions on the part of the Disney studio, related to the type of backlash and discourse with the viewing audience that we discussed at length in Chapter 2. However, we do not see any similar changes over time with regards to compliments to male characters, which speaks to the lack of attention paid to the presentation of masculinity in children's media.

Returning to the wider topic of politeness raised at the beginning of the chapter, we find some initial evidence linking femininity and politeness. It's true that compliments are used by both male and female characters. However, the female characters use compliments as a routine politeness or rapport-building strategy, whereas male characters complimenting one another outside task-based settings is less routine, and at times even framed as a climatically big deal. This suggests to us that although characters of either gender *can* compliment, complimenting as a routine politeness strategy is still associated more closely with femininity. However, compliments are only one of many politeness strategies available for any speaker's repertoire. For the next chapter, we explore directives. With respect to politeness specifically, the decision to phrase directives so as not to threaten someone's face is a common choice that speakers (fictional and real alike) make all the time. Looking at how characters frame their directives on a broad, quantitative scale will provide our next lens into how Disney and Pixar portray politeness strategies in use, and give us another piece of the gender puzzle.

# 5    Directives

Let me rephrase that. Take me up the North Mountain... Please.

Anna, Frozen

### Introduction

Directives are one of the basic building blocks of communication. Directives are defined as speech acts in which a speaker attempts to get the recipient to carry out or refrain from action. Other speech acts we've selected, like insults, compliments, and apologies, are all important for us to function socially with one another – but none of them are quite as common or essential to everyday life as directives. As Goodwin and Cekaite (2013) say, they "constitute a very basic way in which tasks and everyday life get organized" (123).

Directives are a fascinating lens through which to look at gender because their use in everyday life is very closely tied to power. Directives are essentially the request that someone change their course of action to fit the speaker's desire. So, how and when we choose to give such a request has a lot to do with whether or not we think a listener will comply – in other words, how much power we have over them. Formal power structures in school or the workplace, familial relationships, and social hierarchies are all in part constructed through the regulation of directives: the fact that teachers give directives to students freely, but not the other way around, is a fundamental building block of how a classroom works. Less formally, personality traits related to power or assertion (e.g. being passive, aggressive, bossy, demure, and the like) are built and perceived in large part around how and when a speaker chooses to direct others.

Of course, power – formal or informal – can have a lot to do with gender. Women in particular struggle with gaining and holding institutional power, and it has been noted that socially, women can often find themselves trapped between appearing "powerful" or appearing "feminine." In this struggle, some women have begun to police their own (and other women's) use of directives. Currently, the curious can search "How to be an Assertive Woman" on

Wikihow, and find advice like: "Do not make half-statements or add apologies to your requests. For example, do not say to a male colleague, 'If you're not too busy today, would it be possible for you to make those revisions I asked for?' This can come off as a light request. It also may come off as passive-aggressive. Instead, make the request directly. Say something like, 'I need those revisions done by the end of the day'" (Turandot 2020).

Whether this kind of "advice" is accurate or appropriate to give women is a subject for another time. But the fact that the advice exists at all demonstrates the importance of directives in the construction of gender identity, particularly when it comes to inhabiting roles of institutional power. In this chapter, we investigate whether the stereotypes behind directive use are present in our dataset. We'll answer the question of whether male characters formulate directives differently than female characters do. Additionally, we will look closely at whether directives are received differently depending on the gender of the speaking character.

### Background

Directives are formally defined as follows in Searle's 1975 taxonomy of illocutionary acts:

The illocutionary point of these consists in the fact that they are attempts (of varying degrees) ... by the speaker to get the hearer to do something. They may be very modest "attempts," as when I invite you to do it or suggest that you do it, or they may be very fierce attempts as when I insist that you do it ... the propositional content is always that the hearer does some future action. (Searle 1975: 13)

As Searle suggests, although directives have a straightforward intention of inciting actions, they can come in an extremely wide variety of forms. That's because directives are a face-threatening act (FTA) – specifically, one that threatens or damages an addressee's *negative face*, or sense of independent agency by attempting to externally guide their actions (Searle 1975). Face-threatening acts can be handled in a variety of ways, which, according to Brown and Levinson (the progenitors of politeness theory, as discussed in Chapter 4), will vary depending on the relationship or context in which the FTA is uttered.

In the case of directives, speakers have a variety of *mitigation strategies* available to them that help downplay the face threat. These include embedding the directive in a different form (e.g. a question or conditional statement), or using indirect statements to imply the directive without saying it at all. The force of a directive can also be diminished through embellishments or paralinguistic features, like soft whispering tones, politeness (***please** take out the trash*), hedges (*open the window **a little***), and compliments/endearments (*grab me a coffee while you're out, **honey***). Alternatively, speakers have the option to *not* mitigate in any way and instead state their directive outright. They can also choose to use *aggravation strategies* on top of a normal directive to emphasize, rather than downplay, the implicit imposition or threat. Examples of aggravation strategies include insults, raised voices, and even straightforward statements like *that's an order.*

The ways that directives are mitigated or aggravated have social implications. Unmitigated or aggravated directives imply power, because they demonstrate that the speaker believes they may legitimately impose on the addressee (Ervin-Tripp 1976). Mitigation, on the other hand, makes it easier for the addressee to say no or ignore the request altogether, and this increased agency usually implies less hierarchy and/or more solidarity between speaker and hearer. We can see this link between power and directive us in all sorts of social contexts, from parent–child relationships (e.g. Blum-Kulka 1990) to workplaces (e.g. Pearson 1988; Weigel & Weigel 1985) and classrooms (e.g. Davies 2003; Holmes 2013).

There is evidence that gender is a factor for both producing and interpreting directives. Scholars have found that adult women in positions of institutional power tend to enact their power through mitigated more directives than their male counterparts. West (1990) found, for example, that when female doctors in her study gave orders to their patients, they tended to mitigate their commands as a means of minimizing the power difference between themselves and patients. The male doctors in her study, on the other hand, used bald commands and aggravation techniques that emphasized their institutional power.[1]

Parenting techniques often have similarly observable gender differences: fathers tend to be more direct, less polite, more judgmental, and more action-oriented, whereas mothers are more indirect, polite, and compromising (Bellinger & Gleason 1982; Engle 1980; Gleason & Greif 1987). Many researchers have investigated professional settings and have found that female workers often operate by downplaying the institutional power they have (Case 1995; Holmes 2013; Tannen 1996; Wodak 1996). Additionally, we have to consider again that our interest is as much in perception as in actual performance, and women are generally perceived as the more "powerless" gender. Children, for example, perceive both parents as a good deal more direct and authoritative than themselves (Goodwin 1988), but perceive fathers as being more authoritative than mothers (Aronsson & Thorell 1999).

Of course, it's never as simple as "women are nicer than men." Gender is just one of many factors that can influence directive use. For example, urgency or danger has a huge effect on directive form. Common sense, really: if you are

---

[1] See also Cameron (1992) for more on requests, indirectness, and conflict over who is licensed to make requests of whom within the gender order.

urgently hurt and medical attention, you don't ask nicely and quietly for it – you yell, regardless of your gender (Goodwin 2011), Even the originators of linguistic politeness theory observe that in situations of urgency, "imperatives constitute the appropriate and even expected form" (Brown & Levinson 1978).

Marjorie Harness Goodwin (2011) found that situational context can switch expectations for directive use as well. In her ethnography of African-American children at play, she discovered that in open-ended task contexts, young girls worked together in an egalitarian manner, making suggestions rather than commands and being careful not to step on each other's agency; but the same group, when playing "house," adopted a strongly hierarchical structure that closely resembled the boys' group play, with the "mother" at the top of the heap. Others still have found that certain non-gender-based characteristics of an individual, like social status or expertise in the task at hand, are often more important than gender in determining how people form directives (Jones 1992; Vine 2004).

In Disney scholarship, some previous studies have touched on the topic of directives tangentially while analyzing behavioral trends. England et al. (2011) found that a top trait in both male and female Disney characters was "assertiveness," which based on their definition likely includes bald or aggravated directive use.[2] However, the researchers found that when princesses were assertive, it was more often towards animals than other humans. Their conclusions were as follows:

This suggests a fairly submissive and limited way of being assertive, as if they could not assert themselves with other adults, but only when they were mothering, or with those who had less power . . . In contrast to the earlier films, the middle and current films had princesses who were more assertive than in earlier films, and these princesses were assertive towards both people and animals. (563)

England et al. also found that women were more likely to be "tentative," defined as "an experimental manner, uncertain, cautious, seen in behavior or speech" (559). Decker (2010) conducted a study with similar behavioral categories for Pixar movies 1995–2009, and found no significant differences between male and female characters.

All of this leaves us very curious to see how directives work in the Disney and Pixar films. The ideological relationship between gender and directive use, as well as previous behavioral analyses of Disney, suggests to us that female characters may use more mitigation than male characters, a hypothesis we test empirically in this chapter. In addition, directives are so closely tied to power

---

[2] They describe assertiveness as "insistence upon a right claim, the action of declaring or positively stating . . . includes polite assertiveness with a hint of aggression . . . A strong, direct assertion of a position or idea" (2011: 559).

that using directives as a lens will give us a unique view into how Disney and Pixar construct "powerful" characters. This is of particular interest because princesses and queens are, fundamentally, characters with institutional power. The question is, how will they wield it?

## Methodology

The questions we hope to answer in this study include the following:

---

**Key Questions**

- Is there a gender-based difference in who gives and who receives directives in the films?
- What mitigation strategies are used to soften directives? What aggravation strategies are used? Do either of these strategies correlate with gender?
- What other factors, e.g. power/authority, affect directive use? Do these interact with gender in any way?
- How do characters use directives to construct power in conversation?

---

### Data Collection

As with our other quantitative variables, we conducted this analysis from our dataset of 31 Disney and Pixar movies. Every directive in each of the films was collected, and ambiguous cases were discussed until consensus was reached. Ambiguity was fairly common since directives can be extremely indirect, even to the point of being nonverbal. (If you've ever shot someone a dirty look to get them to stop doing something embarrassing in public, you know what we're talking about.) In this case, we tried to understand the illocutionary force implied by the script by tracking if the recipient directly responded to the token in question by carrying out an action and erred on the side of exclusion.

Directives are already a very common speech act, and they become even more so in films that are so action-driven. Scenes are so often composed of determining new courses of action, or yelling at each other during chase scenes, that they're just bursting at the seams with characters telling each other what to do. Our final dataset included 6,904 directives: 2,553 in Disney and 4,351 in Pixar.

### Coding and Quantitative Analysis

A coding system was devised that would allow us to distinguish between plain or aggravated directives and those that use mitigation strategies. This coding

Table 5.1. *Syntactic variation in directives*

| **On-record/unmarked** | |
| --- | --- |
| Bald imperative | ***Warm yourself*** by the fire. |
| Permission statement | ***You can*** start by making yourself more presentable. |
| Want/need statement | ***I want you*** to leave this place. |
| Future statement | ***You will*** wed Jafar. |
| Obligation statement | ***You should*** talk to her. |
| **Indirect/mitigated** | |
| Indirect/hint directive | *I'm stuck. (read: help me)* |
| Collaborative or hidden agent construction | *Oh, a dream!* ***Let's*** *hear all about it!* |
| Embedded/modal construction | ***Will you*** come down to dinner? |
| Example directive | ***I wouldn't*** put my foot there. |
| Conditional statement | ***If*** you listen, they will guide you. |

system is much more granular than those in our other chapters, since it concerns the form of the utterance itself, which can vary widely and on multiple levels. We relied on previous studies to build a detailed taxonomy of directive syntax (Aronsson & Thorell 1999; Ervin-Tripp 1976; Goodwin 1980, 1990; Kendall 2004). We then took inspiration from Ervin-Tripp (1976)'s taxonomy to categorize these different structures into two major categories: "on-record" directives, and directives that are indirect or syntactically mitigated in some way. Grammatical structures and examples are listed in Table 5.1.

We then separately coded for the presence or absence of additional, non-syntactic mitigation strategies. These strategies were also drawn from a variety of previous studies (Aronsson & Thorell 1999; Goodwin 1980, 1990; Kendall 2004). Each directive was coded for presence or absence of the following:

(1) Endearing or deferential address
   *Rex, I could use a hand over here,* **buddy.** *(Toy Story 2)*
(2) Compliment to recipient
   *It seems our little... froggy prince lost his way. And I need your* **generous assistance** *in getting him back. (The Princess and the Frog)*
(3) Hedge or minimizer
   *But if you could do me a* **little favor** *before you leave, um, if you could* **just squish me.** *(A Bug's Life)*
(4) Reasoning for request
   *We have to get closer to Becky* **so she can hear us.** *(Finding Dory)*
(5) Politeness lexicon
   *If you would just stop the winter, bring back summer?* **Please?** *(Frozen)*
(6) Paralinguistic mitigation (soft or whispering tones)

After granular coding was complete, directives were all re-sorted into two primary categories (mitigated and unmitigated). Directives were classified as *mitigated* if they were syntactically indirect, and/or if they used any of the additional mitigation strategies listed above. Otherwise, they were categorized as *unmitigated*.

The background literature suggests that gender is only one factor among many that could impact directive production. So, to control for that possibility, we also coded each directive for various social elements, listed below:

(1) *Urgency*. Situation is "urgent" if someone's life or safety is in danger, or timely compliance is essential to the current task.
(2) *Institutional Power*. Directives were marked if they took place within context of hierarchical institutions (e.g. a classroom, the army, or a palace with royalty present), where the speaker and recipient are both involved in the institution (e.g. a sultan or queen speaking to servants, or a general speaking to his soldiers).
(3) *Goodness*. Disney protagonists and their friends were coded as "good," the villain and their henchmen as "bad," and everyone else was coded as "neutral." Goodness coding is applied to Princess films only. Pixar films didn't reliably have a "good vs. bad" plot structure, and trying to sort characters in this way felt forced or even impossible.

To begin our analysis, we provide a descriptive overview of directives given and received by each gender, broken down by era and compared against proportions of words spoken. In other chapters, we use binomial tests to test the significance of our findings; however, directives have so many factors potentially influencing their use that just comparing frequencies didn't feel particularly helpful.

Instead, to account for the various contextual factors, we ran a set of binomial mixed-effect regression models[3] testing the effects of gender, power, and urgency on the likelihood of directive mitigation.[4] We ran separate regressions for Disney and Pixar; the Disney films also included factors for the Era of the film and the Goodness of the speaker. Both models also included random effects for individual movies and individual speakers within the movies, to account for idiosyncratic character personalities and overall style differences between scripts.

---

[3] For statistically-minded readers: the link function used in our model is logistic.
[4] For statistically-minded readers (again): Please note that the regression was run with mitigation as a base level, meaning that positive coefficients indicate that directives are *less* likely to be mitigated.

Lastly, we include a separate qualitative discussion following up on the results of our quantitative analyses. Our discussion focuses on the particular intersection of gender and institutional power.

## Directive Givers and Receivers

### Who Tells Who What to Do?

The data in Table 5.2 show us that, for the most part, the number of directives given by each gender is very close to the number of words that gender speaks. This is true for the Renaissance (male characters speak 78 percent of words, give 80 percent of directives), the New Age (50 percent of words, 51 percent of directives), and Pixar (74 percent of words, 76 percent of directives). This suggests to us that in these three eras, the frequency of directive use is not really related to gender at all.

As discussed above, directives are a fundamental building block of social life. Features like compliments, insults, or apologies serve social functions that ultimately are kind of optional in everyday life. For example, you could never give any compliments to anyone, and though you might not be well-liked, you could definitely survive in society. Since these speech acts serve primarily social functions, the frequency of their use accordingly varies depending on social factors, gender of speaker and giver among them. Directives, on the other hand, serve a functional purpose that is much more difficult to avoid. This is as true in movies as it is in real life: characters communicate desires, argue, solve problems, collaborate, escape danger, and generally move the plot forward largely through the mechanism of directives. Basically, if a character, you know, *does things*, then they'll be giving directives at some point, regardless of their gender.

This fact is interesting to consider in light of the Classic Era of Disney, which is the only subset where words spoken and directives given don't proportionally match up. Male characters in the Classic Era give more directives than their speech levels would suggest, by a much higher margin than other eras (41 percent of speech, 48 percent of directives), and women proportionally give less. Although the Classic Era does have higher than average counts of female characters, we think these numbers belie the fact that the principal female characters (i.e. the princesses) are passive in their own plots. The male characters of this era also contribute to this imbalance, because the Classic movies (more than any other time period) dedicate a lot of screen time to male royalty. *Sleeping Beauty* and *Cinderella*'s most talkative male characters aren't the princes, but rather the kings, who spend a hearty portion of their screen time bossing around characters in their court. These data suggest a relationship between directive giving and male-coded enactment of institutional authority, which we explore at length later in this chapter.

Table 5.2. *Directives given and received by character gender*

| | Male | | | Female | | |
|---|---|---|---|---|---|---|
| | Total speech | Directives given | Directives received | Total speech | Directives given | Directives received |
| **Classic** | 41% (4,684) | 48% (253) | 48% (253) | 59% (6,710) | 52% (274) | 39% (206) |
| **Renaissance** | 78% (19,756) | 80% (779) | 67% (656) | 22% (5,643) | 21% (202) | 26% (260) |
| **New Age** | 50% (16,899) | 51% (532) | 45% (466) | 50% (16,762) | 49% (509) | 48% (503) |
| **Pixar** | 74% (111,662) | 76% (3,304) | 66% (2851) | 26% (38,950) | 24% (1,028) | 19% (812) |

No binomial tests were run for this chapter.

The totals of directives received in this table are less than 100% in many cases, because the directives are often given to groups of people, and these are not included in our coding schema.

### Predictors of Directive Mitigation

We turn now to the more interesting question, which is whether gender impacts *how* directives are delivered. Our coding of mitigation strategies yielded a total of 720 mitigated directives from Disney and 1,170 mitigated directives from Pixar. These directives make up the minority of the overall directives dataset (28 percent Disney; 27 percent Pixar) The bulk of the directives were unmarked by any particular strategy, syntactic or otherwise (63 percent Disney, 64 percent Pixar). A small number were also found to be aggravated through embellishments or paralinguistic features (8 percent Disney, 10 percent Pixar). Aggravated directives were included in the unmitigated category for the purposes of regression analysis.

Results of our regression analyses are displayed in Tables 5.3 and 5.4. The effect of each individual predictor is discussed below.

> *Gender.* Both models show that male characters are significantly less likely to mitigate directives than female characters. This supports

Table 5.3. *Predictors of directive mitigation in Disney Princess films*

| Category | Level | Estimate (Standard error) | P value |
|---|---|---|---|
| Gender (vs. female) | Male | **0.33** (0.13) | ** |
| Urgent (vs. nonurgent) | Urgent | **1.06** (0.15) | ** |
| Power (vs. NA) | Equal | −0.34 (0.33) | |
| | Down | **0.38** (0.18) | * |
| | Up | **−0.57** (0.20) | ** |
| Goodness (vs. other) | Good | −0.05 (0.14) | |
| | Bad | 0.15 (0.19) | |
| Era (vs. Classic) | Renaissance | **−0.59** (0.18) | ** |
| | New Age | **−0.54** (0.18) | ** |

*p ≤ 0.05; **p ≤ 0.01

Regressions were run with mitigation as a base level. Positive coefficients should be interpreted as *less* likely to mitigate, and negative coefficients as *more* likely to mitigate.

Table 5.4. *Predictors of directive mitigation in Pixar films*

| Category | Level | Estimate (Standard error) | P value |
|---|---|---|---|
| Gender (vs. female) | Male | **0.27** (0.10) | ** |
| Urgent (vs. nonurgent) | Urgent | **0.91** (0.10) | ** |
| Power (vs. NA) | Equal | 0.03 (0.17) | |
| | Down | **0.25** (0.11) | ** |
| | Up | **−0.49** (0.17) | ** |

*p ≤ 0.05; **p ≤ 0.01
Regressions were run with mitigation as a base level. Positive coefficients should be interpreted as *less* likely to mitigate, and negative coefficients as *more* likely to mitigate.

our primary hypothesis of this chapter, which is that gender is a salient factor in determining mitigation strategies.

*Urgency.* Both models show that characters are significantly less likely to mitigate in urgent situations than in nonurgent ones. Both models also show that urgency has the *largest* impact on the likelihood of mitigation of any factor we looked at.

*Power.* Both models show that characters that have institutional power over their addressees are significantly less likely to mitigate their commands compared to characters unaffected by power differences. Conversely, characters who are speaking up a chain of command are significantly more likely to use mitigation strategies. However, there's no significant effect in either dataset when interlocutors are of equal status within a power structure.

*Goodness (Disney Princess only).* The "goodness" of a Disney character has no significant impact on the likelihood of mitigation. Whether a character is a hero, a villain, or just a bystander – it doesn't matter, at least as an independent factor.

*Era.* Compared to the Classic Era films, directives in the Renaissance and New Age eras have a significantly higher chance of being mitigated, independent of any other factors. This result is indicative of changing script styles. Classic Era movies featured minimal, formal dialogue compared to later films, making them feel less like realistic dialogue and more like classical plays (parts of *Snow White* and *Sleeping Beauty* are even written in metered verse.)

The consequence of this style is that mitigation strategies which are common in real-life speech are often eschewed for more straightforward embedded imperatives. The later films, on the other hand, attempt to mimic "real-life" speech, increasing the mitigation rates significantly.

In sum, these results suggest that our two main factors of interest in this chapter – gender and power – both have a significant impact on the mitigation of directives. But we're curious as to what that actually *means* in terms of actual script dialogue. How is power communicated in Disney Princess and Pixar films? And how does gender factor into the way that different characters assume power?

## Qualitative Discussion: Gender and Power

The remainder of this chapter will highlight specific qualitative themes concerning gender and power, using directives as our analytical tool. In the following discussions, we pull individual excerpts from both Disney and Pixar datasets. Each directive in the excerpts is labeled with how it was coded in our analysis (unmarked, mitigated, or aggravated).[5] For mitigated and aggravated commands, we also included the specific mitigating elements (syntax, embellishments, and paralinguistic elements).

### Directness, Politeness, and Gender

Firstly, we found solid qualitative support for our quantitative findings in that direct, unmarked directives in Disney and Pixar are associated with masculinity, and indirect or mitigated directives are associated with femininity. In other words, we can both support and put a finer point on previous scholars' findings that male Disney characters are more "assertive" than female characters (England et al. 2011; Hine et al. 2018).

In some cases, we don't even need to dive into linguistic patterns, because the films make meta-linguistic or meta-behavioral comments that explicitly reinforce the relationship between gender and assertiveness. For example, in one scene from *Mulan* (1997), sidekicks Mushu and Cricket are trying to write an urgent letter to a war general. Cricket pens the letter, which Mushu reads aloud and comments on in Excerpt 5A.

---

[5] We didn't have sufficient space in the chapter to give aggravation its due with a quantitative analysis. But we decided to still include it qualitatively, since aggravating commands ended up being pretty important for how some characters choose to be powerful.

**Excerpt 5A "HELLO, this is the army!" (*Mulan*, 1998)**

MUSHU: Okay, okay, let me see what you've got. From General Li, dear son, **we're waiting for the huns at the pass and it would mean a lot if you'd come and back us up.** *(mitigated; conditional, endearing address; reasoning)* That's very great except you forgot, **"and since we're all out of potpourri, maybe you wouldn't mind bringing up some."** HELLO, this is the army! **Make it sound more urgent, please!** *(mitigated; politeness lexicon)*

Cricket's first draft is filled with mitigation strategies: he embeds the directive in a conditional construction, he provides context and reasoning, and he includes a complimentary address as further embellishment. Mushu then does our job for us, and comments directly on the linguistic construction of Cricket's draft. And in his remarks, we see two elements of our quantitative results reflected. First, he notes that mitigation and urgency don't mix: in Mushu's opinion, the polite tone of the letter works against the urgency of the message. Secondly (and more interestingly) Mushu implies that the message isn't just too casual, but that it's also *girly*, despite the fact that Cricket is coded as male. Potpourri is a feminine-coded object, and by bringing it up in his sarcastic remarks on the draft, Mushu implies that the entire letter sounds womanly, and therefore inappropriate for the moment. The takeaway is that mitigation and femininity are tied ideologically, and both run counter to assertive and urgent messaging.

Pixar also calls out ideological differences between masculine and feminine directive strategies in their film *Inside Out* (2015). The central concept of *Inside Out* is that each character has a cast of sentient emotions in their heads that collectively decide on their actions. One scene in particular uses this technique to draw comic comparisons between strategies of parental authority. The main character, Riley, is at the dinner table with her mother and father. Riley starts sass-talking her parents, which is uncharacteristic behavior, and the parents must decide how to address or correct the behavior. The film juxtaposes two scenes: one, of the mother's internal reaction, visualized as a calm conversation between her five emotions (all female), and the other of the father's reaction, visualized as a war-like hierarchical conversation between his five emotions (all male). The two dialogues are shown below in direct comparison:

**Excerpt 5B "Something's wrong" (*Inside Out*, 2015)**

MOM'S SADNESS: Did you guys pick up on that?
MOM'S EMOTIONS: Oh yeah, definitely.
MOM'S DISGUST: Something's wrong.
MOM'S ANGER: Should we ask her?
MOM'S SADNESS: **Let's probe.** *(mitigated: collaborative)* **But keep it subtle, so she doesn't notice.** *(unmarked)*

| | |
|---|---|
| MOM: | So! How was the first day of school?. . . |
| MOM'S ANGER: | Something's definitely going on. |
| MOM'S DISGUST: | She's never acted like this before. What should we do? |
| MOM'S SADNESS: | **We're going to find out what's happening.** (*mitigated; collaborative*) |
| | But we'll need support. **Signal the husband.** (*unmarked*) |

### Excerpt 5C "Prepare the foot!" (*Inside Out*, 2015)

| | |
|---|---|
| DAD'S FEAR: | Sir, she just rolled her eyes at us. |
| DAD'S ANGER: | What is her deal? Alright, **make a show of force.** (*unmarked*) I don't want to have to put "the Foot" down. |
| DAD'S FEAR: | No. Not the Foot. |
| DAD: | Riley, I do not like this new attitude. . . |
| DAD'S ANGER: | Here it comes. . . **Prepare the Foot!** (*unmarked*) |
| DAD'S FEAR: | **Keys to safety position!** (*unmarked*) Ready to launch on your command, Sir! |
| RILEY: | Just **shut up!** (*aggravated; raised voice*) |
| DAD'S ANGER: | **Fire**! (*aggravated; raised voice*) |
| DAD: | **That's it, go to your room! Now!** (*aggravated; urgency*) |

This scene draws sharp contrasts in gendered behavior on two levels: there are obvious differences in parenting styles on display, but the ways that the parents' emotions themselves come to a solution on what to do with Riley are also extremely divergent. The mother's emotions decide to respond to Riley's sarcasm by probing for more information; her principal emotion, sadness, specifically suggests they "keep it subtle" to avoid any conflict. Amongst themselves, the emotions work cooperatively, offering suggestions and asking each others' opinions. After Riley responds negatively, the mother's emotions become insistent on "finding out what's happening," rather than enacting any discipline. She tries to do so by signaling the father to get him involved in the conversation, a move which is explicitly framed as "needing support."[6]

Once involved in the conversation, the father takes a very different approach. His emotions, to begin with, are organized hierarchically rather than cooperatively, being modeled on a military unit with a commander and a number of subordinate officers. They spend a good deal of time yelling things to each other, which is in contrast with the volume and cadence of the softer board meeting/book club style of the mother's emotions. In terms of parenting, as soon as the father is met with resistance from Riley (in this case, an eye roll),

---

[6] Checking out of emotional or familial conversations is another long-running element of Disney's version of masculinity, as discussed in Chapter 3. *Inside Out* manages to fit a lot of gender stereotypes into this scene.

he chooses to make a "show of force," which is ostensibly a threat, emphasizing the power differences between parent and child. The scene culminates with the father "putting his foot down," with an aggravated directive (realized in-universe as a humorous extended reference to military strikes).

The juxtaposition of these two scenes is obviously meant to be funny. It relies on the exaggeration of perceived gender differences between men and women, and at the same time naturalizes those differences by literally showing us the insides of a male and a female brain. Importantly for us, the comments of each "brain" also naturalize gendered linguistic differences. Female brains "keep it subtle," and male brains "make a show of force." Even more directly than *Mulan*, *Inside Out* communicates that masculinity is associated with aggression, hierarchy, and directness, even when these behaviors aren't situationally appropriate; and femininity is associated with subtlety, indirectness, and collaboration, even when given position of power (in this case, over a child).

### *I'm Still the King: Masculinity and Institutional Authority*

Much has been made in previous literature of how men and women deal differently with formal power, such as being a doctor (e.g. West 1990), a teacher (e.g. Davies 2003), or a boss (e.g. Vine 2004). Disney and Pixar have plenty of male characters in positions of power, making this a rich site of analysis to understand how these films envision masculinity in institutional authority roles.

We found that male leaders in these films are portrayed as natural in their authority roles. They're often established as authority figures early and easily in their narratives. Their linguistic strategies reflect their natural power through their liberal use of unmitigated or aggravated directives.[7] In *Toy Story 2*, Woody, the leader of Andy's toys, opens the movie by walking through Andy's rooms and issuing the following directives in preparation for his leaving on a trip:

**Excerpt 5D "Here's your list of things to do"** (*Toy Story 2*, 1999)

WOODY:    Okay. Here's your list of things to do while I'm gone. **Batteries need to be changed.** (*unmarked*) **Toys in the bottom of the chest need to be rotated.** (*unmarked*) **Oh, and make sure everyone attends Mr. Spell's seminar on what to do if you or part of you is swallowed.** (*unmarked*) Okay? Okay. Good. Okay.

---

[7] In our research, we actually realized that this even manifests in Disney song lyrics and titles: "Dig, Dig, Dig," "Kill the Beast," "Be a Man," and "Kiss the Girl" are all examples of songs in the Renaissance Era named after the male soloist in the song telling someone else what to do. Compare with the Princess's songs, which all fit in the narrative category of the "I Want" song. "Part of your World," "Reflection," "Just around the Riverbend," and "Bonjour" are all declarations of desire, but aren't actually sung as a way to tell anyone else what to do.

In this scene, Woody casually issues a series of unmarked directives to the toys around him. His orders are followed easily and without question. Other male characters in authority positions are similarly characterized in a relatively straightforward way. In many instances, their directives are used more for establishing plot than for establishing anything about their character. For example, Chief Powhatan in *Pocahontas* addresses his people with unmitigated directives, and in doing so, also tells the audience important plot information:

**We will call on our brothers to help us fight.** (unmarked) These white men are dangerous! **No one is to go near them.** (unmarked)

Commands like these don't really stand out, nor do they tell us anything about Powhatan's relationship with authority. That's the point: authoritative male characters are so status quo that their directives just fade into the background.

When authoritative male characters *are* challenged, their response is usually to use unmitigated or aggravated directives to establish hierarchical dominance in the scene. We already saw that masculine authority figures (even informal ones, like fathers) can use these strategies, like the father in *Inside Out*. But combine fatherhood with a formal leadership role like royalty, and the exaggerated dominance can become even more dramatic. Take, for instance, two examples of parent–child arguments between princes/princesses and their kingly fathers in 5E and 5F:

**Excerpt 5E "Nowadays I'm still the king" (*Sleeping Beauty*, 1959)**

HUBERT:     A peasant g-g-girl? You're going to marry a... Why Phillip, you're joking! isn't he? **You can't do this to me!** *(unmarked)*
            **Give up the throne, the kingdom, for some, some nobody?**
            **By Harry, I won't have it.** *(aggravated: insult)*
            You're a prince, and **you're going to marry a princess!** *(unmarked)*
PHILLIP:    Now father, you're living in the past.
            This is the fourteenth century. Nowadays...
HUBERT:     **Nowadays I'm still the king, and I command you to come to your senses.**
            *(aggravated: command)*

**Excerpt 5F "As long as you live under my ocean" (*The Little Mermaid*, 1989)**

TRITON:     They're dangerous.
            Do you think I want to see my youngest daughter snared by some fish-eater's hook?
ARIEL:      I'm sixteen years old— I'm not a child anymore—
TRITON:     **Don't you take that tone of voice with me young lady.** *(unmarked)*
            **As long as you live under my ocean, you'll obey my rules!**
            *(aggravated: command)*

ARIEL:     **But if you would just listen—** *(mitigated: conditional)*
TRITON:    **Not another word—** *(unmarked)* and **I am never, NEVER to hear of you going to the surface again.**
           **Is that clear?** *(aggravated: raised voice, command)*

In both of these exchanges, the kings are frustrated that their children have expressed interest in a romantic partner that they have not approved. The dialogue, which in both cases comes directly after the revelation of this fact, begins with a questioning and invalidation of the child's reasoning. Subsequently, both father characters take the discursive move of emphasizing institutional power differences, rather than making familial connections or emphasizing solidarity. They do so by invoking either their own royal authority (*my ocean*) or their child's institutional royal status (*You're a prince*). Both children respond to this by challenging authority once again. In response, both kings further aggravate their directives, emphasizing in particular that their directives are nonoptional commands. In these cases, aggravation and hierarchical dominance triumph over mitigation strategies that otherwise could be used to defuse the situation.

### Even Princesses Say Please: Femininity and Institutional Authority

Compared to the cast of male leaders, there relatively few female characters in authority roles in Disney and Pixar films. In the Princess movies, most mother figures are absent, which means there are few queens, as compared with the kings we just analyzed. Pixar also has comparatively few female characters in institutional authority, and only two or three are protagonists – Joy from *Inside Out*, Queen Elinor from *Brave*, and arguably Princess Atta from *A Bug's Life*. These characters stand out from the many male leaders of Disney in that their relationship with authority is *not* taken for granted by the narrative. Their method of maintaining authority tends to be less direct, and the act of convincing another to do something, or overcoming a challenge to their authority, can become a plot point or a humorous beat instead of just background noise.

One great example of this more feminine-coded leadership style is shown by Joy from *Inside Out*. Early in the movie, she, much like Woody from the *Toy Story* series, is established in a leadership role as the head of Riley's emotions; but unlike Woody, she is shown having to work to convince people of her ways, even though she's theoretically in charge. In one exchange, she tries to get another female character, Sadness, to stay out of the way after causing some trouble in their mutual work space:

**Excerpt 5G "Atta girl"** (*Inside Out*, 2015)

JOY:       Oh— Sadness! I have a super important job just for you.
SADNESS:   Really?

| | |
|---|---|
| JOY: | **Mmm-hmmm. Follow me**. *(unmarked)* |
| SADNESS: | What are you doing? |
| JOY: | *[draws chalk circle around sadness]* And... there. Perfect. This is the circle of Sadness. **Your job is to make sure that all the Sadness stays inside of it.** *(unmarked)* |
| SADNESS: | So... you want me to just stand here? |
| JOY: | **Hey, it's not MY place to tell you how to do your job.** *(mitigated: indirect)* **Just make sure that ALL the Sadness stays in the circle.** *(mitigated: hedge)* See? You're a pro at this! *(compliment)* Isn't this fun? |
| SADNESS: | No. |
| JOY: | Atta girl. |

In this conversation, Joy demonstrates several stereotypically feminine directive strategies, particularly in her last line. She uses a hedge (*just make sure*) to downplay the directive, compliments both her (*you're a pro*) and the job she's assigned (*I have a super important job . . . Isn't this fun?*), and uses a friendly tone that attempts to convince, rather than demand. She even explicitly downplays her own authority in the space by saying *it's not my place to tell you how to do your job*, even though, by the logic of the movie, it literally is her place.

As discussed above, many male characters react to questions to their authority by doubling down on strategies that emphasize hierarchy and authority. But when female characters have to enforce directives to subordinates, they often display a certain reluctance to do so. In *A Bug's Life*, for example, Princess Atta is in a meeting with some of her council members (Thornie and an unnamed council member, both male), when she is confronted by the main character Flik, who interrupts her and starts a conversation against her wishes:

### Excerpt 5H "Flik, please" (*A Bug's Life*, 1998)

| | |
|---|---|
| FLIK: | This is my new idea for harvesting grain. No more picking individual kernels. You can just cut down the entire stock! |
| ATTA: | Flik! **We don't have time for this.** *(mitigated: indirect)* |
| FLIK: | Exactly. We never have time for ourselves cuz we spend all summer harvesting for the offering. But my invention will speed up production. |
| ATTA: | Another invention? |
| FLIK: | Yeah, and I've got something for you, too. |
| ATTA: | **Flik...** *(mitigated: indirect)* |
| FLIK: | Since you're gonna be queen soon, you can use this to oversee production. **Doctor Flora, if I may...** *(mitigated: indirect)* Just an ordinary blade of grass and a bead of dew. Right? |
| ATTA: | **Flik, please.** *(mitigated: indirect, politeness)* |
| FLIK: | Wrong! It is, in fact, a telescope! |
| ATTA: | **It's very clever, Flik, but—** *(mitigated: indirect, compliment)* |
| FLIK: | Hello, princess. My, aren't you looking lovely this morning! Not, of course, like you would need a telescope to see that... |

| | |
|---|---|
| THORNIE: | **Alright, listen!** *(aggravated: raised voice)* The princess doesn't have time for this! You want to help us fill this thing? **Then get rid of that machine, get back in line, and pick grain like everybody else!** *(aggravated: raised voice)* |
| COUNCIL MEMBER: | Like everybody else! |
| ATTA: | **Please, Flik. Just go.** *(mitigated: politeness, hedge)* |

In this scene, Princess Atta has absolute institutional authority over everyone around her – especially Flik, who by the movie's own description, is a "nobody" civilian ant. Despite this, Flik approaches her without permission and begins talking with her (and over her) about his new inventions. Atta shows increasing discomfort throughout the scene, but her attempts to get him to stop talking are indirect to the point of incompletion, and some are further mitigated by politeness and compliments (*Flik, please; it's very clever*). She doesn't actually even get an entire directive into the conversation until the final line, which is mitigated twice over (*Please . . . just go*). Ultimately, it's not Atta at all, but her two council members – both male – who actually change Flik's behavior, and use a string of unmitigated commands to do so.

Queen Elsa from *Frozen* is another female leader who experiences a direct challenge to her authority, in this case on the issue of her sister's marriage. The conversation is public, happening in the middle of her coronation ball, and all the more face-threatening for it. Although Elsa is characterized as more strong-willed than Anna, she also resists emphasizing her authority in response to a public challenge:

**Excerpt 5I "My answer is no" (*Frozen*, 2013)**

| | |
|---|---|
| ELSA: | **Wait.** *(unmarked)* **Slow down.** *(unmarked)* **No one's brothers are staying here.** *(unmarked)* **No one is getting married.** *(unmarked)* |
| ANNA: | Wait, what? |
| ELSA: | **May I talk to you, please. Alone.** *(mitigated: embedded, politeness)* |
| ANNA: | No. **Whatever you have to say, you— you can say to both of us.** *(unmarked)* |
| ELSA: | Fine. **You can't marry a man you just met.** *(unmarked)* |
| ANNA: | You can if it's true love. |
| ELSA: | Anna, what do you know about true love? |
| ANNA: | More than you. All you know is how to shut people out. |
| ELSA: | You asked for my blessing, but my answer is no. **Now, excuse me.** *(unmarked)* |
| HANS: | **Your Majesty, if I may ease your—** *(mitigated: embedded, address)* |
| ELSA: | **No, you may not.** *(unmarked)* **And I— I think you should go.** *(mitigated: embedded, hedge)* **The party is over. Close the gates.** *(unmarked)* |

Elsa's lack of aggravating techniques in example 5I is striking compared to the kings' strategies in examples 5E and 5F. Elsa begins by expressing her concern with on-record syntactic structures, which Anna immediately challenges.

Elsa then responds not by asserting her dominance, but by offering a face-saving out to Anna, mitigated with politeness (*May I talk to you please. Alone*). When Anna challenges this as well, Elsa reasserts her directive (*You can't marry a man you just met*). Anna becomes agitated, and begins to insult Elsa in a raised voice, which Elsa responds to by maintaining an even tone rather than aggravating her commands in any way (*You asked for my blessing, but my answer is no*). She even mitigates and stutters through her command to Prince Hans to leave. In both these cases, we see royalty who should have absolute power opt for strategies of maintaining solidarity instead of emphasizing the existing hierarchy

The exceptions to this trend are, perhaps predictably, the villainous royals and mothers of the Disney Princess line: the Evil Queen (*Snow White*), the Evil Stepmother (*Cinderella*), Maleficent (*Sleeping Beauty*), and Mother Gothel (*Tangled*).[8] Although goodness has no independent quantitative effect on whether or not directives are mitigated in the dataset as a whole, we would be remiss if we didn't point out the pattern of unmitigated (or even intensely aggravated) directive strategies employed by these characters. In an expository scene in *Snow White*, for example, the Evil Queen orders the princess's death in the following manner:

**Excerpt 5J "You will kill her" (*Snow White*, 1937)**

QUEEN:    **Take her far into the forest.** (*unmarked*) **Find some secluded glade where she can pick wildflowers.** (*unmarked*)
GUARD:    Yes, your majesty.
QUEEN:    **And there, my faithful huntsman, you will kill her!** (*mitigated: address*)
GUARD:    But, your majesty, the little princess!
QUEEN:    **Silence!** (*aggravated: raised voice*) You know the penalty if you fail. (*aggravated: threat*)

Here, unlike "nice" rulers discussed above, the Queen begins with unmitigated directives and tolerates no discussion from her subordinate. When the guard challenges her, she does what we see "good" male rulers do: she shuts down the challenge and emphasizes the hierarchical difference in power, in this case through threats.

### Yes, Dear: Femininity and Domestic Authority

While female characters don't often hold positions of institutional power in Disney, they do commonly inhabit roles of domestic authority. This has been

---

[8] The Disney villainesses are the most obvious examples, but others are to be found. The Pixar movies have a way of characterizing older women in positions of authority as severe and/or unpleasant. Roz, the slug-secretary from *Monsters, Inc.* and Dr. Hardscrabble from *Monsters University* both are portrayed in this way, for example.

noted in Towbin et al. (2004), who found in a thematic analysis that women were domestic and likely to marry, while men were likely to have nondomestic jobs. We bring this up in a linguistic context because it seems to be the case that although female characters resist expressing hierarchical institutional authority, they do not have the same discomfort when it comes to domestic situations. Consider, for example, Excerpt 5K from *Snow White*, whose princess is infamous for being hyperfeminine and passive:

**Excerpt 5K "Let me see your hands" (*Snow White*, 1937)**

| | |
|---|---|
| SNOW WHITE: | Uh uh uh, **just a minute.** (*mitigated: hedge*) Supper's not quite ready. **You'll just have time to wash.** (*mitigated: indirect*) |
| ALL DWARFS: | Wash? |
| GRUMPY: | Hah! Knew there's a catch to it! |
| BASHFUL: | Why wash? |
| HAPPY: | What for? We ain't goin' nowhere. |
| DOC: | Tain't new year. |
| SNOW WHITE: | Oh, perhaps you have washed. |
| DOC: | Perhaps we— yes, perhaps we have. But when? Uh, you said, when? Why, last week— uh month— year— why recently. |
| ALL DWARFS: | Yes, recently. |
| SNOW WHITE: | Oh, recently. **Let me see your hands.** (*unmarked*) **Let me see your hands.** (*unmarked*) Why, Doc, I'm surprised. Come on. **Let's see them.** (*mitigated: collaborative*) Oh, Bashful, my my my! **And you?** (*unmarked*) Tsk, tsk, tsk! Worse than I thought. Oh! How shocking. Tsk, tsk, tsk! Goodness me, this will never do. **March straight outside and wash, or you'll not get a bite to eat.** (*aggravated: threat*) |

Snow White begins by mitigating her requests to the dwarfs, as she has done up to this point in the film. However, as they challenge her on an issue of cleanliness in the context of the kitchen, she transforms, delivering on-record commands and raising her voice. She criticizes the dwarfs (*Worse than I thought*), shames them (*Why Doc, I'm surprised*), and at the end of the dialogue, delivers one of the only two threats in the entire movie (*. . . or you'll not get a bite to eat*). She is also the only one to deliver directives in this scene, despite the fact that she's a guest and it's her first evening in the dwarfs' house. Her actions more closely resemble a male with institutional power, presumably as a direct result of her domestic, mothering role.

It's worth noting that her voice is somewhat infantilizing towards the dwarfs in this exchange; her scolding is particularly reminiscent of a maternal parent– child relationship (Aronsson & Thorell 1999; Bellinger & Gleason 1982; Kendall 2008). The implication here may be that the root of the linguistic expression of domestic authority is actually found in constructing a kind of pseudo-motherhood to the men around them. Indeed, some studies of real-life speakers have also documented women in positions of power purposefully calling on "maternal discourses" to construct their sense of authority (Kendall 2004, 2008; Wodak 1996). We also want to re-raise Goodwin's finding that girls adopted hierarchical play style when playing "house," and the girl playing the "mother" was the one who could give others orders.

Other female characters also create authority by indexing some maternal or domestic identity. Most notably, Queen Elinor of *Brave* (2012) is portrayed as a knowledgeable and effective ruler, but many of her authoritative moments come from positioning male rulers (including her own husband) as rowdy boys. In one scene, for example, a fight breaks out between the leaders of four warring clans, and a massive brawl ensues. Lord Fergus begins by egging on the fight, but is interrupted by a meaningful look from his wife, Elinor:

**Excerpt 5L "Show a little decorum" (*Brave*, 2012)**

| | |
|---|---|
| FERGUS: | **Catch 'em!** *(unmarked)* **Catch 'em!** *(unmarked)* **Bash the wee little D—** *(unmarked)* *[Elinor glares at Fergus.]* *(mitigated: indirect)* **Oh alright. That's it! Now, that's all done! You've had your go at each other, show a little decorum.** *(aggravated: raised voice)* **And no more fighting!** *(aggravated: raised voice)* <br> *[Fighting resumes, Fergus joins.]* <br> *[Elinor finds the four lords and drags them to the front of the hall by their ears.]* |
| LORD MACINTOSH: | I didn't start it, it was he who— my lady queen. I feel terrible. My humblest apologies. |
| LORD DINGWALL: | Sorry. |
| LORD MACGUFFIN: | We mean no disrespect. |
| FERGUS: | Sorry, love. I... I didn't— but— yes, dear. |

It's arguable, but we'd make the case that the first directive meant to stop the fighting isn't from Fergus, but from Elinor herself; her glaring look at Fergus is clearly meant to prompt his action to stop the fighting, with which he immediately complies. Elinor here is being doubly indirect: first, by using nonlinguistic means, and second, by using her husband to achieve her true goal, which is to stop the fighting. Fergus' attempt, on the other hand, is direct, unmitigated, and further aggravated by raised voice and accusatory gestures. Like *Inside Out*, *Brave* derives humor on several occasions by these comparisons between male and female authoritative strategies.

The directives that Fergus yells out prove to be ineffective, and fighting breaks out again almost immediately. Unable to control himself, he also joins the brawl. At this point, Elinor loses patience, cuts through the crowd to find the four kings, and drags them to the front of the room by the ears. Once at the front, they stand sheepishly facing her, muttering apologies, the film purposely calling to mind the image of young chastised boys. Her husband delivers a comic punchline saying *Sorry love. I... I didn't— but— yes, dear.* In this scene, Elinor is characterized as the only leader in the room with real power; however, the film humorously positions her not as a stateswoman, but as a mother and wife. The final line of the exchange being *yes, dear* solidifies the connection between her power and her role as a domestic authority.

### *Female Assertion as Exceptional*

Finally, we want to turn our attention toward the Disney Princess movies in particular, and briefly discuss a trend we've noticed in the New Age princesses. As discussed in Chapter 2, the New Age films in particular have a complicated and at times even paradoxical relationship to the idea of "empowered femininity." On one hand, the princesses of this era are more agential and authoritative than any of their predecessors (Hine et al. 2018). But on the other hand, the New Age movies attempt to embrace femininity, and sell their heroines as more traditionally feminine than the Girl Power princesses of the 1990s. One of the results of this balancing act is that New Age princesses do assert themselves, but the linguistic portrayal of the assertion suggests that there is something difficult or even unnatural about enacting authority. The underlying implication is that the princesses in these films are uncomfortable and unused to wielding direct, unmitigated power, even if they've been royalty-in-training their whole lives.

In fact, this is a surprisingly formulaic dynamic in New Age films. *Tangled*, *Frozen*, and *Moana* all feature scenes in which the female character must convince the male lead of the film to come on an adventure with her. The scenes uniformly feature what we would call a "wind-up" from the princess as they try to psych themselves into being authoritative,[9] only to be met with casual resistance from their co-lead.

In *Tangled*, Rapunzel meets her love interest Flynn because he accidentally stumbles into her tower, and she knocks him unconscious and ties him up. The following excerpt takes place after Flynn wakes up, tied to a chair:

**Excerpt 5M "I never break that promise"** (*Tangled*, 2010)

RAPUNZEL:   Huh. Okay, Flynn Rider, I'm prepared to offer you a deal... tomorrow evening they will light the night sky with these lanterns. **You will act as my guide,** (*unmarked*) **take me to these lanterns,** (*unmarked*) and **return me home safely.** (*unmarked*) Then, and only then, will I return your satchel to you. That is my deal.

FLYNN:   Yeah. No can do. Unfortunately, the kingdom and I aren't exactly "simpatico" at the moment. So I won't be taking you anywhere.

---

[9] In *Moana*, the "wind-up" is particularly striking. She literally practices her command to her co-lead, Maui, for an entire montage as she crosses the sea.

| RAPUNZEL: | Something brought you here, Flynn Rider. Call it what you will: fate, destiny... |
| FLYNN: | A horse. |
| RAPUNZEL: | So I have made the decision to trust you. |
| FLYNN: | A horrible decision, really. |
| RAPUNZEL: | **But trust me when I tell you this.** (*unmarked*) You can tear this tower apart brick by brick, **but without my help, you will never find your precious satchel.** (*aggravated: threat*) |
| FLYNN: | Hmm-mm. Let me just get this straight. I take you to see the lanterns, bring you back home, and you'll give me back my satchel? |
| RAPUNZEL: | I promise. And when I promise something, I never ever break that promise. Ever. |

In this dialogue, Rapunzel theoretically should easily position herself above Flynn. After all, he's tied to a chair; his agency has been completely removed. But instead, she seems awkward and unsure of her own authority. She makes a series of unmitigated directives, which the viewer sees her physically prepare herself for by taking deep breaths and assuming stilted, overly confident body language (the wind-up, and the pitch!). However, he does not accept this positioning, challenging and insulting her after almost every comment. The movie's tone depicts this juxtaposition of their two dispositions as comical – Flynn sits in his chair, collected and suave, while Rapunzel gets more flustered as the conversation goes on. She finally finds an authentic voice of authority in the final line, but it is centered on her merit; she's still convincing Flynn to listen to her, rather than either of them assuming that she has any power.

*Frozen* has a very similar scene when princess Anna meets her love interest Kristoff for the first time. Anna, like Rapunzel, aims to convince Kristoff to escort her on an important mission. And, like Flynn, Kristoff coolly challenges her authority, as seen in Excerpt 5N.

**Excerpt 5N "We leave now" (*Frozen*, 2013)**

| KRISTOFF: | Oh, it's just you. What do you want? |
| ANNA: | **I want you to take me up the North Mountain.** (*unmarked*) |
| KRISTOFF: | I don't take people places. |
| ANNA: | Let me rephrase that... *[throws payment toward Kristoff]* **Take me up the North Mountain... Please.** (*mitigated: politeness*) Look, I know how to stop this winter. (*mitigated: indirect, reason*) |
| KRISTOFF: | **We leave at dawn...** (*unmarked*) **And you forgot the carrots for Sven.** (*mitigated: indirect*) |
| ANNA: | *[throws carrots at Kristoff's head]* Oops. Sorry. Sorry. I'm sorry. I didn't — Hm— hm. **We leave now. Right now.** (*aggravated: urgency*) |

Once again, the scene opens by showing Anna "wind up" for her role as an authoritative figure. She pauses before entering the conversation, literally shakes her body like an athlete would to warm up, and barges in. Just like

Rapunzel, her initial command comes out stilted and awkward. And, like Flynn, Kristoff calmly denies Anna's request, thereby also denying her bid for authority.

Anna tries again to establish her role as royalty; she makes no attempt to convince or reason, but instead issues her command, this time raising her voice. This seems to be effective at first in that Kristoff is surprised, but willing to comply. However Anna is deeply uncomfortable by her own display of authority, and immediately mitigates with politeness lexicon (*please*) and reasoning (*I know how to stop this winter*). Kristoff responds with reluctant compliance but then immediately takes a position as leader by establishing the time of departure. Anna once again tries to establish herself as dominant by acting cool and collected, but fails in a comedically awkward way by accidentally hurting Kristoff and stumbling through mitigation and apology in an attempt to repair the interaction.

Even though Disney has representations of powerful, assertive women in film, the fact that effort and exceptionalism consistently surround the act of assertion complicates this representation. To be clear, there is nothing inherently wrong with mitigating a directive. The problem is that when female characters in authority positions do it and male characters in comparable positions don't, it sends an ideological message about the connection of authority to gender. Disney seems to imply that there's something about femininity that renders more direct forms of authority or dominance awkward, uncomfortable, and/or funny. In this way Disney movies maintain a discourse of femininity that links women with passivity, mitigation, and difficulty establishing direct dominance, despite the fact that the princesses appear "stronger" in newer films.

## Conclusion

Analysis of directives in Disney ended up being an extremely fruitful avenue through which to look at intersecting ideologies of gender and power in Disney. As expected, the issuing of directives is very common in these films, and because they are an essential plot element, it makes sense that their frequency is unrelated to gender. However, the use of mitigation as a politeness strategy is, in fact, strongly correlated with gender in both Disney and Pixar, independent of other important contextual variables such as urgency and institutional power ($p < 0.01$ for both datasets).

Unpacking these gendered patterns further with qualitative data, we find complicated intersections between gender and institutional power. Our model shows that authority makes mitigation less likely, which makes sense. But qualitatively, we find male authority and female authority are framed differently. Male authority is shown as hierarchical, direct, and aggressive; female authority is shown as subtle, and based on persuasion, suggestion, and collaboration – a pattern which echoes research findings on real-life behavior across a number of contexts.

Even more troubling is the subtle way that authority in general is portrayed as natural for male characters and unnatural for female ones. Yes, a queen may have more leeway to tell you what to do than a peasant, but that doesn't mean she likes it. In both Disney and Pixar we find female characters in authority who resist issuing directives (e.g. Atta, Elsa), or who have to work up the courage to issue them (e.g. Moana, Anna) and then often seem flustered when they actually get the directive out. No such hesitations are seen when male characters are in similar positions.

The one time when authority is shown as natural for female characters is in a domestic/maternal setting. Dealing with children, or characters acting like children, is really the only context where female characters can wield authority without hesitation. Or at least this is true for "good" women; although goodness was not quantitatively correlated with mitigation strategies, we still see some qualitative trends of villainous female characters using unmitigated and aggravated directives while in positions of power with greater ease and impunity than heroines.

In aggregate, we end up seeing a discourse of femininity that is at odds with authority, and a discourse of masculinity at home in it. Relatedly, politeness strategies once again are the purview of femininity more than masculinity. In the next chapter, we examine yet another angle of politeness and gender by considering its inverse: impoliteness. This chapter was all about how characters mitigate face threats to others; so what happens when characters aim to *cause* face threats instead? In the following chapter, we examine insults, a common impoliteness strategy, and explore how patterns of impoliteness can further fill out our picture of gender discourses in the media.

# 6    Insults

Fools! Idiots! Imbeciles!

Maleficent, *Sleeping Beauty*

## Introduction

In the previous two chapters, our focus has been on various types of politeness strategies. We've asked questions about who gives more compliments and who tends to mitigate face-threatening directives more, and have so far found that the widespread ideological link between politeness and femininity is indeed reinforced in Disney and Pixar. That is, female characters are portrayed as using politeness strategies more often and more easily, whereas male characters are portrayed as more comfortable speaking without them. But what about the opposite situation – when a speaker's goal isn't to maintain the social order, but rather to disrupt it? In this chapter, we examine this question by looking at insults.

In broad strokes, an insult are a speech activity that *invokes the negative characteristics of the recipient*. We say "in broad strokes," because "insults" (as a speech act) don't actually have a strongly agreed upon definition, and they are often not even studied on their own, but rather subsumed into wider categories of speech and behavior: impoliteness, rudeness, aggression, disaffiliative humor, and other theoretical categories spanning multiple nonlinguistic fields including education, psychology, and sociology.[1]

But to nail down the concept for our own purposes, we're considering insults as an *impoliteness strategy*. Impoliteness strategies are utterances "by means of which the speaker intends (rather than happens) to inflict face-damage" (Dynel 2015). In other words, they've got to be (or at least sound) mean. But to just stop at "mean" or "face-damaging" would be a disservice to

---

[1] If you want to read more about this fascinating tangle of studies, check out Dynel's (2015) piece "The Landscape of Impoliteness Research."

impoliteness, since it actually serves interesting and nuanced functions within our social fabric.

Looking at insults specifically, Mateo and Yus (2013) posit that they actually have three primary social motivations. The first is, naturally, just to cause offense. Offense itself can be for a variety of purposes: causing conflict, emphasizing power differences, building social distance, making a joke, and the like. In addition to offense, insults can be used as a backwards form of praise. Mateo and Yus say that this is achieved linguistically by "transforming the negative and insulting original overtones into positive and praising ones. In this type of context, an utterance such as *You fucking bastard!* would mean *You are a great guy!*" (Mateo & Yus 2013). Relatedly, insults (along with other forms of impoliteness) can function to promote bonding, by showing that the relationship is close enough to be 'real' and not hinge on politeness strategies; as McDiarmid et al. (2017) put it, the more an utterance is "highly disruptive if used seriously in a public setting," the more the "playful exchange . . . is a signification of their shared history" (McDiarmid et al. 2017).

Although insults (and impoliteness generally) can serve these positive social purposes, these acts are still face-damaging on their surface. This makes using them a bit like playing with linguistic fire. Purposely injecting face-damaging utterances into a conversation, for whatever reason, brings the risk of being misconstrued and/or socially punished, and so it matters a lot who's saying them, to whom, and with what purpose. This is where gender may begin to play a role.

## Background

### Are Insults a Guy Thing?

Past research has provided some evidence linking masculinity and impoliteness. There are quite a few scholars who have documented that men and boys tend to use impoliteness strategies frequently in their daily lives in order to assert themselves (Goodwin 1990), enact playful aggression against each other (Eder 1990), and to settle disputes without becoming violent (Kochman 1983; Labov 1972). Sociolinguists have also documented practices of ritual insult, such as *playing the dozens*, among young African-American men (e.g. Labov 1972; Rickford 2000). However, Goodwin watched childhood interactions between young girls and boys and concluded that "conflict is as omnipresent in the interaction of females as in that of males" (Goodwin 2003, cited in Mills & Mullany 2011: 61) And Eder (1990) also observed adolescent girls from lower-income backgrounds engaging in ritual insults. In the world of education research, there are a range of studies documenting the rise in relational aggressive behavior in young women, also arguing that "girls may be as aggressive as boys if gender specific forms of aggression are considered" (Moretti & Odgers 2002: 3). So while we can say there's more *documentation* of masculine impoliteness, this may be due at least in part to a confirmation bias of the existing ideological link between masculinity and impolite behavior.

That being said, research to date also suggests that insults (and impoliteness more broadly) have different social implications depending on gender. For some men, insults not only serve as tools of aggression and conflict mediation, but also as important vessels for masculine solidarity and bonding. Male ice road truckers, for example, use insults (as well as expletives and impolite humor) to establish solidarity with each other and to diffuse tension or embarrassment in social settings (Mullany 2011). In another study, McDiarmid et al. (2017) interviewed adolescent Australian men and found that they understood insults to serve a variety of functions in their social group, and they recognized insult frequency as a signifier of closeness and intimacy. Kiesling (2005) theorizes that insults among men are a form of extreme social indirectness: in all-male contexts, the competition and aggression inherent in insults can take on the indirect illocutionary force of desire and affection. This solves what Kiesling calls the "male homosocial double bind" of expressing desire for male friendship while still appearing independent and heterosexual, which he posits are two key tenets of dominant masculine ideology. Essentially, insults help straight men in some cultures be friends, while avoiding the feminine implications of open affection (which as we saw in Chapter 4 is still very much a taboo).

Women, on the other hand, do not seem to use insults so openly as a tool for mediating affection; perhaps they don't need it, because modern femininity allows for more open homosocial affection and doesn't produce the same "double bind" that masculinity does (again, see Chapter 4). There's also evidence that women are less likely than men to use direct impoliteness strategies like insults for the purpose of offense in the public sphere or in mixed-gender company, opting instead for more indirect forms of aggression (Ringrose 2006).[2] Mills (2002) theorizes that this is because women are judged by different standards than men when it comes to impoliteness: it's precisely *because* femininity is associated with politeness that overt impoliteness is judged more harshly.

---

[2] To our point earlier, we're not sure whether this is because women don't do this, or whether it's because no studies have been conducted on women's insults in private, intra-gender contexts. We would very much like to see this done. Anecdotally, both authors identify as women and do a fair amount of insult-as-bonding with their respective same-age female friends, and occasionally with each other as well.

Consequently, women have to be more strategic in their use of impoliteness strategies in order to achieve social goals. Mullany (2008) found in a recorded business meeting that the women present in the meeting banded together to be impolite to a man in the meeting, showing that women were certainly not incapable of using impoliteness strategies. But she also found that in interviews after the fact, the men working at the office judged this behavior harshly, and saw the women as manipulative, irrational, or using their gender and sexuality to get free passes. In another study, Cheung and Sung (2012) looked at an exchange on an episode of the reality TV show *The Apprentice* where a female project manager insults another female contestant at the show. Donald Trump, upon hearing this comment, marks this behavior as impolite and inappropriate, and criticizes her for it relentlessly throughout the episode. These studies, though limited in scope, support Mills' theory that women's impoliteness is both heavily marked and open to criticism.

Importantly, as we noted in Chapter 1, these hegemonic ideologies of (im) politeness and gender are largely based on the stereotyped behavior of white, middle-class women. In other words, these are the women who will find it the most socially advantageous to adhere to these norms (Mills 2002), while women in ethnically or economically different communities may have linguistic practices that directly clash with these norms. For example, linguists have described a number of discourse patterns such as reading, signifying, and instigating (which is associated particularly with women's discourse), that are used for specific purposes within black communities (see e.g. Green 2002; Morgan 2021). Some of these patterns could overlap with our categorization of insults in the right context but would presumably have a different meaning or function that was community-specific. However, white society has a way of interpreting speech by people of color through a racist lens; historically, Black American women in particular have been stereotyped as "angry" or "aggressive" in mainstream media.[3] These differences in linguistic practice become particularly salient when considering the (predominantly white) screenwriters' portrayals of insult use in characters of different ethnicities.

## *Insults and Gender in the Media*

Insults (and impoliteness practices generally) are hard to track in real life. They're rare, because people generally have a vested interest in maintaining social cohesion rather than wrecking it; and when insults are used for bonding,

---

[3] See e.g. Harris and Hill 1998, Brooks and Hébert 2006, and Gammage 2015 for more on racist stereotypes of African-American women in the media.

it's usually in intimate settings beyond the reach of most formal studies. Consequently, a lot of impoliteness scholars have already turned to scripted media as a site of inquiry. Scripted media is absolutely lousy with impoliteness, because impoliteness drives conflict, and conflict drives story. The severity and consequences of impoliteness strategies in narrative are also often heightened for the sake of drama; this leads some scholars to believe that fictional impoliteness can even highlight or reveal social processes more readily than real-life versions (Dynel 2015). Additionally, impoliteness in scripted media creates a huge opportunity for creativity and humor. Characters often say things that seem extremely face-threatening or hurtful to the addressee, but the fictional recipients are written to respond with less offense than a real person might, allowing the audience to enjoy the creativity and humor of impoliteness without the story world falling down around them (Dynel 2013; Pillier 2013).

Current research on impoliteness in scripted media doesn't cover gender differences very comprehensively. But what's there suggests results in line with observed real-life differences in impoliteness use. Al-Yasin and Rabab'ah (2018) conducted an analysis on the *Fresh Prince of Bel-Air* and found that male characters used impoliteness strategies significantly more than female characters, and that the difference was especially large when considering insults. In a survey of appearance-based comments in 104 prime-time TV episodes, Lauzen and Dozier (2002) found that while female characters overall received the most comments about their appearance, male characters were significantly more likely to insult each other than female characters. In this chapter, we explore whether the existing media portrayals of impoliteness extend to Disney and Pixar.

## Methodology

As in other chapters, our main interest is whether ideologies of gendered behavior are reproduced in these features:

---

**Key Questions**

- Is there a gender-based difference in who **gives and receives insults** in the films?
- Does the **social function of insults** vary by the gender of the giver?
- Are the patterns of insulting, and their relationship to gender, **similar or different in the Disney and Pixar films**?

---

Insults were collected manually from a total of 31 films from Disney and Pixar. For the purposes of the study we based our collection on Dynel's definition:

An insult is a distinct type of speech activity encompassing remarks which invoke negative characteristics of the target. (Dynel 2015)

We used this as a jumping-off point, but with some key distinctions. Firstly, we include negative characteristics about someone's possessions, ideas, and behaviors under the broad umbrella of "the target," which seems only fair given that our compliment data also considers these valid subjects. In addition, the form that insults took was rather wide, including conventional insult forms (e.g. *you little brat!*), overly pointed or negative criticisms (e.g. *You think you could shoot him? Not aiming like that, you couldn't*), insulting directives (e.g. *Get a grip, Jafar!*), and indirect or "mock" forms of impoliteness, such as sarcasm (e.g. saying *how impressive* to a disastrous performance). Using these criteria, insults were collected and double-checked by four undergraduate coders, and any edge cases were discussed until a consensus was reached. This produced a total of 1,259 insults (478 in Disney, and 781 in Pixar).

Our first analysis is an overview of how many insults are given and received by each gender, and whether trends in giving and receiving have changed over time, particularly over the broad span of the Princess movies. As in previous chapters, we control for the gender imbalance in screen time by comparing ratios of insults given and received against the ratio of words spoken in aggregate by each gender. In a world where gender has no bearing on impoliteness strategies, we might expect the ratios of insults given and received to more or less mirror how much each gender is on screen; we use binomial tests to test this hypothesis, comparing the number of insults given and received by each gender against the expected outcome set by their speech ratios.[4]

We also coded each example for the social function of the insult, which we modeled after Mateo and Yus's (2013) proposed taxonomy of functions, shown in detail in Table 6.1.

For the purposes of analysis, we collapse praise and bonding insults into a single "inoffensive" category that we compare against the offense category. We compare these motivations against the gender of the speakers and recipients.[5]

---

[4] With our caveat that that speech amount is not a perfect measure of onscreen time, but gives us as good of a stand-in measure as any to compare against.

[5] Some readers may be asking, "what about the insult topic?," since we looked at compliment topics in such depth. But it turns out that insults in our dataset are generalized statements at a much higher proportion than compliments, and aren't as easily mappable: for example, *She's hopeless* or *Good luck marrying her off!* could be an insult on intelligence, or on character, a skill, or a general statement. So while there's certainly plenty to say about insult topics, we're going to leave them aside for now and concentrate instead on the intent and function of the speech act of insulting more broadly.

Table 6.1. *Functions of insults*

| Function | Description |
| --- | --- |
| Offense (O) | The utterance is intended to cause pain or damage face. Recipient receives the utterance as face-damaging. |
| | E.g. *Fools! Idiots! Imbeciles!* (*Sleeping Beauty*) |
| Praise (P) | The utterance is negative on its face or includes insulting language, but the illocutionary force is complimentary. |
| | E.g. *That punk actually did a good job.* (*Cars*) |
| Bonding (B) | The illocutionary force of the utterance is face-damaging, but the giver uses it to promote or indicate solidarity. Recipient does not take offense. |
| | E.g. *I'm Yao, King of the Rock, and there's nothing you girls can do about it.* (*Mulan*) |
| Unintentional (U) *Added for our dataset* | Recipient character takes something as an insult that clearly wasn't intended that way, usually for comedic effect. |
| | E.g. *Hey, hey, don't worry about my ice business… worry about your hair!* (*Frozen*) |

## Insult Givers and Receivers

### *Who Gives and Receives Insults?*

Our results, reported in Table 6.2, show the proportions of words spoken by each gender compared to the proportion of insults characters of each gender give and receive. In three out of the four eras, male characters give the substantial majority of all insults.[6] In the Classic Era, the discrepancy between words spoken and insults given is the smallest: male characters speak 41 percent of the words and give 45 percent of the insults, and the results of our binomial tests show that the 4 percent difference is not significant. However, in the Renaissance Era, there is a significant difference, with male characters they speak 78 percent of the words but give 82 percent of the insults. The gender gap is the most stark in New Age movies, where male characters speak 51 percent of the words, and they give 69 percent[7] of the insults. In Pixar, the difference is smaller but still significant, with male characters speaking 74 percent of the words and giving 80 percent of the insults. Female characters correspondingly give fewer insults than predicted based on how much they talk in every era. The proportional difference reaches statistical significance in

---

[6] Keep in mind that these percentages won't quite add up to 100 percent, since in every film there are a small number of tokens that were given by (or to) a group of characters of multiple genders, or a character of indeterminable gender.

[7] Nice.

Table 6.2. *Insults given and received by character gender*

| | Male | | | Female | | |
|---|---|---|---|---|---|---|
| | Total speech | Insults given | Insults received | Total speech | Insults given | Insults received |
| Classic | 41% (4,684) | 45% (29) | 42% (27) | 59% (6,710) | 55% (36) | 57% (37) |
| Renaissance | 78% (19,756) | **82%*** (170) | 75% (155) | 22% (5,643) | 18% (37) | 24% (49) |
| New Age | 50% (16,899) | **69%*** (141) | 47% (96) | 50% (16,762) | **31%*** (63) | 50% (103) |
| Pixar | 74% (111,662) | **80%*** (586) | **81%*** (589) | 26% (38,950) | **19%*** (142) | **14%*** (102) |

* Proportion is significantly different than predicted based on proportion of words spoken ($p < 0.05$).

the New Age and Pixar movies. And again, the proportional gap is lowest in the Classic Era.

Results concerning the gender of the recipient show that male and female characters in Disney Princess movies do not have any significant differences between the amount they speak and the amount of insults they receive. That is to say, the amount that each gender is insulted matches with the amount that they're on screen, more or less. Given that there is a gender gap in insults given but not in insults received, we can conclude that male characters in Disney receive fewer insults than they give, and female characters correspondingly receive substantially more insults than they dole out. This discrepancy is again largest in the New Age films, where females give only 31 percent of insults, but receive 50 percent.

Pixar films do not follow the same pattern: male characters receive significantly more insults than predicted based on the amount they speak (74 percent of words spoken vs. 81 percent of insults received) and female characters receive significantly less than predicted (26 percent of words spoken vs. 14 percent of insults received). For male characters, the rate of giving and receiving insults is almost identical (80 percent given vs. 81 percent received). The fact that male characters both give and receive insults at such higher rates is a topic we will cover at length later in this chapter.

### The Insult Gender Gap

Given what we know of real-life speech communities, it seems unsurprising that Disney and Pixar films generally reproduce the idea that men give more insults than women. In fact, the only surprising fact was that the Classic Era was the exception, given that the gender roles presented in those early films are the most "traditional." But upon further inspection, we found that the relative balance between insults given by male and female characters is largely explained by the fact that the Classic movies have female villains. Out of the 36 total insults given by female characters in the Classic Era, 26 of them were given by villains of the films. Comparatively, only five insults in this era are given by a princess – all by Cinderella, and four out of those five are to her family cat. The only real insult that she gives is about her stepsisters' terrible singing. and this is when they are out of the room, when she asks her animal friends if she should *interrupt the, uh... music lesson?* Her pause is just weighty enough to be considered insulting, but it's about as indirect as you can get. More direct female insults are the purview of villains and wicked stepsisters. This trend suggests to us that although there is representation of female insulting in the Classic Era, it's not necessarily a speech act that reflects well or even neutrally on its giver; insults are used to characterize women as cruel, out of control, or angry.

The Renaissance and New Age eras have few female villains compared to male villains; with the largest factor contributing to female characters giving insults basically eradicated, the gender gap between male and female insults appears. Granted, in these new eras, the princesses also insult (18/36 female insults in the Renaissance and 30/63 insults in the New Age are given by the princesses). This presumably reflects Disney's efforts to make their princesses more empowered and sassy instead of being totally demure the entire time. So in these two eras we have Belle telling Gaston that he is *positively primeval* (*Beauty and the Beast*), Princess Tiana calling her love interest, Naveen, a *spoiled little rich boy* (*The Princess and the Frog*), and Anna telling Hans that *the only frozen heart around here is yours* (*Frozen*). These quips paint the princess characters with a sense of wit and imbue them with some oppositional energy to the patriarchal world they're put in; as Do Rozario (2004) puts it, "they're just a little bit bad" (44).

But even though princesses insult people, it doesn't do much to close the gender gap which widens substantially in the Renaissance and New Age eras. While female characters insult occasionally, it doesn't hold a candle to the large amount of casual insults that male characters tend to give, regardless of whether they're good or bad, major or minor, young, old, or anything else. Indeed, in the New Age movies, masculine heroic personalities seem to be actually character-ized by their frequent use of insults. Of the insults given by male characters in the New Age movies, 104/141 are from the heroes, whether it's because they're fast-talking charismatic types who use insults for humor (like Flynn Rider or Naveen) or more taciturn cranky characters (like Kristoff or Maui). A sample of a New Age, insult-ridden conversational style is shown in Excerpt 6A. In this scene from *Moana*, Maui teaches Moana an old nautical skill called "wayfinding."

**Excerpt 6A "Muscle up, Buttercup" (*Moana*, 2016)**

MAUI:     If you wear a dress, and you have an animal sidekick... you're a princess. **You're not a wayfinder. You'll never be a wayfinder. You will never be a wayf—** *[Moana blows a dart in his direction.]* Really? Blowdart in my buttcheek. **You are a bad person.**

MOANA:    If you can talk, you can teach. Wayfinding. Lesson one... hit it.

MAUI:     Pull the sheets. Not the sheets. No. No. No. No. Tried that one already. **You're measuring the stars, not giving the sky a high-five.** If the cur-rent's warm, you're going the right way.

MOANA:    It's cold. Wait, it's getting warmer. *[Notices that Maui has peed in the water.]* Augh, that's disgusting!

MAUI:     **Enjoy your beauty rest?** You know, a real wayfinder never sleeps. So they actually get where they need to go. **Muscle up, butter cup.** We're here.

In this montage, practically every utterance from Maui to Moana contains at least one insulting factor. Whether it's a vocative (*buttercup, princess*), a mockery of her skill (*not giving the sky a high-five*), or just a straightforward negative evaluation (*You are a bad person*), he takes every chance he can get to jab at her, despite the fact that not only is he supposed to be teaching her, but also that he's an ancient demigod and she's a young girl. Importantly, this is not portrayed as a villainous trait. In fact, for all these protagonists, insults are actually part of their heroic and comedic personalities. In this way, the New Age movies do the most out of any Disney era to naturalize insults as a masculine trait.

As for Pixar, since those films rely much less on hero–heroine pairs like the ones we've been talking about, the dynamic is a little different. Insults are again given disproportionately by men; the female characters who do manage to get a top billing, though, do use insults, much like the newly feisty princesses, but in a different way from their male counterparts. We'll discuss the nuances of gender and insults in Pixar in more detail below.

## Insult Intent

### The Functions of Insults in Disney

Tables 6.3 and 6.4 show the distribution of the intent behind insults, according to the gender of the giver and receiver. Across the board, offense is the largest motivator in our dataset: 82 percent (392/478) of all insults in Disney movies and 79 percent (574/731) in Pixar movies were intended as offensive. Researchers of real-life speech communities have found at least impressionistically that offensive insults are not nearly so common as this. People in real life are more choosy about causing open offense, and the maintenance of social norms requires receivers to, at the very least, pretend that an insult is "all in good fun" most of the time (Dynel 2013; Mateo & Yus 2013). But in scripted media, writers are free to create stories and relationships where openly causing offense doesn't hurt social ties between characters. Consequently, the proportion of offensive insults here is much higher than research on real-life communities would lead us to expect. But even with this element of freedom, some

Table 6.3. *Insult intent and gender in Disney Princess films*

|  | Male-to-male | Male-to-female | Female-to-male | Female-to-female |
|---|---|---|---|---|
| Offensive intent | 80% (163) | 82% (103) | 86% (61) | 91% (58) |
| Inoffensive intent (praise, bonding) | 17% (34) | 7% (9) | 8% (6) | 6% (4) |
| Unintentional | 4% (8) | 10% (13) | 6% (4) | 3% (2) |
| Total | 205 | 125 | 71 | 64 |

* $\chi^2 = 16.25$, p $\leq$ 0.01

interesting gender patterns reveal themselves in who gives offensive and inoffensive insults.

Table 6.3 on insult intent in Disney Princess movies by gender shows a few interesting patterns. As mentioned above, the sheer amount of insults intended for offense across the board does indicate a different social reality in the films than in real life. However, the data *are* consistent with documented gender ideologies in that 17 percent of male-to-male insults were not intended for offense – over twice the rate of any other giver/receiver pair. Disney movies have a pattern of showing male characters – heroes and villains alike – insulting each other to demonstrate solidarity and indirectly praise each other. For example, the Englishmen in *Pocahontas*, and in particular the two burly characters Ben and Lon, commonly call each other names like *half-wit*, *idiot*, and *nutter* as a part of their relationship. We can see this kind of playful antagonism in the opening lines of the film, between Ben, Lon, Thomas (a third member of the crew) and hero John Smith:

### Excerpt 6B "Of course he is, you half-wit" (*Pocahontas*, 1995)

| | |
|---|---|
| LON: | Hey, look! Is that Smith? |
| BEN: | That's him, all right, **the old sea dog.** |
| THOMAS: | Captain John Smith! I've heard some amazing stories about him. |
| LON: | Are you coming on this voyage, too? |
| BEN: | Course he is, **you half-wit.** You can't fight Indians without John Smith. |
| JOHN SMITH: | That's right. **I'm not about to let you boys have all the fun.** |

In these first five lines of the movie, Ben calls John Smith an *old sea dog* and Lon a *half-wit*, all while smiling in excitement. John Smith comes on board and immediately joins in the banter; though it's not a direct insult, *I'm not about to let you boys have all the fun* is also playfully antagonistic. All three of these jabs are meant to establish the characters not as enemies, but as old friends, reflecting the way that insults can be used in real life to establish close friendships between men.

In *Brave*, insults are used between male characters not only to maintain rapport, but to actively re-establish it after it has been broken. In this climactic moment near the end of the film, shown in Excerpt 6C, the four heads of the Scottish clans have been leading their men in battle against each other when Merida comes in to try and repair their relationships.

### Excerpt 6C "I was aiming at you, you big tumshie" (*Brave*, 2012)

| | |
|---|---|
| MERIDA: | Our kingdom is young, our stories are not yet legends, but in them a bond was struck. Our clans were once enemies. But when invaders threatened us from the sea, you joined together to defend our lands. You fought for each other. You risked |

|                    | everything for each other. Lord McGuffin, my dad saved your |
| :----------------- | :---------------------------------------------------------- |
|                    | life stopping an arrow as you ran to Dingwall's aid.        |
| LORD MACGUFFIN:    | Aye, and I'll never forget it.                              |
| MERIDA:            | And lord Macintosh, you saved my dad when you charged in on |
|                    | heavy horse and held off the advance. And we all know how   |
|                    | Lord Dingwall broke the enemy lines.                        |
| LORD MACINTOSH:    | With a mighty throw of his spear!                           |
| LORD DINGWALL:     | **I was aiming at you, you big tumshie.**[8]                |

In this exchange, Merida convinces the men to stop fighting by reminding them of the ways they've supported each other in the past. As the tone in the room becomes less violent, Lord Macintosh joins Merida in praising Lord Dingwall. Dingwall responds by calling Macintosh a "tumshie" and claiming that he was "aiming at him" even though, according to the story, he clearly wasn't. But he says this with an affectionate tone, and it is received by not only Macintosh but the entire listening crowd (all male characters) with a warm chuckle. This humorous jab seems to be relying on the behavioral pattern found in real male speech communities wherein insults can take the place of praise in a kind of "social irony" (Kiesling 2005; Mullany 2011).

Female characters, on the other hand, barely ever engage in this kind of playful ribbing – especially with one another. It's true that this is partially an artifact of there being so few female characters to talk to one another, but it's also a result of it not being depicted as part of female personalities and relationships, outside of a few specific examples. Princesses are "sassy" with their friends occasionally: Ariel, for example, teases her friend Flounder a few times by telling him to not be *such a guppy*. Pocahontas' best friend Nakoma affectionately calls her a *show-off* after watching her do a flashy dive off the top of a cliff. But these are limited compared to how frequently we see male characters bond using affectionate antagonism.

Perhaps the best indicator of this gendered divide in Disney movies is in *Mulan*.[9] In *Mulan*, the titular character spends a lot of the movie posing as a man named Ping, and so the characters around her treat her as such. (As a reminder, we even coded insults and other speech samples from male characters to "Ping" as male-to-male examples, since we assume the characters would be speaking according to the implied gender.) In one comic scene, Mulan is taking a bath in the lake when three other soldiers (Ling, Chien-Po,

---

[8] Apparently "tumshie" is a colloquial Scottish term for calling someone gullible, empty-headed, or an idiot. It is derived from the phrase "tumshie-head," meaning "turnip-head," which refers to carved turnip jack-o-lanterns. The more you know!

[9] Honestly, we're so lucky that *Mulan* exists. It's basically a hand-held tour through what Disney thinks gender roles are. You'll have to forgive us for mentioning it so much, but we just can't resist.

and Yao) also come to bathe and run into her. Mulan is trying to escape the situation and Ling stops her, asking to make amends from an earlier fight:

**Excerpt 6D "King of the rock" (*Mulan*, 1998)**

| | |
|---|---|
| MULAN/PING: | Oh hi guys, I didn't know you were here. I was just washing, so now I'm clean and I'm gonna go. Bye, bye. |
| LING: | Come back here. I know we were jerks to you before so let's start over. |
| | Hi, I'm Ling! |
| CHIEN-PO: | And I'm Chien-Po. |
| MULAN/PING: | Hello Chien-Po. |
| YAO: | And I am Yao, king of the rock. **And there's nothin' you girls can do about it.** |
| LING: | Oh, yeah? Well, I think Ping and I could take you. |
| MULAN/PING: | I really don't want to take him anywhere. |
| LING: | Ping, we have to fight! |
| MULAN/PING: | No we don't. We could just close our eyes and swim around. |
| LING: | C'mon **don't be such a g—** Ouch! Something bit me. |

What's interesting about this scene is that the main way that Yao and Ling try to engage "Ping" in a new bond of friendship is through insults (Yao calling them "girls"), and combat (Ling encouraging them to fight). Ling in particular responds to Yao's taunt very positively, playfully striking a fighting pose and nudging "Ping" to join in on the fun. Mulan is in a tough position, given that she's naked and far from the shore, and so attempts to get out of the situation. But the strategy that Disney writes for her to get out of it is heavily gendered, in that Mulan confuses and misconstrues Ling's comment, not acknowledging his social bid at all (*I don't want to take him anywhere*). When Ling pushes the point she resists the bid again (*We could just close our eyes and swim around*). Although her resistance serves a plot purpose, it also serves a humorous one, based on tension between the perceived masculine tendencies to rough house, and how those tendencies are mysterious and unnecessary from a stereotypically feminine point of view.

### The Functions of Insults in Pixar

Table 6.4 shows us that Pixar's relationship to gender and insulting is similar to Disney's in some ways, and different in others. Overall, insults with obviously inoffensive intent are much more common in Pixar movies than in Disney movies: the lowest proportion of inoffensive intent out of any pairing (16 percent) is about on par with the highest proportion found in Disney (17 percent).

In some similarity to Disney, male-to-male insults are by far the most *numerous* out of any giver–receiver combination, both overall and for inoffensive insults in particular. And just like in Disney, male Pixar characters who

Table 6.4. *Insult intent and gender in Pixar films*

|               | Male-to-male | Male-to-female | Female-to-male | Female-to-female |
|---------------|--------------|----------------|----------------|------------------|
| Offensive     | 82% (390)    | 80% (63)       | 58% (66)       | 77% (17)         |
| Inoffensive   | 16% (75)     | 16% (13)       | 40% (45)       | 18% (4)          |
| Unintentional | 2% (9)       | 4% (3)         | 2% (2)         | 5% (1)           |
| Total         | 474          | 79             | 113            | 22               |

* $\chi^2 = 35.57$, $p < 0.01$

are friends with one another often use insults to establish solidarity with one another, to praise one another, and even to reconcile after fights. In the beginning of *Monsters, Inc.*, we are introduced to best friends Mike and Sulley as they make their way through their morning routine. Just like Ben and Lon in *Pocahontas*, their closeness is partially shown by their willingness to insult and mock one another. As they walk to work, they have the following exchange about a commercial that Mike was recently featured on:

**Excerpt 6E "Monstropolis's Most Wanted" (*Monsters, Inc.*, 2001)**

MIKE:     I'm telling you, big daddy, you're going to be seeing this face on TV a lot more often.
SULLEY:  Yeah? **Like, on "Monstropolis's Most Wanted"?**
MIKE:     Ha ha ha ha. **You've been jealous of my good looks since the fourth grade, pal.**

In this scene, both characters exhibit the air and body language of cheerful discussion. Mike tells Sulley about something he's proud of, and Sulley, with a grin, insults him by implying he'll become a criminal. Mike responds by laughing and insulting him back about his appearance. In this early scene, trading witty jabs seems to act as a shorthand to show the audience their close relationship. Other male-to-male buddy pairs have similar dynamics (such as Woody and Buzz once they're friends in the *Toy Story* franchise, or Mr. Incredible and Frozone in *The Incredibles*).

But the thing that makes Pixar's insults stand apart from Disney's is that it's not male-to-male insults, but rather female-to-male insults, that have the highest rate of inoffensive intent, at a whopping 40 percent. We can attribute this to two major factors. First of all, Pixar does feature a few male–female buddy pairs, such as Marlin and Dory in *Finding Nemo*, Hank and Dory in *Finding Dory*, and McQueen and Cruz in *Cars 3*. In these cases, the female characters in the pairs do insult their male counterparts with relative regularity. Dory addresses Marlin with multiple gently teasing vocatives throughout *Finding Nemo*, including *Mr. Grumpy Gills*, *Mr. Bossy*, *Mr. Smarty Pants*, and *Old Man*, for example.

Female-to-male insults are also a result of flirting. Insulting to show roman-tic solidarity or interest is a bit more common for Pixar wives, girlfriends, and love interests than it is for the Disney princesses. At the start of *Finding Nemo*, for example, we see Coral and Marlin interact briefly before Coral is killed: he asks her, *Do you remember how we first met?* to which she quips, *I try not to.* Sally, from the *Cars* franchise, also teases McQueen remorselessly as part of their romantic relationship, often calling him *Stickers* as a reference to the fact that he has decals on the front of his car instead of real headlights. Example 6F shows a scene in *Cars 3* wherein Sally goes to cheer up McQueen after a defeat. In doing so, she also gently mocks his living conditions, as a way to show solidarity and inject humor into the serious conversation:

**Excerpt 6F "Don't fear failure" (*Cars 3*, 2017)**

SALLY:   Don't fear failure. Be afraid of not having the chance. You have the chance. Doc didn't. And you can either take it or you can do what you've been doing. Sitting. In here. For months. And by the way, I love what you've done with the place. **I mean the monster movie lighting and the musky air freshener. And don't let anyone tell you you're not working that primer because... Wow, I have never found you more attractive.** And now that I've been in here for a couple minutes, **the stench... I'm getting kind of used to it.**

Sally's behavior, along with that of Dory, Cruz, and the other playfully insulting female characters, represents a strong deviation from Disney princess movies, where there are only six female-to-male intentional insults not meant for offense in the entire dataset. Granted, this trend isn't consistent across Pixar movies. Joy and Sadness from *Inside Out*, Jessie and Bo Peep from *Toy Story*, Atta from *A Bug's Life*, Colette from *Ratatouille*, and Violet and Mrs. Incredible from *The Incredibles* are all female characters who do not engage in playful teasing much if at all, despite sharing significant screen time with male characters. So while this trait is still predominantly a masculine one in Pixar movies, due to the sheer number of masculine insults, it's interesting (and perhaps encouraging) that some movies leave it open to female characters as well.

### Verbal Slapstick: Gender and Framing Offense

Earlier we mentioned that the number of offensive insults in these movies is likely much higher than you would find in a real-life conversation or relation-ship. Now we want to spend some time looking closely at those offensive insults, because not only do they make up the bulk of the data here, but they also hide some fascinating qualitative nuance in how masculinity and femininity are portrayed. As discussed earlier, genuine offense is so much more common in scripted media because insults and other forms of impoliteness give screenwriters a lot to work with. On one hand, insults can instigate conflict, or can easily shorthand tension between two characters. And on the other hand, there's also a huge humorous potential here. Writers will pen insults between characters that are obviously offensive to all involved, and sometimes even escalate to physical violence, but in a way that implies it's all for laughs and we, the audience, don't have to take it too seriously. Call it verbal slapstick humor, if you will.

What we noticed is that this verbal slapstick approach does not seem to be equally applied among male and female characters. In particular, we observed that in both Disney and Pixar, insults given by male characters (especially to other male characters) are more likely to be framed humorously than insults given by female characters. Take, for example, the scene in *Monsters, Inc.* we mentioned earlier. Directly after the comment about "Monstropolis's Most Wanted" in Excerpt 6E, Mike and Sulley begin arguing about whether to walk to work or take Mike's car. The following exchange occurs:

**Excerpt 6G "Give it a rest, will you, butterball" (*Monsters, Inc.*, 2001)**

MIKE:     Hey, hey, hey, hey, hey! Where are you going? What are you doing?
SULLEY:   Mikey, there's a scream shortage. We're walking.
MIKE:     **Hey, genius,** you want to know why I bought the car? Huh?
SULLEY:   Not really.
MIKE:     To drive it! You know, like, on the street?
SULLEY:   **Waa, waa, waa, waa, waa.**
MIKE:     ...With the honk-honk and the vroom-vroom and no walking involved.
SULLEY:   **Give it a rest, will you, butterball?** Come on, you could use the exercise.
MIKE:     I could use the exercise?! **Look at you. You— ya— you have your own climate!**

Mike, from the beginning of this exchange, is not laughing. He clearly wants badly to take his car. He raises his voice immediately while repeatedly yelling *Hey!* and even physically clinging to his car. Sulley is unbothered by his friend's being upset, and even mocks his negative reaction, by imitating a baby crying. But Sulley also loses his patience at the end of the exchange, saying *Give it a rest, will you, butterball?* He's now glaring at Mike in this exchange. Mike responds with an insult to Sulley's physical appearance, which by Sulley's expression, he takes pretty personally. If we heard this exchange, at this volume, on the street, we'd be concerned; we might even think about intervening. But then the scene cuts, and next thing you know, they're walking alongside each other like nothing happened. The fact that this somewhat hostile exchange is sandwiched between more friendly jostling and future friendliness implies to the audience that these kinds of insults, between (male) friends, are basically the status quo, and they're nothing to bat an eye at.

The *Monsters, Inc.* example is on the tame side of the spectrum. Disney male characters often mix this kind of "verbal slapstick" with actual, physical slapstick, doubling down on the idea that male-to-male violence of any kind is just part of the whole masculinity thing. At the end of *Beauty and the Beast*, friends Lumière and Cogsworth, who frequently argue and insult each other throughout the movie, try to end their feud in the final scene of the film:

**Excerpt 6H "Shall we let bygones be bygones?" (*Beauty and the Beast*, 1991)**

COGSWORTH:    Well, Lumière, old friend. Shall we let bygones be bygones?
LUMIÈRE:       Of course, *mon ami*. I told you she would break the spell.
COGSWORTH:    I beg your pardon, old friend, but I believe I told you.
LUMIÈRE:       No you didn't. I told you.
COGSWORTH:    You most certainly did not, **you pompous paraffin-headed pea-brain!**
LUMIÈRE:       *En garde*, **you overgrown pocket watch!**

As Lumière says "En garde" at the end of this exchange, they both literally assume guard position (from fencing) and begin to punch at each other. Despite the physical violence involved, the cartoonish exaggeration of this masculine-coded behavior allows the audience to consider this not a serious fight; in fact, it seems to be meant as a moment of comic relief during the denouement of the film.

Verbal slapstick and physical slapstick are mixed often, especially in the Classic Era Disney movies. *Snow White*'s gang of dwarfs tumble on top of each other, hit each other, and call each other names like *fool*, *warthog*, and *doodlebug* throughout the run of the film, never with any real repercussions. In *Sleeping Beauty*, the two kings argue about where their children will move once they're married, which devolves into King Stefan calling King Hubert a *pompous blustering old windbag* and Hubert responding by brandishing a fish (which he drunkenly thinks is a knife) at Stefan and declaring, *This means war*. And in *Cinderella*, the King accuses his Duke of *sabotage* and being a *traitor* for not being able to find Cinderella, while swinging a sword at his head and trying to kill him. And though some of these scenes have legitimate tension between characters, they all have a comic tone. After all, what are some face-destroying insults and a few death threats between friends?

Looking at the offensive insults that occur between female characters paints a drastically different picture. They seem far less likely to be used for humor; instead, a greater proportion of them are for dramatic effect, or to establish legitimate hostility between characters. Take the Classic Era of films, for example: there are 23 female–female "offensive" insults in those early movies, and every single one of them is from a hero to a villain or vice versa. There are a few that could be considered witty, as with the stepsisters' mockery or some of Maleficent's quips in *Sleeping Beauty*. But there is a distinct difference between a witty comment and a humorous scene. In the opening dialogue of

*Sleeping Beauty*, for example, Maleficent shows up to the royal hall unannounced:

**Excerpt 6I "How quaint, even the rabble" (*Sleeping Beauty*, 1959)**

MALEFICENT:      Well, quite a glittering assemblage, King Stefan. Royalty, nobility, the gentry, and, **how quaint, even the rabble.** I really felt quite distressed at not receiving an invitation.

MERRYWEATHER:  **You weren't wanted!**

MALEFICENT:      Not wa...? Oh dear, what an awkward situation. I had hoped it was merely due to some oversight. Well, in that event I'd best be on my way.

In this scene, Maleficent delivers the perhaps "funniest" female-to-female insult in the Classic Era, by calling the three good fairies rabble.[10] But no one is laughing. Ominous music swells with Maleficent's arrival, signaling danger to the audience. The crowd is deathly silent, Merryweather reacts with open hostility, and everyone else is afraid.

Later Disney movies aren't quite as stark, but still, insults from female characters tend to be framed as signs of tension or high drama. In *Mulan*, there are only five female-to-female insults – two of them come from the ruthless matchmaker from the start of the film. Mulan's disastrous visit to a matchmaker ends with her publicly insulting Mulan by saying *You are a disgrace! You may look like a bride, but you will never bring your family honor!* In *Beauty and the Beast*, Belle directly insults Gaston, and no one else. A few times these comments are light-hearted and humorous, specifically because she is insulting him without his realizing it (using big words he can't understand, e.g. *Gaston, you are positively primeval*). She only openly insults him once through defending the Beast, saying, *He's not the monster here, you are!* This insult is part of the dramatic final act of the movie, and ends up getting her locked away while Gaston attacks the Beast. Jasmine in *Aladdin* similarly only utters direct insults that she really means, and usually they cause dramatic shifts in the plot: even when insulting Aladdin, she tells him he's just like *every other stuffed-shirt, swaggering peacock I've met* and tells him to jump off a balcony, which she means as a full-throated rejection of his advances.

One might argue that the lack of screen time for female characters could make for less opportunity for humorous female-to-female antagonism. But where we do have such pairs, with plenty of opportunity for bonding insults and/or verbal slapstick, it doesn't occur. Anna and Elsa from *Frozen* are

---

[10] We don't think that it's a coincidence that Maleficent is witty. We think it's a sign of camp, a linguistic element of queer-coding. For more on the subversive elements of her dialogue, check out Excerpt 8B.

sisters, and could have such a relationship, for example. But the only direct insult Anna gives another female character in either film is when she tells Elsa that she doesn't know anything about love and *only knows how to shut people out*, which (a) is super harsh, and (b) goads Elsa into causing an eternal winter. And in *Brave*, the first and only direct exchange of insults between Merida and her mother Elinor has Merida telling her mom *You're a beast* and *I'd rather die than be like you*, which culminates in Elinor burning Merida's prized weapon and causing Merida to run away. In short, when female characters really mean to insult people, it *works*. Instead of being brushed off cartoonishly, they have results closer to what we would expect in the real world for insults of this magnitude. They cause damage to and potentially destroy relationships.

### The Exceptions: Female Characters outside the Politeness Border

That being said, there are a few important exceptions to the "polite woman" pattern that we want to discuss. The first of these exceptions is old women. The older female characters of Disney and Pixar tend to live outside the standards of feminine politeness: they insult others at far higher rates than other female characters, with little to no consequence. Some of these older characters are villains, of course, whom we might expect to be mean and insulting.[11] But older female characters who are neutral or even heroic tend toward the same behavior. Take the three fairies from *Sleeping Beauty*: not only do they insult Maleficent, but they're some of the only characters in the Classic Era to insult each other in a nonoffensive way. For example, in one scene, two of them try to cooperate on making a dress for Princess Aurora (one modeling and one sewing), and have this exchange:

> Merryweather: It looks awful!
> Flora: That's because it's on you, dear.

Grandma Fa from *Mulan*, Grandmother Willow from *Pocahontas*, Mama Oldie from *The Princess and the Frog*, E from *The Incredibles*, Abuelita from *Coco*, and Lizzie from *Cars* are all characters who insult their compatriots. And they're all either comedic on purpose – like Grandma Fa telling Mulan to *add a cricket just for luck, and even you can't blow it!* – or framed by the movie as funny, like when Lizzie tells another resident of Radiator Springs that McQueen's *new road makes this place look like a dump*. Whether the character intended humor or not, movies tend to frame insults from older female characters as harmless fun.

---

[11] In fact, all the female villains of Disney and Pixar are older, which is a problematic pattern in and of itself. See Do Rozario (2004) or Davis (2006) for a more substantial discussion.

The other exception is that of ethnicity. You'll notice that the older characters above are majority characters of color (or coded as such), with the only exceptions being the three Fairies and Lizzie from *Cars*. Even aside from age, there are a selection of female characters of color in the New Age and Pixar films for whom insulting is both common and more likely to be treated as "not a big deal." Cruz Ramirez, the central character of *Cars 3*, was mentioned earlier in this chapter as the female character who gives the most purposely inoffensive insults; we'll add here that she's also the single biggest giver of insults overall among female characters. Many of her insults to McQueen ride the line between bonding and offense, but are treated in the same slapstick way that male-to-male insults are treated:

> He's obviously an imposter. He looks old and broken down with flabby tires.
> These young guys are great and all, but I like a challenge.
> In fact, I call you my senior project.
> We need to loosen those ancient joints.

Cruz far outstrips every other female character in this particular trait, and it's difficult to ignore the fact that she's coded as Latina through her name and the vocal performance provided by Latina comedian Cristela Alonzo.

It's not immediately obvious how this pattern interacts with what we know about portrayals of Latinx characters in the media. As Brooks and Hébert (2006) note, most of the study of Latinx representation has focused on men, but there is evidence to support a trend of "Latinas being portrayed as exotic seductresses [Holtzman, 2000], as tacky and overly emotional [Valdivia, 1995], and as the hypersexualized spitfire [Molina Guzmán & Valdivia, 2004]" (2006: 303). None of these seems to encompass the portrayal of Cruz.

One possibility is that the screenwriters simply are treating female characters of color, including Latinas, as less feminine/polite overall. Géliga Vargas (1999) in talking about the actress Rosie Perez, and the various roles she has played as a Puerto Rican and black actress, describes her as "[giving] voice to the 'take no shit,' 'give me mine' icon of the inner city Latina" (118). While the character of Cruz may not quite rise to this level, the fact that she is cast as a personal trainer suggests a more tough, less traditionally feminine characterization in general.

We also want to call attention to Tiana from *The Princess and the Frog*, the only Black princess. Out of all the princesses, Tiana has the most openly antagonistic relationship with her prince, and insults him throughout most of the runtime of the movie. Below is a sample of Tiana's insults to Naveen:

> It was a costume party, you spoiled little rich boy!
> Keep your slimey self away from me!
> The prince charming here got himself turned into a frog by a voodoo witch doctor.
> You're a no-count, polandering, lazy bump on a log.

> This stick in the mud has had to work two jobs her whole life while you've
> been suckin' on a silver spoon chasin' chamber maids round your... your
> ivory tower!
> *[Sarcastically]* Oh, you poor baby.

Not all these examples are equal in intent: the earlier insults (*you spoiled little rich boy*) happen in the context of agitated arguments, and indicate legitimate contempt towards Naveen, while later insults (e.g. *Oh, you poor baby*) are more gently mocking and even flirtatious as their bond grows. Part of their conflict, as several of these examples show, is also set up in context by their different social classes; she is a hard-working waitress and he grew up with servants. But importantly, the conflicts between Tiana and Naveen are easily repaired as the movie moves on – their conflict is usually coded by the film as fun tension and banter, even when the characters intend harm to one another.

Princess Moana's relationship with her companion Maui is similarly hostile at times, while still retaining a comedic tone. At one point, for example, Maui comments that their adversary, Tamatoa, *loves bragging about how great he is*, and Moana retorts, *You two must get along swell*. Moana and Tiana stand apart from the white princesses of the era (Rapunzel, Anna, and Elsa) in this regard: these three may banter or flirt with those around them, but rarely does it take the form of open insult. Rapunzel, for example, only insults Flynn once, and she does so only indirectly by asking Maximus the Horse whether he's *tired from chasing the bad man [Flynn] all over the place.*

It's possible that this pattern is some kind of coincidence, and that the movies starring characters of color just happened to be the same movies that featured a more comedic buddy-comedy tone. After all, there are some movies that have female characters of color who don't frequently or casually insult others (e.g. *Pocahontas*, *Aladdin*, *Mulan*), although none of these are Black or Latina characters. And there are a few movies with White characters who do insult a fair amount (e.g. *Finding Nemo*, *Brave*). That being said, since representation of female characters of color is so rare, the choice to bring similar character dynamics to all three movies, with Black, Latina, and Pacific Islander leads, tells us that this might not be a coincidence. As we've said, we cannot give this question the time and depth of analysis that it deserves, but we note it as yet another example of the intersectionality of race and gender that positions women of color outside the mainstream discourse associated with gender. And we hope other scholars with the relevant expertise will someday shed a clearer light on Disney's contributions to this discourse.

## Conclusion

Overall, the data we collected for insults reflect a good deal of what we might have predicted, in that they (for the most part) portray insults as associated naturally with masculinity. In all except the Classic Era, we find male characters using proportionally more insults than expected. And across the three Disney eras, they gave a larger proportion of the inoffensive/bonding type insults than expected based on screen time. Both the Disney and Pixar films double down on the link between casual impoliteness and masculinity by treating even offensive insults as humorous verbal slapstick. Male heroes insult those around them with impunity, and it's framed by the films as roguish or humorous, without affecting the overall positive presentation of the character. In addition, the films often show insults as part of how men build relationships with each other, particularly in Pixar's buddy movies. Much of what we've found seems to harken back to Kiesling's (2005) concept of "social indirectness," the masculine strategy of using conflict language or impoliteness as an indirect signifier of solidarity instead of risking more direct displays of positive emotion or homosocial desire.

The relationship of insults to female characters and femininity is more complicated, and also varies more across the different groups of films. The female characters in the Classic Era support the notion that "nice girls" don't use insults (except possibly to a cat), and that using direct insults as a woman is associated only with villainy. As we enter the Renaissance and New Age eras, the princesses become a bit more feisty, and do sometimes use insults, but they are generally of the offensive type and deployed much more seriously than those used by male characters, which are often framed as humorous. Female characters insulting others isn't typically seen as "funny" in Disney. The clear exceptions to this rule are older characters, where the "sassy old lady without a filter" trope seems to be alive and well. There is also some evidence that the more recent characters of color (e.g. Tiana, Moana) have more of an impolite air to them, both with serious insults and teasing or flirtatious ones.

In the Pixar films, in contrast, we find a wider range of insults used by female characters. As in other places, we find that women are underrepresented in Pixar, but once they make it to the screen, they seem to be treated with a bit more nuance. In some films, female characters take on the "buddy" role (as with Cruz or Dory) and use more bonding insults with their male counterparts. But even here, female characters rarely use insults to bond with each other.

Taken together with the previous data on compliments, the results presented in this chapter round out a particular view of gendered ideologies on language use and expressiveness. Discourses of masculinity in Disney and Pixar sanction insults as an expression of emotion, but portray more straightforward forms of affection as less common and/or less desirable. For femininity, the opposite discourse is upheld: politeness forms (like compliments or mitigation strategies) are framed as easy, natural, and/or desirable ways to express feeling, and it's insults that have negative consequences. Of course, insults are just one part of the larger category of impolite speech, just as compliments and directives only partial representations of politeness; but even though our individual analyses are narrow, the data we have collected so far point to a cohesive ideological divide in the linguistic practices of male and female characters. For one final piece of the puzzle, we turn in the next section to apologies. Given the gender differences in how characters use insults – deliberate tears in the social fabric – how will Disney and Pixar portray characters as they attempt to mend the social fabric instead?

# 7    Apologies

Jessie: Oh, Woody, we were wrong to leave Andy. I... I was wrong...
Mr. Potato Head: Jessie's right, Woody – she was wrong!

*Toy Story 3*

## Introduction

We have chosen to put the insults and apologies chapters next to each other because these two features are the ones that have the closest relationship with the idea of face and face-threatening acts. If insults represent a deliberate (potential) tear in the social fabric, apologies represent a deliberate attempt to mend that tear. In comparison with directives, with their strong functional component, the role of apologies is more fully social. Apologies are a way of conducting politeness and preserving interpersonal relationships. As Holmes (1990) says:

An apology is primarily and essentially a social act. It is aimed at maintaining good relations between participants. To apologize is to act politely, both in the vernacular sense and in the more technical sense of paying attention to the addressee's face needs [Brown & Levinson 1978, 1987]. (Holmes 1990: 156–157)

Inasmuch as women are disproportionately expected to be "polite," as we have discussed at various points throughout the book, we might expect to find a connection between apologizing and femininity. Indeed, this does seem to be the case with mainstream imaginings of gender roles. As Deborah Cameron puts it, when reflecting on trends in language policing, "'Sorry' may have been the hardest word for Elton John, but to women it [allegedly] comes as naturally as breathing."[1] This connection is what we will be exploring in this chapter.[2]

---

[1]  https://debuk.wordpress.com/2016/07/28/sorry-but-its-complicated/
[2]  A relevant anecdote: When asked to give potential examples of gendered differences in speech in a language and gender class, one of our students said she felt as though (as a woman) she apologized unnecessarily for things such as being in the same aisle as someone else at the grocery store.

What is an apology? For our definition, we've chosen to use the one from Holmes (1990: 159):

An apology is a speech act addressed to B's face-needs and intended to remedy an offense for which A takes responsibility, and thus to restore equilibrium between A and B (where A is the apologizer, and B is the person offended).

The most obvious version of this is, of course, to say *sorry*, or *I apologize*. However, apologies have multiple potential elements, not limited to just an explicit expression of apology (aka an illocutionary force indicating device, or IFID). Apologizers can also explain or account for their wrongdoing (e.g. *I wasn't expecting it to be you*), accept blame (e.g. *It was my fault*), offer to repair or redress (e.g. *We'll replace it for you*), or promise a change of behavior (e.g. *It won't happen again*) (see Cohen & Olshtain 1981 or Holmes 1989 for the full taxonomy). Linguists studying apologies often recognize any combination of these things to be an apology, as long as the fundamental force of addressing face needs and restoring balance is present.

When it comes to our data, we have found that apologies, though fascinating, present some challenges that other speech acts in this book have not. First of all, they're rare. Apologies only happen to redress wrongs, unlike other speech acts that are chosen at the speakers' discretion (e.g. compliments, insults) or *must* be spoken to get things done (e.g. directives). The sample size is therefore much smaller, making patterns more difficult to discern. Secondly, the social implications of apologizing more or less, or of varying the form of an apology, are not agreed on by scholars. Does it make you deferent or polite to apologize a lot? Can it make you look weak? And how do these perceptions vary according to speaker gender? While we may not have specific hypotheses about the connection of apologies to gender to start from, we suspect that apologies will show some gendered patterns, if only because of their connection to politeness, so we will use quantitative and qualitative methods to look for these patterns.

### Background

Previous work on apologies in various languages has focused on a number of factors, including the format of the apology itself (both syntactically and pragmatically), the context, and the social identity and relationship of the speaker and hearer. In terms of form, there has been a good deal of work on the type of apology strategy that is used, such as expressions of embarrassment or offers of reparation (e.g. Bataineh & Bataineh 2008; Sugimoto 1997). There's also been significant study on the severity of offense, and the relationship of offense to apology form (e.g. Holmes 1989; Schumann & Ross 2010). Most relevantly for our purposes, a number of studies of apologies have focused on gender, either alone or in combination with other factors.[3]

As with other studies that focus on gender, there is a range of reliability and a number of factors that may or may not have been handled with sufficient nuance. But in addition, the previous research on gender and apologies in English has produced more conflicting results than we found with our other speech acts. Deutschmann (2003), for example, found no overall differences by gender in his book-length study of apologies in British English; the factors he found to be most significant were age and social class (younger and middle-class speakers apologized more) as well as status differences (where, surprisingly, people were more likely to apologize downward in status, rather than upward). Similarly, Abedi (2016) found that the native English speakers in their study used the same types of apology strategies, regardless of gender, although their focus was on types of strategies rather than overall frequency.

Ogiermann (2008) compared male and female speakers of English with each other and also with male and female speakers of Russian. The results of this study perfectly encapsulate the complexities of apology research. It's a difficult study to even summarize because many of the factors showed no differences by gender, while others were discussed as "trends," and a few were actually statistically significant. The one clear conclusion Ogiermann reaches is that differences *between* the two languages/cultures were much more frequent and significant than differences by gender within a single language.

In contrast, Holmes, whose work we cited in discussing compliments,[4] found very clear differences in the frequency of apologies by gender in New Zealand. Holmes (1989, 1990, 1993) looks at a corpus of 183 apologies in New Zealand English, exploring their functions, strategies, and structures, as well as some sociolinguistic factors, including gender. She reports that about 75 percent of all the apologies were given by women, and that women *received* about 73 percent of the apologies as well. Status was a factor, in the expected direction, with people apologizing more to those above them in rank. Severity of the offense played a role as well, with the women in her study being more likely to apologize for offenses in the "light" category, while the men in her group were more likely to apologize for a more weighty offense.

---

[3] For example, studies have included speakers with different status or power levels (e.g. Deutschmann 2003; Holmes 1989), age (e.g. Deutschmann 2003), native-speakers vs. non-native speakers (e.g. Abedi 2016), or speakers of different languages (e.g. Bataineh & Bataineh 2008).

[4] And in fact, at least some of the same students were doing data collection for both of her studies.

Holmes' findings are similar to those of a more recent study on apologies and gender differences that was conducted by psychologists at a Canadian university (Schumann & Ross 2010). They found that female participants did, in fact, apologize more than male participants, at least according to self-report. However, in a separate follow-up study, they found evidence to suggest that this was because the men perceived offenses as less severe. In other words, male and female participants in the study were equally likely to apologize when they felt they had given offense; male participants just had a higher bar for what type of offense was severe enough to merit an apology.[5]

The use of "non-apology strategies" is particularly interesting from a pragmatic viewpoint. Despite the name, non-apology strategies are not incompatible with an apology; they can be tacked on in an attempt to reduce the degree of blame, even when an apology is issued. Kampf (2009) conducted a detailed study of political leaders issuing apologies (or facsimiles thereof) for global and political events or for comments they made on the record. He constructs a taxonomy of the different strategies the leaders use to apologize while shifting blame (such as "blaming the victim" or expressing a willingness to apologize without actually apologizing).[6] Bataineh and Bataineh (2008), in their study of gender and non-apology strategies, found that the men in their study used non-apology strategies more frequently than women. They also report that the women in their sample apologized more overall than the men in the group. At the same time, both groups used the same basic apology strategies, although in slightly different proportions.

In sum, these studies show that the relationship of apologies to gender (at least for English) is complicated. Women apologize more, except when they don't; men and women apologize for different things, or they apologize for the same things, but use different strategies; or they use the same strategies in different proportions. That being said, there is a through-line underneath the murk. While there were studies that showed no gender differences, there were none that showed male participants apologizing more; if there was a difference, it always skewed toward female participants. Women also seem more likely to make apologies for light offenses, and less likely to try to shift blame.

One key component in the relationship of gender to apologies is their explicit role in the maintenance of good social relationships. It's not that

---

[5] Just one more reminder to stay skeptical about the generalizability of this conclusion. The only demographic information we have about the participants is their ages and presumed genders, and that they are students at the University of Waterloo, 66 total in the first study and 120 in the second.

[6] Gender was not something he included in the study, though.

men somehow don't care about social relationships. In fact, we saw in our earlier chapter on male characters' use of insults that even a feature that looked like it might be negative or face-threatening could be used to do positive work in a relationship. At the same time, there is a recognized imbalance in the amount of "emotional labor" (a term associated with the sociologist Arlie Hochschild) that women are expected to do. Cameron (Cameron 2016) ties this concept explicitly to apology behavior:

The aim of an apology is to maintain or restore harmony. Apologising says: "I accept that I have given (or might give) offence, I regret that and I ask for your forgiveness". By implication it also says: "your feelings matter to me: I understand that you may feel bad and I want you to feel better". In that sense apologising can be seen as a form of emotional labour, part of the work of managing your own and others' feelings. And willingness to perform emotional labour is one of the most basic things that's expected of women just because they are women. Even when they're not explicitly cast in a caring role (like "mother"), women are routinely expected to pay attention to others' feelings, and pour oil on troubled waters when harmony is threatened. (Cameron 2016)

We are also interested in the mention of mothers, which was significant in our study of directives, and which we will return to in the qualitative analysis. For now, this perspective encourages us to see if in fact there are quantitative differences in apologies, where female characters apologize more frequently, as well as continuing to look into what apologies are being used to do.

## Methodology

These are the questions we will focus on for our analysis of apologies:

---

**Key Questions**

- Is there a gender-based difference in who **gives and receives apologies** in the films?
- Is there a gender-based difference in the **format or structure of apologies**?
- Are there other ways in which gender interacts with the use of apologies in social contexts; for example are there **certain types of offenses** that only male or only female characters apologize for?

---

Using our dataset of 31 films, and the general methods that have already been discussed, we extracted all examples of apologies according to Holmes' definition listed above. We also followed Holmes in looking at the function of the utterance in context to see if remediation was the goal, even if a speaker doesn't include an explicit apology, since a wide range of forms can be used for remediation. This means that we counted some utterances that did not include a verb like *apologize* or the word *sorry*, or an explicit expression of apology. Here are two examples:

ANNA:     Whoa... I'll replace your sled and everything in it. And I understand if you don't want to help me anymore. (*Frozen*)
MOANA:    Oh! I didn't mean... I wasn't... what? They're calling me, so I gotta... Bye. (*Moana*)

In the first, Anna offers to redress the wrong, and in the second, Moana provides the beginning of an expression of lack of intent. In neither case is there a direct expression of apology. Still, both utterances clearly were intended to serve as apologies in the context of the scene.

Following the same methodology as with the other discourse features, we excluded sarcastic apologies where it is clear to the speaker, hearer, and audience that no remediation was really intended. On the other hand, we included examples where we felt the speaker was somewhat insincere, but it had all the surface characteristics of a true apology. Any ambiguous cases were discussed until a consensus was reached. We collected a total of 351 apologies (117 in Disney and 234 in Pixar).

As with our other linguistic variables, we used binomial tests to compare the number of apologies given and received by each gender against the proportion of male vs. female speech in each era. Although we kept track of both givers and receivers, previous research has focused primarily on who gives apologies, and that will be our focus as well. Because of the small sample size, as well as the conflicting results from previous studies, we decided to add another quantitative measure here as well: ranking individual characters by their total number of apologies, to see if this analysis revealed gendered or other patterns.[7] We also rely more extensively on qualitative study in this chapter than in others.

For the qualitative analysis, we extracted all the apologies by male characters and by female characters (for Disney and Pixar) and looked for recurring patterns in either (a) the nature of the offense, or (b) the form of the apology itself that were linked to gender. Given that several studies (e.g. Bataineh & Bataineh 2008) found gender discrepancies in non-apology use, we also combed through our data for non-apology strategies and paid attention to the gender of the speaker. The strategies we looked for in this part are taken from

---

[7] We initially wanted to include the severity of the offense as a variable, but quickly discovered that the contexts for apologies in the films were so different from the parallel real-life contexts that they weren't comparable at all. In Holmes' data, for instance, the most serious type of offense is heavy, for which the example given is "causes someone to miss an important engagement" (1999: 203). Our "heavy" offenses routinely included things like publicly humiliating another character, banishing them from the kingdom, or almost causing them to die.

Kampf (2009) and Bataineh and Bataineh (2008) and encompass both lexical choices and discourse strategies, including:

- blaming the victim (*I'm sorry if someone took my words out of context*)
- apologizing for the style in which something was worded (*I'm sorry if the way I said this was insensitive*)
- using a verb with pragmatic functions other than apology (*I feel sad that this happened*).

Below we discuss the trends we found to be interesting at both quantitative and qualitative levels.

## Apology Givers and Receivers

### Apology Givers and Receivers

While we will present the quantitative results of our analysis below, the numbers are relatively small (117 in Disney and 234 in Pixar), since apologies are much less frequent in both conversation and plot structure than some of our other features, like directives.[8] Still, these numbers can serve as a helpful backdrop for our subsequent qualitative analysis.

In Table 7.1. are the results of apologies by gender for the three eras of Disney Princess movies as well as the Pixar dataset.

Because the numbers are small, we did not expect to find the statistical significance that we found with insults. Nonetheless, and somewhat to our surprise, some of the numbers, as can be seen in bold in the chart, did reach a basic level of significance according to a binomial test.

First, we see a notable difference among the Disney eras. In the Classic Era, the apologies given by each gender correspond almost exactly to the amount of overall speech. There are only a total of 10 apologies, though, so we hesitate to say anything about them, except that in theory it would be possible for them *all* to be given by female characters and that's not what we find. In the Renaissance Era, though, we see a striking (and statistically significant) drop in the proportion of apologies given by male characters, relative to their total speech, with a corresponding jump in the proportion given by female characters. Male characters gave only 62 percent of the apologies despite speaking 78 percent of words; female characters gave 38 percent of the apologies, while speaking 22 percent of words. These numbers did cross the threshold into significance via the binomial test.

As we turn to the New Age films, once more the results parallel much of what we have already found in previous chapters. These films offer an

---

[8] Although to be fair, Holmes' (1989) corpus which we referenced only had 183.

Table 7.1. *Apologies given and received by character gender*

| | Male characters | | | Female characters | | |
|---|---|---|---|---|---|---|
| | Total speech | Apologies given | Apologies received | Total speech | Apologies given | Apologies received |
| **Classic** | 41% (4,684) | 40% (4) | 50% (5) | 59% (6,710) | 60% (6) | 40% (4) |
| **Renaissance** | 78% (19,756) | 62%* (26) | 81% (34) | 22% (5,643) | 38%* (16) | 19% (8) |
| **New Age** | 50% (16,899) | 43% (28) | 46% (30) | 50% (16,762) | 57% (37) | 52% (34) |
| **Pixar** | 74% (111,662) | 68%* (159) | 63%* (147) | 26% (38,950) | 32% (74) | 26% (62) |

* Proportion is significantly different than predicted based on proportion of words spoken ($p < 0.05$)

overall "correction" from the gender-stereotyped excesses of the Renaissance Era, but not entirely. Male characters give 43 percent of apologies, while speaking 50 percent of words; female characters give 57 percent of the compliments while speaking 50 percent of words. This discrepancy is more moderate than that of the Renaissance and does not reach statistical significance.

And finally, Pixar. As with some of the other variables, such as compliments, the Pixar data pattern most closely with the New Age data, the era they most closely overlap with in terms of chronology. Male characters apologize slightly less than expected: they give 68 percent of the apologies while speaking 74 percent of words. Female characters, on the other hand, give 32 percent of apologies while speaking 26 percent of words. The difference between speech amounts and apologies given is significant for male characters, but not for female characters.

The overall frequency of apologies by male or female characters provides some degree of support for the idea that apologizing is associated with performance of femininity, although not dramatically so, suggesting that there may be more important factors at play here than gender. One such factor is likely to be the importance of specific plot elements, since, as mentioned, apologies only occur in the context where some perceived harm has occurred (well, mostly . . . we will get back to that in our discussion below). The types of harms that can occur vary widely across the films, from Hank the octopus' "inking" in the pool (*Finding Dory*) to Merida's accidentally turning her mother into a bear (*Brave*). As we see from these examples, many of them are also unlikely to be situations that occurred in the studies we cited as background. So we will need to supplement these large-scale trends by looking in detail at individual characters and scenes for other factors that affect the use of apologies, which we will return to in the qualitative analysis below.

### *Top Apologizers*

Another quantitative element that we thought might set an interesting stage for our qualitative analysis was to look at the total number of apologies given by individual characters to see who apologizes the most. We wondered if some characters might apologize frequently as part of their overall characterization (and if this might correlate with gender). Table 7.2 gives a list of all the characters who apologize at least five times in our dataset. Because some of them appear in more than one movie, we give a separate total by movie for these characters as well. Ultimately, though, the number of movies they are in is not as much of a factor as one would think. There are plenty of characters who appear as the lead in multiple movies and never apologize at all. And our "top fish," Dory, would still be at the top of the list even if she had appeared in

Table 7.2. *Top apologizers in Disney and Pixar*

| Apology Num | Character | Film |
|---|---|---|
| 22 | Dory (F) | *Finding Nemo* (2003), n = 7 |
|  |  | *Finding Dory* (2016), n = 15 |
| 14 | Anna (F) | *Frozen* (2013), n = 12 |
|  |  | *Frozen II* (2019), n = 2 |
| 12 | Marlin (M) | *Finding Nemo* (2003), n = 8 |
|  |  | *Finding Dory* (2016), n = 4 |
| 11 | Flik (M) | *A Bug's Life* (1998) |
| 10 | Mater (M) | *Cars 2* (2011), n = 8 |
|  |  | *Cars 3* (2017), n = 2 |
| 10 | Sulley (M) | *Monsters, Inc.* (2001), n = 6 |
|  |  | *Monsters University* (2013), n = 4 |
| 8 | Rapunzel (F) | *Tangled* (2010) |
| 8 | Sadness (F) | *Inside Out* (2015) |
| 7 | Aladdin (M) | *Aladdin* (1992) |
| 7 | Lightning McQueen (M) | *Cars* (2006), n = 2 |
|  |  | *Cars 2* (2011), n = 3 |
|  |  | *Cars 3* (2017), n = 2 |
| 7 | Woody (M) | *Toy Story* (1995), n = 2 |
|  |  | *Toy Story 2* (1999), n = 4 |
|  |  | *Toy Story 3* (2010), n = 1 |
| 6 | Flynn Rider (M) | *Tangled* (2010) |
| 5 | Mr. Incredible (M) | *The Incredibles* (2004) |
| 5 | Linguini (M) | *Ratatouille* (2007) |
| 5 | Mike Wazowski (M) | *Monsters, Inc.* (2001), n = 3 |
|  |  | *Monsters University* (2013), n = 2 |

only one movie. As you can see from the table, the list includes both male and female characters, solidifying our growing sense that apologizing is not clearly marked as feminine language. Male characters predominate on this list, as they do in the overall data.

Pixar's "New Men" (Gillam & Wooden 2008; Jeffords 1995) seem to be well represented on the list, which is worth thinking about. As noted in Chapter 2, the male leads in the Pixar films have been described as being more sensitive and community-oriented than the older, more macho-style heroes like the traditional Disney princes. Our top list includes Sulley and Mike (*Monsters, Inc.* and *Monsters U*), Marlin (*Finding Nemo*), Bob (*The Incredibles*), Woody (*Toy Story* series), and McQueen and Mater (*Cars* series). And Aladdin, who is often cited as a less aggressively masculine prince (Li-Vollmer & LaPointe 2003) is up there as well.

Elements of this list also support our contention that apologies are very plot-driven compared with other factors we have been studying. For example, Flik, the accident-prone inventor in *A Bug's Life*, kicks off the action in his film by losing the offering to the grasshoppers on which his entire community depends. Similarly, Sadness in *Inside Out* precipitates a crisis by accidentally touching certain memories and sending them to core storage, something she doesn't consciously want to do but seems unable to control. Not every character's behavior necessarily works this way. The point is that some plot structures may create contexts that lead inevitably to apologies, and in this sense, we would expect gender to be a secondary concern, so the result that the overall number of apologies is not always significantly different by gender makes sense.

At the same time, the number of apologies in a single movie by each of these two top female characters (Dory, 15; Anna, 12) is substantially higher than for any of the male characters, suggesting that a higher than average quantity of apologies may be more clearly associated with a feminine-marked style. While it's true that plot-driven actions seem to be the main influencer of apologies, Dory and Anna are distinctive in how often they're shown apologizing for actions that are inconsequential to the plot. Six of Anna's 12 apologies in *Frozen*, for example, are throw-away lines apologizing for some clumsiness, including bumping into someone, trying to move through a crowd, accidentally hitting Hans, or accidentally throwing a bag of carrots at Kristoff. Dory has a similar issue, as discussed in the next section. This suggests to us that apologizing as a routine politeness strategy may be influenced by the gender of the speaker, even though apologies for plot-driven offenses are not.

## Qualitative Discussion: Apologies on a Sliding Scale

In our qualitative analysis, we looked for recurring themes that appeared within apologies by male characters or apologies by female characters, particularly with respect to either the nature of the offense or the form of the apology itself. We were interested in whether a more detailed and context-driven analysis might uncover gendered patterns and ideologies that the larger analysis had missed, particularly with respect to severity or other aspects of the offense.

In addition, we considered the question of whether one utterance might be more or less of an apology than another. Our quantitative analysis was based only on those examples that fit the criteria for an apology described earlier; we excluded all the other utterances. However, Murphy (2019) uses experimental data to argue convincingly that apologies are not always clearly delineated phenomena but instead should be modeled with a prototype at the center and other potential examples of the phenomenon getting progressively further away as various factors change. So it may be worth looking at "how apology" the utterances by male or female characters are.

*Sorry, I Have a Head Injury: Apologizing without an Offense*

The first pattern that recurred and that was clearly tied to gender was apologizing for something where the speaker had no control over the event. The severity scale from Holmes (1989) had three categories of offense, from severe to light, with light including things such as bumping into someone. The lightest offenses often included things that were entirely accidental or due to misunderstanding, but Holmes does not report any examples where the person apologizing had no control at all over what took place. The more we looked at the data, the more we found numerous examples where it seemed odd for the character to apologize, for a variety of reasons. And spoiler alert: the characters who did this were overwhelmingly female.

First of all, our top scorer, Dory, apologizes repeatedly for having short-term memory loss. This does cause inconveniences for the listeners sometimes, but she does it (1) frequently and (2) even in situations where it's not clear that any problem was caused for the receiver. A good example is this scene with Hank the octopus from *Finding Dory*.

**Excerpt 7A "What tag?" (*Finding Dory*, 2016)**

HANK:     If I just take your tag, I can take your place on the transport truck then you can
          go back inside and find your family. All you have to do is give me the tag.
DORY:     What tag? *[looks]* There's a tag on my fin!
HANK:     How could you forget you have a tag on your fin?
DORY:     Oh no. **I'm sorry. I… I suffer from short-term memory loss**.

So in this case, the harm from the memory loss actually is only to Dory (forgetting she has a tag on her fin). Hank can see the tag perfectly well. Maybe she is apologizing for his confusion? But whatever a "light" offense consists of, this seems to us to be a notch below that.[9]

Similarly, another high scorer on Table 7.2 is Sadness from *Inside Out*. Like Dory, Sadness repeatedly apologizes for an essential quality that she has no control over and that is in fact her raison d'être: being sad. Here is an example:

**Excerpt 7B "I went sad" (*Inside Out*, 2015)**

JOY:      Oh, it's that time in the twisty tree, remember? The hockey team showed
          up and Mom and Dad were there cheering. Look at her, having fun and
          laughing. I love this one.
SADNESS:  Mmm. I love that one too.
JOY:      Atta girl! Now you're getting it!

---

[9] We also have some serious concerns about this pattern with respect to ableism and portrayals of disability. And we wonder if the pattern would be the same if the character had been a male fish. Perhaps a future film will answer this question.

SADNESS:   Yeah. It was the day the Prairie Dogs lost the big playoff game. Riley
missed the winning shot. She felt awful. She wanted to quit. **Sorry. I went
sad again, didn't I?**

JOY:       I'll tell ya what. We can keep working on that when we get back. Okay?

SADNESS:   Okay.

Here, Joy (the embodiment of one of Riley's emotions, and de facto Team
Leader) is trying to teach Sadness to be more positive. In the end, the film
performs a moral plot twist, in which it reminds us that all emotions are an
essential part of life, and Sadness turns out to be essential to saving the day.
But before that point, her apologies for being sad are treated as perfectly
reasonable. In fact, in the excerpt above, Joy doesn't even entirely accept her
apology, but rather reframes it as something along the lines of "ok, but try
harder next time."

It's notable to us that Dory and Sadness are both in their own ways
representing mental illness or disability, Dory explicitly having short-term
memory loss, and Sadness in many ways coded as clinically depressed. In
Excerpts 7A and 7B, both characters apologize specifically for these facets of
their existence, which suggests to us that ableism may also play a role in how
these characters are depicted. While exploring this issue in more detail is out of
scope for this project, we would be excited to see future scholars examine the
relationship of gender and disability in these films.

In quite a few situations, a female character apologizes for something that is
actually a male character's fault. A perfect example comes once again from
Dory, this time in *Finding Nemo*:

**Excerpt 7C "The trench" (*Finding Nemo*, 2003)**

DORY:      Trench, through it, not over it. I remember. Hey, hey! Hey! Hey! Hey, wait
up, partner. Hold on. Wait! Wait—wait! I got, I gotta tell you something. . .
whoa. Nice trench. Hello! Okay, let's go.

MARLIN:    Bad trench, bad trench. Come on, we're gonna swim over this thing.

DORY:      Whoa, whoa, partner. Little red flag goin' up. Somethin's telling me we
should swim through it, not over it.

MARLIN:    Are you even looking at this thing? It's got death written all over it.

DORY:      **I'm sorry, but I really, really, really think we should swim through.**

MARLIN:    And I'm really, really done talking about this. Over we go.

Here, it is actually Dory who has the pertinent information, which is that it is
safer to swim through the trench rather than over it, even if she doesn't
remember why. And Marlin is going to regret his mistake soon enough. But
Dory ends up apologizing, for something that isn't entirely clear. Because he is
wrong? Because she is contradicting him? Because she is reasserting her
position? And he responds snarkily and dismissively because at heart Marlin
is a big mansplainer, or fishsplainer, or whatever.

These examples are all drawn from Pixar, but we see this pattern in Disney as well. In *Beauty and the Beast* there is a scene where Gaston (that ultimate symbol of toxic masculinity) comes to Belle's house to try to convince her to marry him. She uses one politeness strategy after another to turn him down, culminating in a self-deprecating apology: *I'm very sorry, Gaston, but I just don't deserve you.* After he leaves, she shares her true feelings with the audience (in song, of course), calling him *boorish* and *brainless* and all the things she doesn't say to him directly. In other words, not even Belle herself really thinks she should be apologizing here, and yet she does.

We did not find this type of pattern used by male characters. The closest we could find was Randy, Mike's roommate in *Monsters University*, who accidentally disappears while Mike is talking to him:

**Excerpt 7D "You just disappeared?" (*Monsters University*, 2013)**

RANDY:    Hey there! I'm your roomie! Name's Randy Boggs! Scaring major.
MIKE:     Oh, what a... Mike Wazowski! Scaring major.
RANDY:    I can tell we're gonna be best chums, Mike. Take whichever bed you want. I wanted you to have first dibs. *[Randy disappears.]* Ah!
MIKE:     You just disappeared?
RANDY:    *[Randy reappears.]* **Sorry.** If I do that in scaring class, I'll be a joke.

It's clear that Randy didn't intend to disappear, so it matches that part of the pattern, but on the other hand it is a reasonable thing to apologize for, since it takes place in the middle of a conversation. But there were no cases of a male character apologizing to someone for something that caused no problem at all or was actually the receiver's fault. So here is a pattern that suggests that there may in fact be a correlation between the severity of the offense and the gender of the apologizer, even if our larger-scale coding couldn't detect it.

## Sorry-Not Sorry: Gender and Non-Apology Strategies

There was another recurring pattern in the qualitative analysis, this one linked with apologies by male characters: the use of non-apology strategies. As we have noted, previous studies that looked at non-apology strategies found that they were more frequent among male participants. Ogiermann (2008) also suggests that the English-speaking male participants in her study are more inclined to provide excuses than female participants, and that they are more direct in denying responsibility.[10] This same pattern of denying responsibility is found among the political leaders that Kampf (2009) studied, who are, as best we can tell since he doesn't give a list of the participants, all men. There

---

[10] Although she notes these as "trends" and not statistically significant.

seems to be an element of power and/or privilege at work here, though it's beyond the scope of what we are doing to fully explore all its ramifications.

For the basic non-apology strategies, we found that in the Disney dataset, all but one of these were issued by male characters. For example, Grimsby, Prince Eric's assistant in *The Little Mermaid*, has been accusing the Prince of having imagined seeing Ariel and made clear that he doesn't think she is real. When he finally sees "Ariel" (who is actually Ursula, the villain, in disguise), he says:

Well, uh— err, Eric. I— it appears that I was mistaken. This mystery maiden of yours does in fact exist. And— and she is lovely.

Here Grimsby is using what Kampf calls "syntactic and lexical means to downgrade his responsibility" by hedging the entire sentence with *It appears that . . .*, as well as having a number of false starts at the beginning. He also uses the verb *mistaken*, which corresponds to what Holmes labels "expression of deficiency," but without an actual illocutionary force indicating device. Not to be outdone, Prince Eric himself also uses this strategy when he first encounters the now-voiceless Ariel and has a one-sided conversation with her. At one point he says to her,

You know, I feel really bad not knowing your name.

This corresponds exactly to Kampf's strategy of "using a verb with several pragmatic functions" instead of a straightforward verb like *I apologize*.

In the Pixar data set as well, it is generally male characters who use the non-apology strategies. A good example is this sequence from *Monsters, Inc.* between Roz and Mike (Wazowski):

**Excerpt 7E "That darn paperwork" (*Monsters, Inc.*, 2001)**

ROZ:   Wazowski, you didn't file your paperwork last night.
MIKE:  Oh, that darn paperwork. **Wouldn't it be easier if it all just blew away?**
ROZ:   Don't let it happen again.
MIKE:  Yes, well, I'll, uh. . . **I'll try to be less careless.**

Here we have a non-apology in the first exchange, which more or less corresponds to a category in Bataineh and Bataineh (2008) of "brushing off the incident as unimportant," suggesting that perhaps there is no actual offense on the table. When Roz continues to scold him, he finally produces an apology that consists of a "promise of forbearance" but without an actual IFID or other explicit expression of regret.

Similarly, the somewhat hapless Flik from *A Bug's Life* uses a number of non-apology strategies. For example, in one scene, Flik has messed up his job of bringing food to the offering stone, and Atta discovers the problem and says, "What did you do?!" Flik replies:

It was an accident?

It is clear in the context that he is genuinely sorry and intends this as an apology. But it falls under Kampf's category of "denying responsibility" and "attributing blame to an external source."

There were only two examples of non-apology strategies used by female characters across the dataset, one from Disney and one from Pixar. The example from Disney occurs in *Frozen II*, where Anna says to Elsa, who has left the room abruptly:

Did we hurt your feelings? I'm so sorry, if we did.

Here, she does what Kampf calls "apologizing for the outcome and not the act," in other words saying she is sorry if Elsa is hurt, but not naming what she may have done wrong, and keeping the whole thing in the conditional. Still it is clearly intended as a genuine apology in the context, and even includes the emphasizer "so." (And, for the record, it turns out that Elsa is upset about something else entirely, so Anna was not off-base to make her apology conditional.)

There is only one female character in Pixar who uses what appears to be a non-apology strategy: Helen from *The Incredibles*. When she and her husband are having an argument late at night, and they realize their children are listening, she says to them:

We're sorry we woke you. Everything's okay. Go back to bed. It's late.

It's a true apology, but the use of the plural we instead of I corresponds to Kampf's category of "blurring the offender," which we saw in Anna's example also.[11] There's a similar example from Jessie of *Toy Story 3* in the epigraph at the beginning of this chapter, although in her case she actually corrects it to a full apology by changing the pronoun.

We don't mean to suggest with this analysis that apologizing is associated only with femininity; male characters can and do apologize. Even in these specific instances, where strategies are used to downgrade the apology in some sense, it's clear that the male characters intended their utterances as apologies. What seems more likely is that male characters are more likely to keep some distance between themselves and their apologies, just as they are more select-ive in who they compliment, and on what, than the female characters.

An interesting example that seems to support this interpretation occurs with Marlin in *Finding Dory* where he seems to be trying to avoid apologizing. In this scene with his son, Nemo, Marlin tries to rationalize away his behavior (telling Dory to "go wait over there and just forget") which has led to Dory's being captured by some marine biologists.

---

[11] It's tempting to suggest that female characters are more likely to apologize in the plural, since it happened in all three cases here, but there are also male characters who do it.

**Excerpt 7F. "It's all my fault she got kidnapped"** (*Finding Dory*, **2016**)

NEMO:       You said that, Dory swam to the surface, and she got taken by some...
MARLIN:     All right, I don't want to hear the whole story again. I was just asking about the one part because, look, **if I said that**... **I'm not positive I did**. **It's actually a compliment** because... I asked her to wait and I said, "it's what you do best." So I... **Oh, it's my fault! It's all my fault she got kidnapped** and taken into whatever this place is. What if it's a restaurant?

The first part of Marlin's monologue sounds very much like one of Kampf's slimy politicians trying to weasel their way out of a jam. It is filled with non-apology strategies like the conditional *if I said that*, and the attempt to reclassify the offense as a compliment. These elements come beforehand, and then there is a sudden shift to a real apology, or at least a direct acceptance of responsibility. Marlin, after all, is one of our top apologizers, and to be clear, in many other instances his apologies are unqualified and sincere. But again, masculinity seems to at least open the door to avoidance of certain behaviors, apologies apparently among them.

## Conclusion

There's a scene in *Mulan* that we found very insightful in terms of our discussion here, and that neatly sums up everything we have been talking about. In it, Mulan (passing as the male soldier "Ping") has started a fight amongst the soldiers when their commanding officer, Shang, shows up.

**Excerpt 7G "Manly urges"** (*Mulan*, **1998**)

SHANG:       I don't need anyone causing trouble in my camp!
MULAN/PING:  Sorry! Uhhhhh... I mean, sorry you had to see that. You know how it is when you get those, uh manly urges and you just have to kill something— fix things— uh, cook outdoors.

Between the first apology (*sorry!*), which seems automatic and genuine, and the rest of the utterance, Mulan-as-Ping changes her physical demeanor, squaring her shoulders and lowering her voice pitch. The rest of the utterance falls more or less under Kampf's non-apology strategy of "apologizing for the outcome" and not for the act (2009: 2264). It also includes an "account," i.e. an explanation of why the offense occurred, which for comic effect invokes exaggerated stereotypes of masculinity involving testosterone and violence. It clearly positions apologies as something associated with women, and something that, if she's not careful, could reveal to the world that Mulan is a woman and not a man.

Our data, both quantitative and qualitative, show that the relationship of apologies to gender is far from direct, no matter how much Mulan believes otherwise. That's not an unexpected result, given how equivocal and inconclusive the literature we reviewed was for this variable, compared to the other ones we have worked with. Both male and female characters apologize, and in a certain proportion of the cases we suspect this is determined more by the specifics of the plot than by gender or any other characteristic of the speaker.

At the same time, we find some patterning at the extremes that seems more clearly linked to gender. While apologizing may not be marked as specifically associated with femininity, non-apology strategies do seem to be mostly used by the male characters. And female characters are more likely to apologize in situations that make us ask, "Why are you apologizing for that?" This is particularly true for the few female characters who also are depicted as having a mental illness or a cognitive disability, which may be reflective of ableist ideologies present in Disney and Pixar as well.

A possible explanation for the gender patterns may be found in the association between femininity and politeness that we discussed in Chapter 4. Women have been held more responsible for maintaining social relations and catering to the face needs of others. Femininity may be tied to a focus on making sure the social harm is repaired, while masculinity involves more of an emphasis on producing the speech act of the apology while (if possible) hedging against the inherent face threat it involves. Apologizing, after all, is both a way of attending to the addressee's face needs, as in the Holmes excerpt, and a face-threatening act for the speaker, as Kampf, for example, points out. We find that, as with compliments, female characters overall use apologies more frequently and with less hesitation, while male characters use them, but with more caveats and possible distancing strategies. And in some parts of the texts, as with the example from *Mulan*, we find hints that apologies may be thought of as associated with femininity in the ideology, even if that doesn't line up particularly well with the behavior of either our characters or people in the nonanimated realm.

We will bring together some of the common themes from these four speech acts and their role in constructing gender when we return to them in our Conclusion; we will also come back to the ever-present topic of politeness. But for the moment, in the next chapter, we turn to something entirely different: queerness in Disney. If you were tired of the binary and the constant modeling of language in these films as having to go with femininity or masculinity, with no other options on the table, then this next chapter is for you.

> I relate much more to Ursula, who lives alone and isolated in her drag queen
> boudoir under the sea, likely reviled for her visible body fat and unsexy
> appearance (I feel you, gurl).
>
> Mark Helmsing (2016: 62)

## Introduction

Up to this point, we have been working within the framework that Disney (and
Pixar for the most part) presents as the default, in which everything is heteronormative and binary, male or female. We've analyzed our data in this way to
match the stance in the films, complicating the narrative occasionally as
needed, but mostly looking at how binary gender ideologies are presented,
which is what drew us to the Princess films in the first place. If little girls have
a fantasy about wearing a fancy ballgown and being swept off their feet by a
man, then Disney has surely played a role in shaping that fantasy over several
generations, and our goal has been to see how that heteronormative view is
expressed linguistically.

But even though the Disney canon is full of heteronormative ideology (see
Martin & Kazyak 2009), there is also queerness to be found in children's films.
In fact, it's worth noting that "known to be queer" characters in Disney have
enough of a presence in popular culture that they are routinely part of conversations we have had with each other, with students, or just with personal
contacts we have talked to. Oh, yeah, I love Ursula, did you know she's based
on a drag queen? I love that part where Scar says he's going to curtsy! An
online search quickly reveals numerous articles or lists with titles such as "18
Disney Characters Who Are Probably LGBTQ."[1] And as with so many other
aspects of media representation, the picture is complicated both by what we
find on screen and by how viewers interpret it through the lens of their own
experiences. So if the rest of the book has been about how Disney presents

---

[1] https://gayety.co/disney-characters-who-were-probably-lgbtq

models of gender normativity, this chapter is on what happens when Disney breaks those patterns.[2]

In recent years, there has been an overt (if minimal) effort by Pixar, in particular, to diversify representations of sexuality, in keeping with changes in social norms, such as the increasing legality of marriage between same-sex couples in the US and elsewhere. As a result, the last few years have produced the first officially recognized queer characters in the Disney/Pixar canon. Most notable among these is Officer Specter in Pixar's movie *Onward* (2020), who plays a minimal role in the film but explicitly mentions her girlfriend in the text of the movie.[3] At a less widely distributed level, Pixar released a short film in 2020 called *Out* that purports to feature the first gay lead character in the studio's history (Romano 2020).

We leave it to the reader to decide whether this handful of characters represents true progress or just a form of rainbow capitalism where Disney and Pixar are making these choices not to expand their repertoire of voices, but solely to make money by targeting queer communities with hints and promises. Linguist Katie Conner tells us, "I have seen and read and been part of discussions of frustration that come from a place where it feels like Disney/Pixar is queer baiting the community at times ... 'will we or won't we' to exploit the hunger for representation to drive up views" (K. Conner, personal communication). In any case, the door to the metaphorical closet is clearly open now, so it will be interesting to see how this pattern develops in the next decade or two.

Our focus here will be on a different group of characters: specifically characters from Disney films who have been coded with queer and/or gender-transgressive traits and celebrated as queer by audiences, but have not been identified as such in the canon of their respective films. Examples commonly cited in the scholarly literature (as well as in numerous online blogs and fan pages) include Maleficent from *Sleeping Beauty* (1959), Ursula from *The Little Mermaid* (1989), Scar from *The Lion King* (1994), and Ratcliffe from *Pocahontas* (1995): all characters who are queer-coded in that they meaningfully deviate from the rigid gender binaries Disney enforces on other characters in the films. And, not coincidentally, all of them are villains.

A number of previous studies have documented how gender transgression and queerness are closely associated with villainy in many children's films

---

[2] A huge shout out to Katie Conner and Robin Queen for their help on this chapter. But if we messed anything up please don't blame these outstanding human beings.

[3] There were some vague forays into this realm in earlier movies, such as the appearance of an arguably gay couple (Bucky and Pronk) in *Zootopia* (2016), or the much-debated detail that Oaken, the trader from *Frozen* (2013), waves to a family that appears to include his husband.

(e.g. Li-Vollmer & LaPointe 2003; Putnam 2013). Putnam sums up this pattern and its implications for ideology:

In contrast to the heterosexist leads, many of the villains display transgendered attributes – depicted as women with either strong masculine qualities or as strangely defeminized, while the male bad guys are portrayed as effeminate, often complete with stereotypical limp-wristed affectation. These repeated motifs become even more disconcerting when they are coupled with the evil machinations for which, well, villains are known. (Putnam 2013: 147–148)

This scholarship has uncovered an undeniable pattern in the way that Disney movies queer their villains, and in doing so, further reinforce heteronormative ideologies in their films. It is this group of **quillains** (a term we have borrowed with great delight from McLeod's [2016] dissertation) that will be the focus of our analysis in this chapter.

Existing studies of queerness in Disney have focused either on visual elements (e.g. costume, hairstyle, body movement) or on behavioral elements on a wider scale (e.g. decision-making, romantic partnership). No work to date has focused on describing the actual linguistic elements that ultimately help turn a character into a quillain. You know our modus operandi by now: we're going to offer linguistics a seat at the table. We will explore whether the gender-transgressive traits of these characters include recurring lexical, syntactic, and/ or pragmatic features. We are particularly interested in whether such features cluster together to form an identifiable queer style, and if so, what that style is being used to do. We hope to add a new linguistic understanding to the ways that gender-transgressive characters coexist with, reinforce, and sometimes subvert the dominant Disney narrative of heteronormative romance.

## Background: Queer Theory

Because queerness is a phenomenon lurking subversively on the margins in Disney, we do not have sufficient data to undertake a quantitative analysis of specific features such as the one that has been the focus of our work up to this point. We turn instead to qualitative methods and approach our data within the framework of queer theory, hoping to provide as nuanced a picture of queerness in these films as possible. Li-Vollmer and LaPointe (2003), who, as we mentioned, have done some of the foundational research on Disney villains, explain how queerness informs their methods and serves as a lens through which they view their data.

Likewise, we invoke queer as part of our methodology. Used thus, queer represents a moment of fissure when that which is normal is thrown into question – a space through which the researcher can locate and relay evidence that problematizes the relation between the normal and the natural. (Li-Vollmer & LaPointe 2003: 92)

Throughout this book, we have been examining the discourse that frames heterosexuality and particular gender roles as natural, and this chapter adds an important piece to that puzzle.

Queer theory calls us to more actively denormalize the ideology of cis/heteronormativity. We do so in part by turning our attention to rich spaces where "normality" and "naturality" are flouted in the context of the media in question; or, as Li-Vollmer and LaPointe put it "by noting and uncovering moments of struggle between images that reinforce heteronormative notions and images that seek to undermine such notions" (2003: 93). We also encourage readers to use a queer theory perspective to think about media representations they are familiar with, including and beyond those discussed here, and experiment with how it opens up new ways of viewing those representations.

Before moving on, we should take a moment to discuss the terms queer and queerness. We are reluctant to give a strict definition of either, since, like many terms within a social construction framework, they are inherently complex and nuanced, as well as subject to change along with shifting social norms and practices.[4] Still, we want to provide some context for what to expect as we work with these concepts throughout the chapter, and for that purpose, we find this passage from Li-Vollmer and LaPointe (2003) useful and relevant:

> We see **queer** as a powerful term that encompasses broad notions of that which is other than or beyond "normal," as well as narrower understandings of individuals and images that can be identified as gay, lesbian, bisexual, transgendered, or transsexual. For the purposes of our work here, we purposefully maintain these multiple meanings and examine representations of villainy as both deviant and as homosexual – in other words, through both a broad and a narrow understanding of queer. (Li-Vollmer & LaPointe 2003: 92)

We also believe that although individual people may choose whether or not they identify with the label "queer," queerness in the abstract is not a binary quality that one either does or does not have. As Motschenbacher and Stegu (2013) put it:

A binary conceptualisation of Queerness as a matter of being either Queer or not Queer is clearly too simplistic to capture the sexual variability that has been documented. It is, therefore, more productive to assume a continuum of Queerness and to accept that concrete behaviours may be *slightly Queer, moderately Queer, highly Queer, Queerer* or *less Queer* than others, etc. (2013: 521; italics in original)

---

[4]  See also McConnell-Ginet (2002) for a detailed discussion of the difficulties of defining "queer."

Their comment is about real people in human societies, but it applies equally well to characters on film. The characters we have chosen to analyze may not strike every reader as equally representative of some idea of queerness, or as fitting along that continuum at all; conversely, some characters we have deliberately excluded may arguably display some characteristics that could warrant their inclusion.

Given that queerness can exist on a spectrum, and can be interpreted both broadly and narrowly, there are many characters and films that can be read as queer which we won't be covering, but will touch on briefly here. Some characters have normative feminine or masculine gender presentation, for example, but are read as queer in a broader sense because they transgress the normative expectations for their gender in ways that resonate with a queer worldview. We have mentioned Mulan (*Mulan*, 1998), numerous times in the discussion thus far, but there are also Elsa (*Frozen*, 2013; *Frozen II*, 2019), and Merida (*Brave*, 2012), sometimes read as queer because of their apparent lack of interest in heteroromantic relationships. Elsa's song "Let It Go" resonated with many queer viewers as a "coming out" song ("Conceal, don't feel, / don't let them know / Well, now they know") and a disavowal of the expectations of a rigid society in favor of self-authenticity, which is a decidedly queer idea when viewed through the right lens.[5]

In any case, our goal is not to make any sort of determination or generate a definitive list of who is and isn't queer in Disney or Pixar, but rather to explore how portrayals of queerness and gender transgression occur and recur across the set of films addressed here. Queer-coding, or the act of subtextually associating a character with queer identities, appears across the Disney canon in a variety of characters. Some of these roles include sidekicks (e.g. LeFou, *Beauty and the Beast*, Wiggins, *Pocahontas*), queer-coded "couples" (e.g. Timon and Pumbaa, *The Lion King*), and minor characters who play with cross-dressing or other forms of gender-crossing (e.g. Pleakley, *Lilo and Stitch*). However, following up with Li-Vollmer and LaPointe's (2003) analysis, we take particular interest in the queer-coded antagonists (the quillains), who easily comprise the largest subset of queer-coded characters. In analyzing the linguistic mechanisms through which quillains are queer-coded, we hope to answer the question: What messages are being encoded for the viewer about those outside a heterosexual norm?

One quick note about intersectionality before we move on. Although we explained in Chapter 1 that we have made the decision to set aside any detailed analysis of ethnicity as being beyond the scope of the current work, we nonetheless must acknowledge the critical intersection of gender, sexuality,

---

[5] Nikolas (2014) extends this interpretation to characters from a wide range of films, including examples like *Pinocchio* (1940) and *Dumbo* (1941).

and ethnicity here. At the moment, queerness in Disney and Pixar is represented predominantly by characters who are also coded as white, although Jafar, for example, is usually read as a person of color. While this may simply be due to a lack of ethnic diversity in these movies overall, we must also be open to the possibility that the same social forces that often marginalize queer people of color in actual human societies are at work here as well.

## Language, Style, and Queerness

The construction and performance of a queer identity, like most things about human beings, is complex and tremendously variable, and does not lend itself to a simplistic analysis at a linguistic level or any other (e.g. Bucholtz & Hall 2004; Kelley 2013; Podesva 2007; Queen 2005).[6] As Livia and Hall (1997) put it:

> An utterance becomes typically lesbian or gay only if the hearer/reader understands that it was the speaker's intent that it should be taken up that way. Queerspeak should thus be considered an essentially intentional phenomenon, sharing some of the echoic or polyphonic structure of irony. (1997: 14)

Much of the linguistic research that exists on queer language has focused on the performance of gay masculinity (e.g. Podesva 2007), with some increasing study of trans identities (e.g. Zimman 2014), but very little recent work on lesbian identities, at least in the US.[7] Furthermore, as discussed in Chapter 1, recent frameworks in sociolinguistic research have found it more productive to focus less on identities and individuals and more on linguistic styles. With this in mind, we will be drawing on two linguistics styles that have been studied fairly extensively, to see if they appear in our datasets: Women's Language, and camp. It is no coincidence that both of these styles are associated with gay male and/or drag queen identities.

Women's Language (WL from here on) is a term drawn from one of the earliest and most cited works on language and gender, Robin Lakoff's book *Language and Woman's Place* (1973). Lakoff gives a list of the alleged features of WL, including things like empty adjectives (*darling, cute, lovely*), tag questions (*It's hot out, isn't it?*), or using hyperbole and exaggeration.[8] The book itself does not provide any actual data from speakers, and numerous subsequent studies found no clear support for any of the features on the list being used more frequently by women than by men. On the other hand, their

---

[6] Neither does a heterosexual identity, for that matter, though that's not our focus in this chapter.
[7] There are a few studies based in the US, like Queen 2005 as well as some interesting work on Japanese lesbians (e.g. Abe 2004).
[8] Also avoiding taboo language. Your authors, who both identify as women, have been marvelously unsuccessful at that one for their entire lives.

use by drag queens as part of their performance of gender (on and off stage) has been documented carefully by Barrett (1999, 2017), Mann (2011), and Calder (2019) among others. So although WL isn't consistently used by women, the style is recognizable as feminine and can be used as a way to invoke a feminine performance (e.g. by gay men in drag).

Another linguistic style associated with a performance of queerness is camp. The work of Keith Harvey (2000, 2002), although reliant on fictional sources for data, is useful nonetheless because it grounds the analysis of camp in previous work on queer linguistics. His analysis also provides a clear connection of the features of this style to their sociopolitical context. Harvey (2002) describes camp in this way:

Camp, as I understand it, is motivated by a playful and subversive take on sign-making that encompasses aspects of register play, reversal of expected outcomes and encodings, and parody. The parodic dimension is particularly important; its main arena being that of notions of femininity. This specific parodic focus (although there are others) accounts for the popular link between camp and 'effeminacy' in male (usually homosexual) speakers. (2002: 1149)

As Harvey points out, camp is a broad stylistic category that encompasses many different styles of language play. In its specific use to subvert gender boundaries, camp shares some connection with WL. Both camp and WL have been documented as used by gay men to subvert gender boundaries, the former by calling attention to and parodying gender performance, and the latter by actively performing a feminine style.[9]

In addition, a number of researchers who have written about queerness in Disney, although they are not linguists, discuss camp in their analysis. Letts (2016) centers camp in his discussion, and sets as his goal, "[to] explore 'camp' Disney with reference to five iconic Disney villains – Ursula, Jafar, Scar, Governor Ratcliffe, and Hades – from films released over eight years" (Letts 2016: 148). Similarly, Helmsing (2016) only mentions camp in passing, but uses the term "diva villains," and describes their "diva pedagogy" as including sassiness, sarcasm, and throwing shade, all of which we consider to be elements of camp, and which we will be looking for in our analysis.

The features of these two styles associated with gay masculinities give us a starting point, much as features identified with the performance of straight masculinities or femininities helped us decide what to explore in the quantitative analyses we presented earlier. Our goal, however, is to look holistically at

---

[9] Harvey also notes that "Camp comments seem often to be part of a performance that is ostensibly directed at an interlocutor while actually having a wider audience in mind" (Harvey 2002: 1156). What could possibly be more suited to a study of characters on film?

a group of characters in Disney[10] that have been coded as queer (see method-ology below) in their texts and examine how their scripted language plays a role in their presentation, and what ideologies are being challenged or reinforced in the process.

## Queering Characters: Male vs. Female Quillains

You may have noticed that the characters mentioned in the discussion of previous research on queerness in Disney have included both male and female villains, and both have been discussed in relation to camp. That raises some interesting questions, because if camp is associated with gay masculinity, why is it being performed by female characters? In this section we look at how queerness interacts with male and female gender categories, what elements of these performances are similar or different, and what ideologies are being enacted through these patterns.

### *Male Quillains*

The most frequently discussed members of the quillain group are male villains whose feminine-coded behaviors and qualities signal that they are "other," e.g. Scar (*The Lion King*), Jafar (*Aladdin*), or Ratcliffe (*Pocahontas*). A good overview of these characters is provided by Li-Vollmer and LaPointe (2003). The physical traits they found that recurred among these villains included slender physiques with long tapered hands, facial features that "invoke trad-itional ideals of feminine beauty," such as slim, narrow faces and shading on the eyes that resembled eyeshadow. They often had long or flowing hair and wore fancy/frilly clothing. Their behaviors included expressive hand gestures, obsession with their appearance/grooming, and discussion of feminine-marked topics such as fashion. They also evidenced an aversion to or avoidance of female characters.

Li-Vollmer and LaPointe describe these features as producing an "excessive display of femininity as a marker of deviance" (2003: 104) and specifically highlight the drag-queen nature of these performances. Interestingly, they note that the feminized physical features occur even where the character is an animal, as can be seen in the contrast between Scar and his more "manly" brother Mufasa. Scar has a thinner body and jaw than his brother, with a flowy mane, hooded/shadowed eyes, and extended, tapering claws.

As expected, we found that when we began looking at the scenes that contained our male quillains, their behaviors contrasted with heteronormative

---

[10] All of them from Disney films. Pixar doesn't seem to have these sorts of central queer-but-not-officially characters. Pixar characters are more likely to be "out" but play a very minor role.

Figure 8.1 Toy figure of Jafar (*Aladdin*, 1992)
Reproduced by permission of Tania Pantoja

ideas of masculinity in unmistakable ways. Ratcliffe, for example, descends a staircase wearing high heels and ribbons in his hair, brandishing a feather boa and singing. The lyrics to his song include the word lovely as well as this part:

> My rivals back home
> It's not that I'm bitter
> But think how they'll squirm
> When they see how I glitter!

Both the glittering and the bitterness hearken to queer sensibilities (see e.g. Helmsing 2016).

Jafar, the evil Vizier in *Aladdin* schemes to marry Princess Jasmine, but makes clear that he is not attracted to her at all, and only wants the power she can confer to rule the kingdom. He shows no interest in pleasing or charming her. In the scene where she pretends to seduce him as a distraction, Jafar seems most interested in the compliments she gives him, rather than in the princess herself, saying, as they embrace, *Now, pussycat, tell me more about. . . myself.*

In keeping with our goal of placing these films in historical context, we noticed that the prototypical male quillains were clustered in the 1990s, mostly in the Renaissance Era. Li-Vollmer and LaPointe suggest that in fact the male villains in these movies evolved specifically to provide a contrast with heroes who had become more sensitive and less unabashedly masculine, at least in comparison with the Classic Era princes.

[M]ale heroes in contemporary films are no longer the epitome of masculinity as machismo . . . We see this in the sensitive (and sometimes self-doubting) characters of Aladdin . . . and Hercules . . ., who seem especially vulnerable and even a bit goofy when around their female counterparts. However, any suggestion of "feminine weakness" in the heroes can be easily dismissed by the appearance of a villain who can better the heroine in womanly display. We suggest that the queered villains may, in fact, become even more feminized as a sort of countervailing presentation of gender that helps heroes maintain their masculinity and male standing. (Li-Vollmer & LaPointe 2003: 104–105)

Their argument resonates with us, and with our tracking of masculinity throughout this book. It is deeply disappointing, nonetheless. We felt encouraged by newer representations of masculinity (particularly in Pixar) that seemed to allow more room for vulnerability and nuance. Yet in this group of Disney films, the ideological message appears to be that it's okay for a man to be less brawny and burly and more sensitive than the Classic Era heroes, but only to a certain degree. Once a character passes that point in performing masculinity, they get labeled as deviant. And a villain. Not okay.

### Female Quillains

There is also a group of female characters who recur in discussions of the quillain category. They are referred to as Mean Ladies by Putnam (2013) and as Diva Villains by Helmsing (2016). And although Li-Vollmer and LaPointe's analysis is only of male characters, they draw a direct parallel to the early Classic Era villainesses like the Evil Queen (*Snow White*). Some of them embody many of the same physical characteristics as the male characters, such as Maleficent, with her long tapered fingers and heavily made-up eyelids. Other female characters, like Cinderella's stepmother Lady Tremaine (*Cinderella*) or Mother Gothel (*Tangled*), are much closer to a heteronormative ideal, although they still diverge from the appearance of the princess in predictable ways. (Check out Lady Tremaine's arched eyebrows and prominent, pointed chin for example.)

And Ursula, even though we have included her with the ladies, is sui generis. To begin with, she gets her credentials as a queer character more explicitly, since, as any true Disney fan probably knows, she is modeled on the drag queen Divine. Her physical body type is also quite different from that of Maleficent, for instance, and some previous researchers have grouped her with the male villains instead (e.g. Letts 2016). In fact, Tinkcom actually pairs her with Ratcliffe (from *Pocahontas*) and interprets their heavier body types as reflecting a "hallmark camp plumpness" (Tinkcom 2002, cited in Letts 2016: 156). In any case, Ursula's larger body is also a clear part of her queerness, contrasting as it does with the trademark (and often critically censured) unnatural slenderness of the princesses.[11]

It is surprising, to some degree, to find that the deviant performance of femininity parallels so closely the deviant performance of masculinity in these villains. After all, if the male villains are presented as too feminine, we might expect the female villains to be presented as too masculine. That's not the case, though (with some caveats, which we will return to later). In fact, Griffin

---

[11] Robin Queen (p.c.) notes that the body type could also be connected to ideologies about stereotypical lesbian appearances.

(2000) argues that the queens of the early movies can be read as queer precisely because they "overtly overperform their gender roles" (2000: 74). Coca (2000), similarly, connects the older and somewhat newer female villains, specifically through invoking the concept of drag:

On the other hand, the Queen from *Snow White and the Seven Dwarfs* and Ursula from *The Little Mermaid* are rather accurate representations of drag, overdoing their 'womanly' roles, wearing excessive makeup, long hair and polished nails. (Coca 2000: 16)

Note that the concept of drag being referenced here is referring to a stylized hyper-performance of femininity often (though not always) performed by men, and not the stylized drag king performance of masculinity that might be the gender-crossing equivalent for women.

So then to some extent, it is a performance of a type of masculinity, but one that involves specifically performing femininity. It's also interesting, and beyond the scope of this book, to ponder exactly how a "drag" type sensibility came to be found in a character from 1939, well before drag culture was visible to mainstream audiences.

In any case, the resulting ideology is discouraging, managing as it does to encompass both sexism (the idea that deviance always involves femininity) and heteronormativity (the idea that any deviation from a narrow hegemonic ideal of femininity has the potential to make you a villain). Furthermore, even in this process of gender-othering in the films, there is a kind of norming of queerness taking place as well. The representation of queer characters relies almost entirely on a gay male version of queerness, erasing lesbian, nonbinary and other identities in the process.[12]

## Methodology

Our questions for this chapter have a slightly different format:

---

**Key Questions**

- Is there a **style of language or set of linguistic features** associated with queer characters, specifically "quillains"?
- If so, what is this linguistic performance **being used to do**? Does it reinforce heteronormativity? Is it subversive? How does it fit with the overall ethos of the Disney films and corporation?

---

[12] The character of Terkina (or Terk), Tarzan's best friend and sidekick from *Tarzan*, represents one of the very few examples discussed in the literature where queerness seems to be packaged as a lesbian rather than gay male identity (see e.g. Letts 2016). Terk is voiced by Rosie O'Donnell, a lesbian comedian and actress.

*Selecting Quillain Characters*

We used our scholarly sources, as well as a handful of popular articles written by Disney fans across the net, to gather a list of queer characters and identify those whose names turned up repeatedly across various formats. We also kept track of the real-life identities of the voice actors, since many of the characters listed here were voiced by queer actors.[13] One important aspect that sets this chapter apart from the rest of our study is that instead of focusing only on the Princess films for Disney, we expanded our scope to the entire Disney film roster,[14] since some of the characters whose names came up most often in our background research on queerness were from outside the Princess films (e.g. Scar from *The Lion King*).

A list of the characters we chose to analyze appears in Table 8.1. As noted earlier, they are all drawn from Disney rather than Pixar films and the majority are from the Classic or Renaissance Eras, although a few, like Tamatoa in *Moana* (2016), are more recent. In each group, there were characters who recurred in almost all the discussions of queerness in Disney (labeled "main"), while others were mentioned less frequently (labeled "secondary").

The main characters all exhibit many of the physical qualities discussed earlier, e.g. tapered fingers, exaggerated lipstick/eyeshadow, etc. Those in the secondary group are less likely to exhibit these markers. Tamatoa, for example, is a giant crab who physically looks unlike Jafar or even Scar. However he comes up in discussions of queer characters, in part because he is based loosely on David Bowie, who performed a vast array of queer, campy characters. In both the male and female secondary groups, the line between what is queer and what is simply a non-normative presentation of masculinity or femininity becomes blurred, although we do not have the space here to give this question the attention it deserves.

*Data Collection*

We began by pulling from the scripts all of the dialogue from the quillains in Table 8.1. We went through the scenes looking for patterns that recurred in the speech of our characters, especially patterns associated with either WL or camp. This allowed us also to analyze their speech in context, including the speech of other characters and any interesting features of the interaction.

---

[13] David Ogden Stiers for example voices characters in eight different Disney films, including both Ratcliffe and his sidekick Wiggins from *Pocahontas*.

[14] Although still excluding straight-to-video, minor league players such as the (absolutely execrable) sequel to *Pocahontas*.

Table 8.1. *Queer-coded characters analyzed*

**Male villains**
Main
Jafar (*Aladdin*, 1992)
Scar (*Lion King*, 1994)
Ratcliffe (*Pocahontas*, 1995)
Hades (*Hercules*, 1997)

Secondary
Shere Khan (*Jungle Book*, 1967)
Chi Fu (*Mulan*, 1998)
Tamatoa (*Moana*, 2016)

**Female villains**
Main
Queen Grimhilde/Evil Queen (*Snow White*, 1939)
Lady Tremaine/Stepmother (*Cinderella*, 1950)
Maleficent (*Sleeping Beauty*, 1959)
Ursula (*Little Mermaid*, 1989)

Secondary
Cruella De Vil (*101 Dalmatians*, 1961)
Yzma (*Emperor's New Groove*, 2000)
Gothel (*Tangled*, 2010)

It is important to keep in mind what Harvey notes about camp: that it is the co-occurrence of a number of features as part of a camp style that is relevant.

No-one claims, of course, that irony is the preserve of gay people. Nor is it suggested that the devices of implicature are rare in "straight speech." If the characteristics mentioned by Livia and Hall are indeed typical of gay and lesbian language use, then we might surmise that this is only achieved through a marked frequency of occurrence and/or *a particularly dense clustering of different features*. (Harvey 2002: 1147; italics ours)

What we will be looking for, then, is not the presence of any individual feature across all (or even some) of the quillains.[15] Rather our focus will be on clusters of features that we find working together to create a style that separates these quillains from the other characters, and that serves some specifically queer function or functions.

Note that because we are working from the ground up here, the format of our results will be a bit different from the presentation in previous chapters. In other chapters we selected a speech act that we already knew would occur, counted it, and looked at how it functioned. Here, we will begin by

---

[15] Nor, for that matter, its absence among the straight characters.

documenting and describing the features of the style that we found, in some detail, and only then move on to the analysis of function.

## The Quillain Language Style in Disney

### *Features of the Quillain Language Style*

We turn now to our central question: How is this construction of queerness reflected in language? Overall, we found that features drawn from camp and WL styles dramatically populated the performances of our queer characters. Among the quillains on our list, all of them exhibited multiple features from those styles.

We should note that though we looked for features of WL, what we found could better be described as "features of women's language as interpreted by drag queens" as in the studies cited earlier. The characters we analyzed flouted exactly those features of Lakoff's original list that the drag queens did, including "not telling jokes" (Hades' entire dialogue is basically one punchline after another) and euphemism or "shying away from coarse expressions" (Barrett 1999). The Evil Queen in *Snow White*, for example, describes the effects of poison in the poisoned apple by saying *Her breath will still, her blood congeal*. Congealed blood is not what we would call a euphemistic description.

There were also features of camp that did not occur or occurred only in very limited environments. For example, pop culture references, which were critical to Harvey's (2002) notion of citationality, are rare in these constructed worlds, since they themselves constitute the type of pop culture being cited. Additionally, there were a few features we found that seemed related to the others but that were not specifically mentioned in the literature on either style, such as faux politeness.

When we put all of this together, the results show that the speech of our quillains exhibits groups of features that cluster together to form a distinct style. We identified five linguistically coherent categories that work together to form what we will call the Quillain Language Style (QLS):

---

**Quillain Language Style**

(1) Playing with register or style
(2) Sarcasm and other humorous verbal aggression
(3) Wordplay or metalinguistic focus
(4) Invocation of femininity (pragmatic)
(5) Invocation of femininity (syntactic or lexical)

---

We present each of these five categories below, with examples taken from our quillains and some brief commentary on their possible function as seen through a queer theory lens. We will provide a more detailed analysis of function in the next section, where we will analyze the language of three specific quillains in detail. But for now, we mainly want to signal how these features work together across a wide range of movies to, as Sedgwick puts it, "smuggle queer representation in where it must be smuggled" (Sedgwick 1994, cited in Helmsing 2016: 60).[16]

## Playing with register or style

Playing with register appears in various forms, including unexpectedly formal or literate register, similar to what Harvey (2000) calls "mock literary" speech, e.g. academic or literary words or superstandard grammar. It also includes characters referring to themselves in third person, or inserting French or another language.

Examples:

> Why! If it isn't my big brother descending from on high to mingle with the commoners. | Scar, *The Lion King*
>
> We mustn't lurk in doorways – it's rude. One MIGHT question your upbringing. | Ursula, *The Little Mermaid*
>
> Oh, dear! Oh, how frightfully upsetting. Had I but known! | Jafar, *Aladdin*
>
> Then you should also know that everyone runs from Shere Khan. | Shere Khan, *The Jungle Book*
>
> Soak it in 'cause it's the last you'll ever see, *C'est la vie, mon ami!* | Tamatoa, *Moana*

These features serve as a way of drawing on a cosmopolitan culture or high art, often paired paradoxically with a "low" topic. They underline the emphasis on appearance, sophistication and luxury that is central to camp, while highlighting the juxtaposition of unexpected elements as a signal of queerness.

## Sarcasm and other humorous verbal aggression

Interestingly, Harvey (2000, 2002) does not list sarcasm as a separate feature of camp (although it's clearly related to some he does list, like irony), but it was one of the most frequent patterns in our data. In addition to sarcasm, we include here catty comments and shade-throwing, as well as teasing or joking that relies on saying something without meaning it. We also include in this group insincere or faux politeness forms, which may not necessarily be humorous in context but are read as ironic or insincere by the viewer.

---

[16] Unfortunately we don't have the data to determine whether or not this smuggling was deliberate. Still, given the history of gay male artists at Disney, it's certainly a possibility.

Examples:

> Oooh. . . I quiver with FEAR. | Scar, *The Lion King*
>
> Be careful, Captain. The General may be your father, but I am the Emperor's counsel. And, oh, by the way, huh, I got that job on my own.| Chi Fu, *Mulan*
>
> I think it's time to say goodbye to Prince Abooboo [=Prince Abu]. | Jafar, *Aladdin*
>
> Rapunzel, look in that mirror. You know what I see? I see a strong, confident, beautiful young lady. [Rapunzel: Hm.] Oh look, you're here too. I'm just teasing! | Gothel, *Tangled*
>
> Oh dear, what an awkward situation. I had hoped it was merely due to some oversight. Well, in that event I'd best be on my way. | Maleficent, *Sleeping Beauty*

Sarcasm and the other features of verbal aggression allow characters to be subversive or point out hidden or dual perspectives or motives. They invite the listener to join in a process of "flipping the script," so that things don't mean what they are supposed to mean, which is a central part of looking at the world through a queer lens. Also, throwing shade is often associated with drag queens in particular.

## Wordplay or metalinguistic focus

Under wordplay we include double-entendres, inversions of rhetorical routines (e.g. deliberately misquoting or switching words in a proverb or saying), humorous metaphors, and metalinguistic commentary on the words themselves.
Examples:

> Well, as far as brains go, I got the lion's share. But, when it comes to brute strength. . . I'm afraid I'm at the shallow end of the gene pool. | Scar, *The Lion King*
>
> Oh, yeah. I wonder if maybe I haven't been throwing. . . the right curves at him, Meg, my sweet.| Hades, *Hercules*
>
> You've heard of the golden rule, haven't you boy? Whoever has the gold makes the rules. | Jafar, *Aladdin*
>
> Well, it's time Ursula took matters into her own tentacles! | Ursula, *The Little Mermaid*

The use of wordplay goes with the long tradition of hidden language practices among marginalized groups. It functions as another way of signaling a duality of meaning, as part and parcel of queerness, along with the witty sophistication that is essential to camp performances.

## Invocation of femininity (pragmatic)

We include here the features of WL related to discourse and pragmatics such as hyperbole and speaking in italics. We see these types of features as functioning in a more subtle way to highlight the performance of femininity than the lexical and syntactic features, which we will discuss next, so we have chosen to keep them in separate groups.

Examples:

> I'm doomed! I should be wallowing in riches right now and I haven't seen so much as a speck! | Ratcliffe, *Pocahontas*
> That was today? Oh, I feel simply awful.| Scar, *The Lion King*
> Oh, no, no, no, no, no. I can't stand it – it's too easy. | Ursula, *The Little Mermaid*
> Oh everyone's talking about it. The whole kingdom! Oh hurry now. He'll be here any minute.| Stepmother, *Cinderella*

The pragmatic features of WL seen here can be used to perform emotional expressiveness, a quality traditionally policed for heterosexual men. They also invoke the drama and theatricality of camp.

## Invocation of femininity (syntactic or lexical)

Here we include specific linguistic features or structures of WL, as per Lakoff, e.g. so-called empty adjectives (*cute, divine, charming*) or other words coded for femininity (*pretty, curtsy*) as well as hedges (*kind of, maybe*) and tag questions (*we did, didn't we?*).

Examples:

> Isn't it just peachy? | Hades, *Hercules*
> Well, Tamatoa hasn't always been this glam. | Tamatoa, *Moana*
> Ohh, I shall practice my curtsy. | Scar, *The Lion King*
> Meg, Meg, Meg, my sweet deluded little minion. Aren't we forgetting one teensy-weensy, but ever so crucial little, tiny detail? | Hades, *Hercules*
> Life's full of tough choices, innit? | Ursula, *The Little Mermaid*

The lexical items like *peachy* and *glam* serve as arrows directly pointing to the queerness of these performances, while some of the others signal femininity in a more indirect way. As noted earlier, the use of features associated with the performance of femininity to signal deviance for male *and* female characters is both interesting and dismaying, and we will attempt to unpack this idea further in the next section.

## Case Studies of the Quillain Language Style

In this section, we analyze selections of dialogue from several key quillains to see how the clustering of these features works to produce the QLS in context. We've chosen to analyze excerpts from three very different quillains – Scar, Maleficent, and Ursula – to show how the use of features from our categories recurs across eras and types, and how language complements (and at times complicates) the previous research that has been done on other aspects of queerness in Disney.

*A Male Quillain: Scar*

Scar (from *The Lion King*) is cited extensively in discussions of queerness in Disney, perhaps more than any other single character. Although Scar is a lion, even in animal form he has the purple eyeshadow that turns out to be typical of so many of our quillains, as well as many of the other physical characteristics listed earlier. He is drawn as longer, slimmer, and darker than his brother Mufasa. Scar is also voiced by a British actor (Jeremy Irons) and we found a good deal of overlap between being gay and being what might be termed "unpleasantly British," though we don't have the space to analyze this connection in detail.

In this scene, toward the beginning of the movie, Scar, the brother of the king, has missed the celebration of the birth of an heir to the throne, an event about which he is decidedly unenthusiastic. He is preparing to eat a mouse he has caught, when the king's assistant, Zazu the hornbill, arrives.

**Excerpt 8A "Missing the Ceremony" (*Lion King*, 1994)**

| | |
|---|---|
| SCAR: | Life's not fair, is it? You see I— well, I. . . shall never be King. And you. . . shall never see the light of another day. [*starts to place the mouse on his tongue*] . . . Adieu. . . |
| ZAZU: | Didn't your mother ever tell you not to play with your food? |
| SCAR: | What do you want? |
| ZAZU: | I'm here to announce that King Mufasa is on his way. . . So you'd better have a good excuse for missing the ceremony this morning. [*The mouse runs away.*] |
| SCAR: | Oh now look, Zazu; you've made me lose my lunch. |
| ZAZU: | Hah! You'll lose more than that when the King gets through with you. He's as mad as a hippo with a hernia. |
| SCAR: | Oooh. . . I quiver with FEAR. [*crouches down, baring his teeth*] |
| ZAZU: | Now Scar, don't look at me that way. . . HELP! [*Scar pounces on the bird, catching him in his mouth.*] |
| MUFASA: | Scar! . . . |
| SCAR: | [*mouth full*] Mm-hmm? |
| MUFASA: | Drop him. |
| ZAZU: | Impeccable timing, your majesty. [*Scar spits the bird out, covered with saliva.*] |
| ZAZU: | Eyyccch. |
| SCAR: | Why! If it isn't my big brother descending from on high to mingle with the commoners. |
| MUFASA: | Sarabi and I didn't see you at the presentation of Simba. |
| SCAR: | That was today? Oh, I feel simply awful. [*admiring his claws*] . . . Must have slipped my mind. |
| ZAZU: | Yes, well, as slippery as your mind is, as the king's brother, you should have been first in line! |
| SCAR: | Well, I was first in line. . . until the little hairball was born. |

MUFASA:   That "hairball" is my son... and your future king.
SCAR:     Ohh, I shall practice my curtsy. [*Scar turns away and starts to exit.*]
MUFASA:   Don't turn your back on me, Scar.
SCAR:     Oh, no, Mufasa. Perhaps YOU shouldn't turn YOUR back on me.
MUFASA:   [*roars and jumps in front of Scar, baring his teeth*] Is that a challenge?
SCAR:     Temper, temper. I wouldn't dream of challenging you.
ZAZU:     Pity! Why not?
SCAR:     Well, as far as brains go, I got the lion's share. But, when it comes to brute strength... I'm afraid I'm at the shallow end of the gene pool.

In this excerpt, Scar's lines exemplify the sarcastic, over-the-top persona of the quillain, reinforced by his body language and intonational patterns. His dialogue is packed with features from each of our categories:

- Academic words: *descending from on high to mingle with the commoners*
- Superstandard grammar: *I shall never be King. And you shall never see the light of another day.*
- Use of French: *Adieu!*
- Sarcasm: *Oh, I quiver with fear.*
- Innuendo/shade: *the little hairball; as far as brains go, I got the lion's share*
- Wordplay: *You've made me lose my lunch; the shallow end of the gene pool*
- Speaking in italics: *Oh, I feel simply awful; I wouldn't dream of challenging you*
- Hedges: *I'm afraid...*
- Tag questions: *Life's not fair, is it?*

Throughout the script, Scar repeatedly deploys these features in crafting his linguistic persona. He waves the Pride flag most dramatically, so to speak, when he uses the term *curtsy*, in the line *Ohh, I shall practice my curtsy*, which is often cited as specific evidence of his queerness in discussions of this topic (e.g. Li-Vollmer & La Pointe 2003).

Using features from across all five categories, and using them liberally, Scar is one of the clearest exemplars of the style we are describing. The density of features that are stylistically associated with gay men, and with drag performance specifically, lends credence to the idea that Disney is using linguistic as well as visual cues to code its villains as queer. Many of the particular features that are arguably used in queer-coding Scar also position him as intelligent or witty (e.g. use of French, academic words, superstandard grammar, wordplay); we will unpack this further below. Moreover, Scar's speaking style, in being campy and performative, also suggests manipulation – the audience is supposed to understand him as not saying directly what he means, thereby hiding his true intentions with wordplay. The use of the QLS helps to frame him for the audience as manipulative and subversive, qualities Disney is thus also associating with queerness.

*A Female Quillain: Maleficent*

In the opening scene of *Sleeping Beauty* (which we highly encourage our readers to watch if they are interested in the topic of this chapter), Maleficent appears as the absolute epitome of camp. Physically, she is tall and slender, with a pointed face, like so many of the male quillains. She has dramatic purple eyeshadow, crimson painted lips, and long, tapered fingers with red finger-nails. Also like many of the male characters, she wears long flowing robes, and speaks with dramatic hand gestures.[17] Her voice is also noticeably deeper than that of the other female characters, especially the fairies and the giggly, teenaged Aurora.

Since the scenes in the older films are shorter in general, we have chosen to include two of Maleficent's. The first scene, like the one above with Scar, involves the celebration of an heir to the kingdom, a princess, as well as the betrothal of this infant girl to the son of a neighboring king for a future arranged royal wedding.[18] The problem here is that Maleficent has not been invited to the celebration, presumably due to her evility (a word we have coined specifically for her), but she shows up anyway. And like all good drag queens, she knows how to make an entrance.

**Excerpt 8B. "Maleficent bestows a gift"** (*Sleeping Beauty*, **1959**)

[*A blow of the wind, the door of the castle swings open. Lightning and thunder. Maleficent appears behind green flames. Her raven floats down onto her scepter.*]

| | |
|---|---|
| FLORA: | Why, it's Maleficent! |
| MERRYWEATHER: | What does she want here? |
| FAUNA: | Shhh! |
| MALEFICENT: | Well, quite a glittering assemblage, King Stefan. Royalty, nobil-ity, the gentry, and, how quaint, [*gestures at the fairies*] even the rabble. |
| | [*Merryweather angrily starts to fly towards Maleficent but is held back by Flora.*] . . . I really felt quite distressed at not receiving an invitation. [*strokes her raven*] |
| MERRYWEATHER: | You weren't wanted! |
| MALEFICENT: | Not wa. . .? Oh dear, what an awkward situation. I had hoped it was merely due to some oversight. Well, in that event I'd best be on my way. |
| | [*continues to stroke her raven demurely*] |
| QUEEN: | And you're not offended, your excellency? |

---

[17] Griffin (2000) argues that the fact that almost her entire body is covered by clothing, including her head, helps to promote a queer reading.

[18] Ew, don't get us started on the antifeminist, heterosexist implications of *that*.

Figure 8.2 Notecard featuring Maleficent (*Sleeping Beauty*, 1959)
Reproduced by permission of Tania Pantoja

MALEFICENT:     Why no, your majesty. And to show I bear no ill will, I, too, shall
                bestow a gift on the child... [*The fairies protect the cradle.*]
                Listen well, all of you! The princess shall indeed grow in grace
                and beauty, beloved by all who know her. But, before the sun sets
                on her sixteenth birthday, she shall prick her finger on the spindle
                of a spinning wheel and die. [*swirls her fingers around her
                scepter as she explains her "blessing"*]
QUEEN:          Oh no!
MALEFICENT:     Ha, ha, ha, ha!
STEFAN:         Seize that creature!
MALEFICENT:     Stand back you fools. [*raises her arms upwards and evaporates
                into a cloud of green fire before she can be apprehended*]

Even though this is a fairly brief excerpt, it still shows quite a number of the
QLS features. They include:

- Academic words: *quite a glittering assemblage, merely due to some oversight*
- Superstandard grammar: *I, too, shall bestow a gift...*
- Irony/sarcasm: *to show I bear no ill will, I, too, shall bestow a gift on the child*
- Faux politeness: *Well, in that event I'd best be on my way*
- Innuendo/shade: *how quaint, even the rabble*
- Speaking in italics: *I really feel quite distressed*
- Empty adjectives: *how quaint, oh dear*

The use of features from WL (italics, empty adjectives) is fascinating here, since
they don't make Maleficent appear more feminine at all. Rather, 40 years before the
premiere of *RuPaul's Drag Race* in 2009, we find an arguably "drag" character (in
this case, one who is performing femininity in order to manipulate her audience).

In the second excerpt, sarcasm, which was less of a focus in the first scene,
comes to the forefront as a core pillar of her language style. In this scene,

Maleficent has imprisoned Prince Phillip[19] and decides to go down to the dungeon and visit him ... wait for it ... *just to gloat*!

### Excerpt 8C "A most gratifying day" (*Sleeping Beauty*, 1959)

| | |
|---|---|
| MALEFICENT: | *[lighting Phillip's face with a candle]* Well, this is a pleasant surprise. I set my trap for a peasant, and lo! *[laughs]* I catch a prince! Away with him.<br>But gently, my pets, gently, I have plans for our royal guest.<br>*[The fairies arrive and find the door open. They see Phillip's hat on the floor.]* |
| FAIRIES: | Maleficent! |
| MERRYWEATHER: | She's got Prince Phillip! |
| FLORA: | At the forbidden mountain. |
| FAUNA: | But we can't, we can't go there! |
| FLORA: | We can, and we must.<br>*[The fairies look in the window to where Maleficent is having a feast, with her 'pets' around a huge fire.]* |
| MALEFICENT: | *[to her raven]* What a pity prince Phillip can't be here to enjoy the celebration. Come, we must go to the dungeon and cheer him up.<br>*[Maleficent walks to the dungeon where Phillip sits chained to the wall.]* |
| MALEFICENT: | Oh come now, prince Phillip. Why so melancholy? A wondrous future lies before you. You, the destined hero of a charming fairy tale come true.<br>*[Maleficent uses her magic stick to depict the following scene.]* |
| MALEFICENT: | Behold, King Stefan's castle, and in yonder topmost tower, dreaming of her true love, the princess Aurora. But see the gracious whim of fate. Why, 'tis the selfsame peasant maid, who won the heart of our noble prince but yesterday. She is indeed most wondrous fair. Gold of sunshine in her hair, lips that shame the red, red rose. In ageless sleep she finds repose. The years roll by, but a hundred years to a steadfast heart are but a day. And now, the gates of the dungeon part, and the prince is free to go his way. Off he rides on his noble steed...<br>*[In Maleficent's imagery, the prince is shown to be extremely old.]* |
| MALEFICENT: | ... a valiant figure, straight and tall, to wake his love with love's first kiss, and prove that true love conquers all.<br>*[Phillip struggles in his chains.]* |
| MERRYWEATHER: | Why, you mean... *[She is pulled back by Flora.]* |
| MALEFICENT: | Come, my pet. Let us leave our noble prince with these happy thoughts. A most gratifying day. *[Outside the dungeon, she locks the door.]* For the first time in sixteen years I shall sleep well. |

[19] Who, by the way, is relatively inept and ends up relying extensively on the three middle-aged fairies to help him slay the dragon, so perhaps feminism isn't entirely absent from this film after all ...

In this brief section, Maleficent unleashes an absolute torrent of sarcasm, and not just any sarcasm, but rather campy, over-the-top, embellished sarcasm. She begins by referring to him as her "guest" and telling her henchbirds that they are going to the dungeon to "cheer him up." She then mercilessly mocks Phillip's supposedly heroic destiny, promising to release him in a hundred years so that he can then go pursue his true love ... as a tired old man.

Her monologue is a master class in campy evility: the smarmy, insincere concern (*Why so melancholy?*), the fake surprise when she sees Aurora in the vision she is showing him (*Why tis the selfsame peasant maid ...!*), the sarcastic encouragement in the name of true love (*a hundred years to a steadfast heart are but a day!*). Not to mention the smug comment about how well she is going to sleep. This campiness sets her apart from the rest of the cast; purposely or not, it also has made her one of the more memorable characters in the film, well-known and liked more than 50 years after her debut.[20] Despite the fact that she pre-dates Scar by 35 years, Maleficent also uses examples from across all five of our categories and uses them in combination with physical behaviors and subversive stances that clearly code her as queer. This is an intriguing pattern to uncover given that Maleficent is also a female character, but seems to be using a style most closely with drag queen performances.

In the methodology section we raised the difficulty of delineating the boundary between non-normative femininity and queerness, which comes to bear here as we consider that Maleficent is also an older woman and potentially just performing an alternate version of femininity. But we think that's not quite it, since part of her character is so specifically the weaponized *performance* of a traditionally feminine style. Maleficent is sarcastic to Phillip through the use of ironic caretaking and emotional labor (cheering him up) – seemingly knowing nods to societal expectations of women. Other older female characters are portrayed in Disney as rude and outside the boundaries of hegemonic feminine norms (see Chapter 6); however, they are positioned as not beholden to or even understanding of feminine norms, whereas Maleficent and other quillains like her enact their aggressive behavior through the careful and knowing performance of those norms. Her language simultaneously sets her outside the ideal of femininity and allows her to use a faux version of that femininity to toy with her victims.

In addition, Maleficent's language is marked by the absence of the discourse practices that we have documented in previous chapters as being associated with femininity. Her use of compliments is sarcastic and blatantly insincere. But more importantly she freely uses those features that are associated with

---

[20] Yes, the live action films of the twenty-first century have a role in this phenomenon as well, but still, the character endures.

both masculinity and power. Her directives are unmitigated or sometimes even aggravated:

> Away with him!
> Come, we must go to the dungeon and cheer him up.
> Stand back, you fools!

In the last example, she uses an insult as well. In each case, the form she chooses is the one we found to be most likely among male characters rather than female ones overall. These patterns are ones that we find with Scar as well, but with his character they were unremarkable because he is male. On the other hand it seems that the female quillains like Maleficent perform (or "overperform") some aspects of femininity, but not the aspects that would be associated naturally with less power. Those aspects (which the princesses adhere to), they flout.

### An Octopus Drag Queen: Ursula

Ursula the Sea Witch (from *The Little Mermaid*) is, as we noted, a bit different from the other quillains, including the female quillains, although she is clearly assigned female gender in the script. She is the only character we know of to be modeled deliberately on a real-life queer individual (Divine, a drag queen). And while some researchers group her with the evil queens of the early movies (Helmsing 2016), others group her with the male quillains like Scar (Letts 2016).

Figure 8.3 (l) Float featuring Ursula (*The Little Mermaid*, 1989); (r) Photo of the drag queen Divine
Reproduced by permission of www.gettyimages.com

While Ursula has a different body type from the other female quillains, as we discussed earlier, she still shows many of the physical features that should be familiar by now: painted lips and nails, eyeshadow (hers is blue but possibly only because her skin itself is lavender, so the usual color wouldn't show up), and extravagant, sweeping hand gestures. In lieu of robes, she has tentacles that swirl and float around her like the skirt of a fancy ball gown. Like Maleficent, she has a deep voice, about which Pat Carroll, who voices her, made a deliberate choice.[21]

She definitely keeps pace with the other quillains in her linguistic features as well. In this scene, Ursula's hench-eels, Flotsam and Jetsam, have led Ariel, the mermaid princess, to Ursula's lair, where Ursula offers her a chance to be human in exchange for giving up her lovely voice.

**Excerpt 8D "Poor unfortunate souls"** (*The Little Mermaid*, 1989)

| | |
|---|---|
| FLOTSAM: | This way. |
| JETSAM: | This way. |
| URSULA: | Come in. Come in, my child. We mustn't lurk in doorways... It's rude. One MIGHT question your upbringing... Now, then. You're here because you have a thing for this human. This, er, prince fellow. Not that I blame you— he is quite a catch, isn't he? Well, angel fish, the solution to your problem is simple [*applies lipstick and blows a kiss*]. The only way to get what you want— is to become a human yourself. |
| ARIEL: | Can you DO that? |
| URSULA: | My dear, sweet child. That's what I do— it's what I live for. To help unfortunate merfolk [*hands clasped at her heart*] — like yourself [*puts a finger under Ariel's chin*]. Poor souls with no one else to turn to. |

[*She sings "Poor Unfortunate Souls."*]

---

[*spoken*]

| | |
|---|---|
| URSULA: | Now, here's the deal. [*grabs Ariel with a scarf*] I will make you a potion that will turn you into a human for three days. Got that? Three days. Now, listen, this is important. [*uses magic to illustrate her point*] Before the sun sets on the third day, you got to get dear, old princey to fall in love with you. That is, he's got to kiss you. Not just any kiss, the kiss of true love. If he does kiss you before the sun sets on the third day, you'll remain human permanently. But if he doesn't, you turn back into a mermaid, and you belong to me. |
| SEBASTIAN: | No Ariel! [*Ursula's eels strangle Sebastian so his voice is cut off.*] |
| URSULA: | Have we got a deal? [*holds Ariel's chin in her hand and puts face very close*] |
| ARIEL: | If I become human, I'll never be with my father or sisters again. |

[21] https://web.archive.org/web/20141107050713/http://www.fast-rewind.com/making_littlemermaid.htm

URSULA:     That's right... But— you'll have your man. [*laughs, shakes shoulders, and shimmies*] Life's full of tough choices, innit? Oh— and there is one more thing. We haven't discussed the subject of payment. You can't get something for nothing, you know.

ARIEL:     But I don't have any— [*Ursula uses a tentacle to cover Ariel's mouth.*]

URSULA:     I'm not asking much. Just a token, really, a trifle. You'll never even miss it. What I want from you is [*points at Ariel's throat, deepens pitch*]... your voice.

ARIEL:     My voice?

URSULA:     You've got it, sweetcakes. No more talking, singing, zip.

ARIEL:     But without my voice, how can I—

URSULA:     You'll have your looks! Your pretty face! [*examines her nails, shrugs*] And don't underestimate the importance of body language! Ha! [*thrusts crudely, whole body moves*]

[*Song resumes.*]

As with the others, maybe even more so, the language in this scene works tightly with other elements of the physical performance. For example, in the last line, when Ursula says *body language*, she moves her ample bottom from side to side suggestively, but also very much in the style of burlesque dancers, a kissing cousin to drag musical performances. And the song itself (which we so regret not having the space to analyze here) is laden with campy gestures and facial expressions.[22] At one point (on the line *on the whole, I've been a saint!*), Ursula puts her scarf over her head and seems to mime being a nun, or possibly simply ... a girl? There is some very complex pointing to the performativity of gender going on here.

The language itself also provides more than enough material for analysis. In terms of our QLS features, we find:

- Superstandard grammar: *One might question your upbringing...*
- Sarcasm: *Life's full of tough choices, innit?*
- Faux politeness: *We mustn't lurk in doorways... It's rude.*
- Double entendre: *And don't underestimate the importance of body language!*
- Speaking in italics: *It's what I LIVE for...*
- Empty adjectives: *dear old princey, dear sweet child*
- Hedges: *just a token*
- Tag questions: *Life's full of tough choices, innit?*

As with Maleficent, the exaggerated use of WL features by a character who is ostensibly gendered female is worth exploring. Our impression is that these features are used to produce a kind of contrastive humor; Ursula's "failure" at

---

[22] Ursula is also the first villainess to have a song of her own, one of the most popular in the entire Disney repertoire.

achieving an ideal feminine appearance (having purple skin and tentacles, but also underscored by Disney's recurrent presentation of being fat as undesirable) is highlighted by her excessive use of supposedly feminine language. It's a clear example of the phenomenon we discussed earlier, where Disney manages to be both sexist and heterosexist (and let's not forget fatphobic) simultaneously.

At the same time, like Maleficent and Scar, Ursula wants to take back some of the power that has been denied to her as an outsider (*banished and exiled and practically starving*, as she puts it), and the subversive nature of QLS fits her character's motivations perfectly. And like them, she selects the discourse practices that are associated with power such as aggravated directives and insults. Although there aren't many examples in this particular excerpt, in other parts of the script, Ursula's directives and insults sound much like Maleficent's:

> Don't fool with me you little brat!
> You pitiful, insignificant, fool!
> Say goodbye to your sweetheart.

Again, she chooses the forms that index power, and that we found, not coincidentally, were more likely to be used by male characters. So while, as we said earlier, QLS relies in part on the performance of femininity, even for female characters, it also encompasses the use of discourse features associated with power, and secondarily with masculinity.

We selected Scar, Maleficent, and Ursula to show that the QLS is, as they say, a thing. It recurs across characters that are quite different in some ways (including their assigned gender), and it works alongside suprasegmental features, visual cues, and body language to create a particular type of performance. So having established that there is a queer linguistic style associated with the quillains, and having walked through the features it uses and the elements of meaning it appears to encompass, we zoom out again to look at implications and broader impacts.

### Discussion: The Complex Implications of the Quillain Language Style

We return now to the second of our main questions for this chapter: What is this queer style being used to do in these films? There has been plenty of previous discussion about the fact that most of the clearly queer-coded characters in Disney are villains, as discussed in our review of the literature above.[23]

---

[23] The recent scattering of "canonically queer" characters in Pixar, on the other hand, are not villains. It takes some effort to see this as progress. It takes some effort to see it at all, since Officer Specter from *Onward*, for example, has only a handful of lines.

Our analysis confirms much of what has already been observed, and also adds a linguistic element to the queer-coding that Disney employs. We looked for, and found, clusterings of discursive features throughout our collection of quillains that have been documented in real life among gay men and in the performances of drag queens.

This finding offers us some insights into Disney's ideological world. First, just as Disney otherizes and vilifies queerness by queer-coding its villains so consistently, the same is true of the linguistic features of the villains' dialogue. The association with the performance of femininity in particular (by drawing on stereotypical elements of WL), especially by male quillains, links villainy with a kind of linguistic gender transgression which stands out as distinctive from the more normative linguistic styles of other characters described in Chapters 4 through 7. The association of this style, and of queerness in general, with villainy continues to reinforce the dominance of heteronormative gender roles, performances, and language.

Another pattern we uncovered is that the QLS is used to characterize both male and female quillains. This is of interest because these features are associated mainly with queer masculinity. Linguistic studies on queer speakers besides gay men are still very few and far between, but we feel fairly confident that the QLS does not fully represent the variety of identities and speaking styles found in LGBTQIA+ communities. In a way, this is another iteration of Disney subtly spotlighting and normalizing a version of masculinity as the default. That normalization tracks historically, both with Disney's overall gender ideology, and also with the history of queer rights movements in the US, in which cis gay men have been by far the most visible subgroup and thereby the most available to stereotype.

Additionally, we believe this phenomenon underscores Disney's ideologies around feminine-coded language practices (shown in Chapters 4 and 5, particularly). The markedness of male characters receiving appearance-based compliments, for example, is underscored all the more when a villain like Jafar actively solicits them (*now pussycat, tell me more about... myself*). The fact that female quillains are also coded as queer for hyper-performing some of these features suggests to us that feminine language styles are only idealized in women when framed as natural. When Maleficent or Ursula use feminine-coded features, it's an obvious, over-the-top performance; although they're using the same features as some female characters, the performativity seems to *distance* them from hegemonic femininity rather than draw them closer. We are looking forward to future scholars examining this particular phenomenon further.

In light of all of this, we certainly don't want to argue that Scar and Ursula are progressive or positive role models. The association of queerness with being "bad" or "other" that these quillains embody has long upheld the hegemony of a heteronormative view in Disney. Ultimately, boy meets girl. Always.

And yet. And yet.

One of the great things about queer theory is its ability to give a different lens to a text, an ability to center nuance and complexity, rather than forcing everything into binary boxes. The quillains are popular in part because they embody some qualities that are very appealing: self-confidence, a sense of humor, cleverness, and, perhaps most importantly, a flouting of social norms. They are the rebels, the schemers, and, in terms of language, the ones who say the things we are all thinking but are too polite to mention. And despite being cast as "deviant" and "other," the queer characters are on some levels more appealing than the heroic or exceptionally beautiful straight characters. There is no shortage of adults (and probably children as well) who want to dress as Ursula for Halloween.[24]

We need to mention again the important role of the viewer in interpreting these films. Describing these characters as appealing "despite" being othered stems from the heterosexist view we attribute to the filmmakers. But for many queer viewers, being framed as deviant may in fact be the point: the quality that is most attractive and relatable to their own life experiences. Helmsing (2016) provides an intimate and personal window into this perspective, including the contrast with heteronormative straight characters. He says of the Diva Villains, as he calls them:

> As a good queer kid, I learned to invest my own fascination and dutiful learning in these animated teachers who performed model lessons in what Halberstam (2011) identifies as the queer art of failure – lessons teaching me how to embrace failure fabulously and how to not relinquish my abjection (of being queer, frail, and weird) that was seemingly keeping me from succeeding in the straight, normal world of Prince Charming and Aladdin. (2016: 60)

Helmsing argues that the female villains in these films serve as teachers and role models to their straight counterparts, much as older queer folks might mentor younger ones with "tough love," and that the quillains perform a similar function for the queer viewer: they offer an alternative to the (unrealistic or unappealing) straight models.[25]

At the same time, queerness is not just for queer kids. The beauty of queer theory is that it offers a way of looking at *all* texts, not just those that focus on a particular type of identity, and it offers that perspective to everyone, regardless of gender or sexuality. Helmsing, in fact, begins his analysis with an anecdote

---

[24] Check Pinterest if you don't believe us.
[25] For a more detailed discussion of the importance of Disney villains to gay men see also Griffin 2000.

about a group of presumably heterosexual girls discussing which princess they would want to be in real life. One of them ends up writing a blog post about wanting to be Ursula instead, where she "argues that unlike 'those silly princesses who are subversive mainly because they're after love, the villains revel in their subversion. Some may call them evil, but I call them fabulous'" (Helmsing 2016: 59).

For straight girls, in particular, the appeal of female quillains such as Ursula or Maleficent is unsurprising. QLS allows these characters to harness and queer the performance of femininity through camp, while also asserting power through the use of features like aggravated directives and insults. In doing so, they offer an alternative way of constructing femininity for the audience. If the princesses mitigate their commands, even in positions of power, the female quillains order others around without concern. If the princesses always strive to be polite, the Diva Villains either eschew this concern completely or actually turn a performance of politeness into a powerful weapon.

Belle, for example, is so unfailingly polite that when the Beast asks her to come to dinner, through the door to *the room in which he has imprisoned her*, she replies *No, thank you*. Now contrast this with Maleficent, whose cause for anger, as we saw above, is that she wasn't invited to a party (upsetting of course, but we would argue at a lower level than being imprisoned). Maleficent responds by pointing out with fake politeness the "awkwardness" of the situation to make everyone uncomfortable, lying about whether or not she is angry, and then putting a curse on an infant! She not only does what she wants without caring what anyone thinks, she actually *performs politeness* as an ironic tool to lull everyone into a false sense of security.

This campy style, which allows for some nod to femininity while embracing agency, subversion and hierarchical power, may appeal to girls and women who feel alienated by mainstream cis/heteronormative gender expectations. Bucholtz (1999) shows how a group of high school girls embrace the marginalized nerd identity in part as a way to push back against the notion that science, math, and intelligence in general are somehow the birthright of the boys. When hegemonic femininity in society is tied ideologically to potentially limiting qualities such as politeness, mitigation, and silence, it makes sense that girls would want instead to be like the villainesses who do whatever the hell they want.

For both male and female villains, then, the use of QLS provides yet another way of subverting the status quo. We read the scene with Scar, for example, as one in which he appears to be both very queer (at least in the gay male sense) and very, very powerful. Particularly for smaller children, he may come off as dislikeable, deviant, even frightening. And this is presumably the "othering" narrative that Disney intended. But for teenagers or adults, queer or otherwise, we suspect there is a healthy amount of admiration there for his wily ways, playful language, and throwing of shade left and right. Even naive Simba adores him. Similarly, Helmsing says of Maleficent, "My queerness was informed as a child by her devastating lines, defenses against the forces of King Stefan's kingdom that render her abject" (2016: 66).

So in looking at the impact of language and queerness in these films, we find both a perpetuation of heterosexism and a countercurrent of rebellion and subversion. And the implications of this perspective, which we are sure can be found extensively among queer, straight, or other Disney fans, are clear: the perpetuation of the heterosexist fantasy and the reinforcement of Disney's conservative values has not been entirely successful. As Helmsing concludes:

If one identifies with or cheers for the villains, then in part Disney's intended ideological lessons have failed … the diva villains consistently lend themselves to queer appropriations and pleasures, opening up scenes of affective engagement with the (presumably heterosexual) family-friendly fare Disney sells. (2016: 60)

At both a personal and academic level, the arguments that Helmsing makes for the power of queerness in Disney is formidable.

Interestingly, there is very little discussion of this sort about the canonical queer characters, such as Officer Specter, above. Nobody seems to want to be Oaken for Halloween. This may be the result of how little space such characters take up. Or it may be that they lack the over-the-top rebellion and excitement that the quillains bring to the table. Of course, showing canonically queer characters as being relatively ordinary is not a bad thing, and is in fact much preferable to showing them as being only happy performing in high heels and a feather boa. It remains to be seen, if in fact queer characters become a regular feature of children's animated films, how that will change the landscape for the role of queerness in Disney. We would be delighted if a future edition of this book required us to rewrite this entire chapter, focusing more on the range of language features that the "ordinary" queer characters exhibit. Fingers crossed.

# 9 Conclusion

## A Tale as Old as Time (Now Streaming on Disney+)

---

> We just make the pictures, and let the professors tell us what they mean.
>
> Walt Disney, cited in Bell, Haas, and Sells (1995)

So here we are, at (almost) the end of a long, complicated journey through the world of Disney and Pixar. While each chapter contains its own independent analysis, the chapters also work together to paint a larger picture of the linguistic ideologies constructed by these studios. And for the most part, it hasn't felt like we were describing the happiest place on earth. We will use this last section to show how the features and patterns we have been looking at come together to tell, if you'll forgive the reference, a tale as old as time.

### Gender and Representation

*Women Should Be Seen and Not Heard . . . and Actually Not Even Seen*

Disney and Pixar have a problem with their representation of women. They're not alone in this, of course.[1] But after all of our analysis we can confidently say that there are way fewer female individuals on the screen than there are in the world, and they talk less than their fair share. Often much less. To remind you of how stark this is:

> All of the Disney Princess and Pixar films we studied have more male than female characters.

Old? New? Yes and yes. All. Disney comes closest to equal representation with small casts, such as the ones in the Classic Era movies. *Moana*, one of the

---

[1] The Geena Davis Institute on Gender in Media has documented this discrepancy across a wide range of children's media content. See e.g. Smith 2008.

few recent princess movies to have something close to parity in terms of the gender of the characters, seems to achieve it by this exact same route. There are only 10 characters who speak in *Moana*, compared with 45 in *The Princess and the Frog*, for example. But as the cast gets larger, so does the discrepancy. Pixar similarly has large casts which tend to vastly overrepresent male characters. Both studios have improved since the 1990s, and yet, they still haven't managed a single balanced cast.

If we measure the number of words spoken, we find a similar discrepancy; in the majority of the movies, female characters speak less. Some readers may find that unsurprising, but the truth of the matter is that it wasn't an obvious conclusion to us. We fully expected that female characters might dominate speaking time in the Princess movies, because the films are so clearly geared towards little girls. In the Renaissance films particularly, the main characters were supposed to be paradigms of empowered femininity. But actually, the Renaissance movies of the 90s – known for their Girl Power attitude – are the least balanced of them all. We also find that in Disney, male leads tended to be dominant in conversation with their female co-leads, from 1937 all the way up to the present day.

The New Age and Pixar movies are more of a mixed bag than the older eras, but still tend towards giving female characters short shrift. In *Frozen*, with not one but *two* princesses, male characters' speech still dominates. Still, this is one area where some change is evident. In the New Age films as a group, the amount of speaking time for male and female characters is equal overall. For Pixar, male characters speak more in aggregate across the studio's films, as expected given that male characters make up 75 percent of the roster. However, in more recent films that feature two strong female characters working together, such as Merida and her mother in *Brave* (2012), or Joy and Sadness in *Inside Out* (2015), female characters actually do get more speaking time than male characters.

In terms of the discourse of the films themselves, Disney and Pixar also both have a preponderance of female characters who are judged by other characters to be overly talkative. Disney and Pixar frame women as better communicators and facilitators who are naturally adept at processing emotions verbally and keeping conversation rolling. Male characters, on the other hand, are more commonly portrayed as overly taciturn and either incompetent in or actively resistant to verbal communication. The qualitative framing works together with the quantitative imbalance in speaking time to communicate an unfortunate message about gender. Women speaking less and/or playing facilitative roles to men is normalized, and the framing of women as chatty implies that even the amount that female characters *do* show up is too much.

## Discourses of Gender Difference

### *Aladdin Is from Mars, Jasmine Is from Venus*

That last pattern provides a good opportunity for us to return to a concept we discussed in Chapter 1: the discourse of gender difference and the conceptualization of men and women as two fundamentally different sides of one binary coin. This "men are from Mars, women are from Venus" mentality pervades modern culture.[2] Our conclusion is that it also pervades Disney and Pixar. We discussed in Chapter 1 that filmmakers, and those in animation particularly, have a certain freedom to work in an ideological world rather than a realistic one. This allows them to package what is (in reality) a complicated, shifting gender performance into a strict naturalized binary. On the basis of our findings, we would argue that just as Disney and Pixar use visual cues to construct binary gender (unnaturally skinny waists and giant eyes for women, beefy muscles and square jaws for men), they also use linguistic cues to construct that same binary.

This effect is revealed clearly by our quantitative results. We examined five linguistic elements throughout this book, and in each case, we uncovered statistically significant differences between the two binary genders of Disney's world. The fewest differences were found in apologies, which might be due to the small sample size, since qualitative differences were also present. We will discuss these results in more depth throughout the rest of this chapter, but we want to step back and say: that's a lot of differences. Significant discrepancies across so many features ladder up to two distinct styles of speaking that are scripted for the majority of characters, at least in broad strokes. This pattern of difference is enough in and of itself to build an ideology of binary difference, though it may fly under the radar for most audiences.

Qualitatively, we also found that these features are evaluated or treated differently depending on the gender of the speaker. The differing evaluations often come from other characters in the movies, e.g. characters being put off by male characters caring about their appearance, but not by female characters doing the same. Evaluations also were found in the language of film and in the framing of different linguistic acts to the audience: for example, insults given by female characters usually only occur in the context of grave conflict, whereas insults given by male characters are more likely to be framed as humorous. Both levels of evaluation work in tandem to model how audiences should evaluate men and women speaking in real life.

---

[2] Just check out the toy aisles at Target.

There are also a multitude of instances in these films where Disney and Pixar go more on record about the alleged differences between the two binary genders. One of the subtle but noticeable ways is through direct comparison of gendered speech styles and behaviors – scenes where humor or drama is derived from male and female characters acting wildly differently from each other. We've given examples of this type throughout the book: women verbally processing while men silently observe (*Tangled*, Chapter 3), men roughhousing while women roll their eyes (*Brave*, Chapters 5 and 6), men aggressively asking for what they want while women flounder to find the words (*A Bug's Life*, Chapter 5), little girls receiving appearance compliments while boys receive skill compliments (*The Incredibles*, Chapter 4), and others. We discussed at length two different dinner table scenes (one from *Inside Out* in Chapter 5, and one from *The Incredibles* in Chapter 3) which both portray strikingly stereotypical speech patterns for the mothers and fathers and directly compare them for the sake of humor. And *Mulan* notably bases its entire plot on gender difference: the bulk of the tension in the film is based on the idea that men and women are so different that the behavior of the soldiers in the camp is alien to Mulan, who has to figure out how to blend in.

Occasionally, Disney and Pixar provide even more explicit metacommentary in support of binary gender differences. Ratcliffe says, *A man's not a man unless he can shoot.* The Genie tells Aladdin *A woman appreciates a man who can make her laugh!* Mulan's family sings to her that good women are *calm, obedient* (and possess *a tiny waist*). We also see attempts to talk openly, and more critically, about gender roles from time to time. Tiana in *The Princess and the Frog* gives Naveen a hard time about expecting her to cook for him and makes him get up and mince mushrooms. Merida from *Brave* rebels against the expectation to marry, and complains that she doesn't want to wear the (very princessy) dress her mom has picked out because it's uncomfortable. But in the end, these scenes still highlight the alleged gender differences by bringing them up in this way.

It's also worth calling out one more time that the stereotypical gender discourses we are referring to here are constructed through a frame of whiteness. Alongside the linguistic ideologies that are communicated, we find some racializing of behaviors that fall "outside the lines" – women of color and impoliteness, Jewish men and talkativeness, etc. These don't necessarily expand the norm, though; they just stereotype that group as *unable* to achieve the norm. Like the queer characters, who often serve the purpose (for the filmmakers at least) of carving out a negative space around the young cis-het gendered characters, characters of different ethnicities are sometimes positioned to solidify whiteness as the default. So please bear that in mind as we describe the gendered ideologies we uncovered in the next few sections.

## Ideologies of Femininity

### Femininity and Politeness in Disney

We've brought up at various points that dominant language ideology tends to link politeness and femininity closely together, and that connection bears out strongly in our results, especially for the Disney Princess films.

> Female characters are disproportionately polite: even though they speak less, they use more of the various markers that highlight a concern with maintaining the social fabric.

This ideology is reflected in a number of the individual variables we measured, especially in the patterns listed below:

- Although male and female characters give about the same proportion of directives, the ones female characters give are much more likely to be mitigated in both Disney and Pixar.
- Compliments are used between female characters as part of a routine positive politeness strategy.
- Female characters give proportionally fewer insults than male characters, especially to each other, and these insults are less likely to be treated as humorous.
- Female characters often apologize for events outside their control or that do not cause any harm.
- Female villains insult more than female heroes, and mitigate their commands less, suggesting a link between impoliteness and transgressive or immoral women.

The through-line for all of these patterns is that female characters are depicted as attending to face needs more than others. Women being nice is presented as the easy, natural thing to do in most cases. It's particularly telling that female characters in homosocial settings (like *Frozen*) tend to be even more polite with one another than with male characters.

Ironically, Disney, at least, pays a fair amount of lip service to the idea that women shouldn't have to be polite – that a Girl Power character shouldn't care what other people think. And yet, the polite behavior of princesses is rarely challenged. Belle's polite rejection of Gaston, Elsa's discomfort with issuing orders, and numerous other scenes we have discussed underscore the screenwriters' and filmmakers' perspective that politeness is natural for women. At the same time, male characters from the Beast to Mike and Sulley are presented as naturally impolite, and yet they aren't judged particularly harshly for their behaviors. Repeatedly, Disney (and Pixar to a lesser extent) gives toxic masculinity a pass, and frames the female characters as being responsible for everyone's face needs.

### Intersections with Femininity: Maturity, Domesticity, Authority, Evility

Disney sets up a few exceptions to the assumption that women are polite, but in a sense these exceptions serve to reinforce the connection between hegemonic femininity and politeness in Disney's gender ideology. For example, as we saw in Chapter 6 on insults, older female characters are allowed to break the rules. In fact the "sassy older woman with no filter" trope is alive and well in both Disney and Pixar. Characters like Grandmother Willow (*Pocahontas*), Grandma Fa (*Mulan*), and Lizzie (*Cars*) are allowed to issue bald directives or insults, and here their use is perceived not as actually impolite, but as humorous. Even the three fairies in *Sleeping Beauty*, who are almost nauseatingly sweet and good most of the time, insult each other playfully as they get ready for Aurora's birthday party.[3]

A related pattern involves female characters in a maternal role. In our analysis, we find that motherhood seems to suspend some of the polite language behaviors female characters otherwise tend to use. For instance, while female characters rarely use non-apology strategies (as the male characters do), there are a few instances where they use them in talking to their children, as in the example in Chapter 7 involving Helen from *The Incredibles*. Similarly, Mrs. Potts in *Beauty and the Beast* gives plenty of unmitigated directives to her son, Chip. This pattern extends not just to actual mothers, but also to female characters who take on a symbolic maternal role. We saw an example in Chapter 5 with Snow White, who gives unmitigated directives to the dwarfs when she is telling them to wash their hands. Never mind that these are presumably old men (since their hair is generally white), or that she is a 14-year-old visitor in their house. She steps in as the mom, and part of how she constructs her maternal personality is through directness and even impoliteness.[4] Yet in contrast with older characters' impoliteness, these examples are not framed as humorous; they're treated as unremarkable. The implication here is that domestic or maternal authority is a kind of power (perhaps the only kind

---

[3] Although a full discussion of age as a social factor is outside our scope, one way of interpreting this pattern is that polite femininity is the responsibility of the young, and older women are released from the burden because they are framed as no longer sexually desirable in these films.

[4] And, by the way, the fact that none of these seven men, who have presumably been surviving perfectly well on their own in the forest, would think to wash their hands without help from a woman sets things up nicely for decades of the discourse of gender difference. And don't get us started on emotional labor.

of power) that is natural for women; the authority they naturally carry in those spaces enables them to use linguistic strategies that they otherwise avoid.

We might expect formal or institutional authority to be a similar mitigating factor that allows female characters to be less polite. After all, you don't have to say please if you're the queen, right? According to Disney, you do. Our analysis in Chapter 5 suggests that both Disney and Pixar frame female characters as being uneasy with taking a position of power (Anna, *Frozen*; Rapunzel, *Tangled*), or attempting to mitigate that power with their linguistic choices (Elsa, *Frozen*; Joy, *Inside Out*). The good queen who uses her power most freely is Elinor from *Brave*, and while we thought she might be a counterexample at first, we quickly realized that she is the only one on this list whose main role in the plot is as a mother. And in fact even when she is dealing with the unruly skirmish among the kings and lords, and not her actual children, the film frames her as drawing on a maternal (rather than royal) authority to take control of the situation.

It's important to us to emphasize that Disney and Pixar are not only drawing connections between femininity and politeness, but they're also *moralizing* those connections – being a good girl or woman means being polite. The villainesses, though, flout the politeness rules repeatedly, often dramatically. Maleficent's ordering everyone around is an essential part of her character; at the end of her first scene, she disappears in a plume of smoke with one last aggravated directive: *Stand back, you fools!* As we saw in Chapter 8, this style is related to Disney's version of queerness. Unfortunately, we can't separate queerness from being a villain, at least in the Disney films. In any case, though, we end up with gender-nonconformity and bad moral character linked both to each other and to the failure to meet politeness expectations.

There's one further wrinkle to this association between being good and being polite for female characters. Sometimes the evil villainesses are *so* evil that they actually use politeness as a weapon to manipulate others or hide their motives. Mother Gothel (*Tangled*) compliments Rapunzel as part of her elaborate mind games. Ursula (*The Little Mermaid*) not only performs politeness throughout her manipulation of Ariel, but she actually draws Ariel into her lair in the first place by *accusing her of being rude*.[5]

In sum, then, the ideal woman in Disney is young, sweet, and uncomfortable with authority. Also acceptable are being a mom or being a sassy grandma. She only speaks a lot if she is a princess, and even then she is careful not to speak more than the prince/beast/male sidekick. And if you're a good girl, you can never be too polite. A lot of the absolute worst, most double-bindy instances of

---

[5] We are pretty sure this isn't the message that Disney intended, but we'd like to point out that there is in fact an excellent lesson to be learned here: ladies, don't let worrying that someone might think you're rude get you into a dangerous situation! Use your voice!

linguistic policing are directed at female characters in these films, through the framing of femininity.

### Femininity in Pixar

Pixar's female characters have more leeway to challenge the politeness norms, but they still reproduce some strongly gendered patterns. For many of the features we looked at, our analysis of Pixar documented the same results we see in Disney, in that female characters are framed as polite much more often than male characters. They apologize more, mitigate directives more, and are more likely than male characters to be complimented on their appearance. Dory in *Finding Nemo* continually apologizes for having a brain injury.

On the other hand, there are situations where Pixar's female characters seem to have more linguistic options than their Disney counterparts, even if they're not mothers or sorceresses. To begin with, there is more variability across Pixar movies in the amount of female speech than there is with Disney; in some movies female characters speak less than expected, but in others they actually speak more. (Which is a good thing: that means that there's no one clear gender-based expectation of how much female characters should talk.) Moreover, in the context of romantic relationships, Pixar ladies can be more impolite for the purposes of flirting, even if it sometimes veers into the realm of a "one of the guys" male fantasy. Some of the female characters, like Cruz from *Cars 3*, play the role of buddy without the romance, and use the language that goes with it, such as bonding insults.

And an area where Pixar does much better at representing femininity than Disney is in the context of authority. While the *Frozen* franchise sisters may seem reluctant to grab the wheel, Colette in *Ratatouille* is all business. In fact, some of Pixar's lead players, like Colette, or Helen in *The Incredibles* seem closer to the strong, empowered female characters that Disney was supposedly aiming for with its new wave of princesses. So it's a mixed bag for Pixar, but at least some of their (admittedly infrequent) female characters go against the overall trends binding femininity to politeness. We hesitate to laud Pixar too much on the variety of female characters, though, given that in total they still only make up 25 percent of their overall character cast.

### Ideologies of Masculinity

### Male Freedom and Masculinity as Default

We turn now to our findings with respect to masculinity. We know that the pressures of linguistic ideologies fall disproportionately on women in real life, but that there are also plenty of stereotypes about men's language floating around out there as well. Masculinity is both more dominant in our datasets (with more characters and more talking time), and more variant (even if only because so many of the minor characters are male). Our results show that these films overall uphold socially dominant interactional practices as part of masculinity, as illustrated by a number of patterns:

- Although male and female characters give about the same proportion of directives, male characters are much less likely to mitigate their directives, in both Disney and Pixar, independent of other social variables.
- Male characters are conversationally dominant in the films, and yet they aren't framed as too talkative.
- Male characters apologize proportionally less than female characters in both the Disney Renaissance Era and Pixar, and are also much more likely across the board to use non-apology strategies.

These patterns underscore the linguistic privilege that men still hold in the off-screen world.[6] When viewers see that male characters don't apologize as much, for example, or are less likely to mitigate, it reinforces the ideology that it is fine for boys and men in real life not to do these things. Qualitatively we found that male characters are likely to be in positions of power and are shown as taking on the linguistic trappings of authority very easily. Unmarked directives don't appear to make them uncomfortable, as they did for the female characters, and aren't met with any resistance from the characters they interact with. We noted earlier that differing evaluations and judgments of linguistic behaviors were used to reinforce the discourse of gender difference. Unsurprisingly, these judgments fall disproportionately on the behaviors of female characters: overall, male characters are *not* judged negatively for the same linguistic behaviors that *are* judged negatively in female characters, which clearly mirrors language policing in real life.

### Male Violence and Vulnerability

As we discussed in Chapter 2, lots of parents are worried that their daughters will get harmful ideas about how to behave from Cinderella or Snow White. We hear much less about those who are worried their sons will get harmful ideas from the Beast or Prince Eric, or from any of the wide array of Pixar's male protagonists. Maybe we need to turn the volume up a bit on that one, though, because it's pretty alarming. Male characters may have more freedom

---

[6] The privilege we are referencing here accrues primarily to white, straight, cis-gendered men in the real world. We have less analysis of intersectionality with male characters (for example looking at ethnicity) than we do with female characters. But still, even male characters who are coded as Jewish are treated differently, for example by being presented as speaking too much.

in their linguistic performances in some ways, but in others, Disney and Pixar construct a rather restrictive ideology of masculine language behavior, which reifies toxic and damaging ideas of what it means to be a man.

Here are some of the patterns related to masculinity that we found particularly concerning:

- Generally, it is taboo for male characters to receive compliments on their appearance, except within the narrow bounds of heterosexual romantic relationships. It is especially taboo to receive them from other male characters.
- Male characters can (and do) aggravate directives with insults or threats of violence.
- Male characters give more insults than female characters, and between male characters, insults are often used for bonding.
- Male-to-male insults are more likely to be framed humorously than with other dyadic pairs, even if they offend the recipient.

First of all, the data from the films we analyzed appear to confirm Kiesling's (2005) observation that friendships between men have powerful stories and rules around them. Particularly with each other, male characters are depicted as very comfortable with impoliteness, from insults to aggravated commands to straight-up threats of violence. All of those are framed as a natural part of male relationships, and not a big deal.

Male buddy teams, like those that are so prominent in Pixar, often bond through insults in a way that female character pairs don't. Basically, it's preferable to show that you like another guy by calling him *a big tumshie* (or whatever the equivalent is in your dialect of English) instead of giving him an actual compliment (*Brave*, Chapter 6). Male buddies use faux insults as bonding events; they also use real insults, where someone gets angry, but these are still presented as humorous for the audience. Note that the few female–female buddies don't do this. This gendered pattern suggests that two men insulting each other is hilarious, but two women insulting each other constitutes high drama, presumably because the expectation is that women will be polite (especially with one another).

As a counterpart to the idea that female characters can't be too polite, it's tempting to say that male characters can't be too rude. That's not quite right. Male characters do get called out at times for behaving rudely, but it's surprising how far they can go before that happens. For example, the Beast not only issues unmitigated and aggravated directives to Belle, he even calls attention to this behavior himself by saying, *You will join me for dinner. That's not a request.* And that's all before he starts threatening to break down the door. You may be thinking that his behavior isn't framed as a positive thing in the movie, and that would be true. But it's not framed as unacceptable either.

It's framed, we would say, as unfortunate, a miscalculation, someone who doesn't know any better and needs tutoring from the clock and the teapot about how to be nicer, a running theme in the movie. But even during these speech events, the Beast is seen as basically a good guy with some issues. His linguistic behavior is framed as bad because it's socially awkward and unlikely to achieve the desired effect, not because of what it really is: abusive.

In general, male characters even when they are heroes or framed as good, are still more likely to be portrayed as poor communicators (like Riley's dad, in the dinner table scene from *Inside Out*) or prone to violence and solitude (like the Beast). Wooden and Gillam (2014) were right to point out that the male characters in Pixar aren't setting very positive models for young boys. We find it upsetting that male aggression (linguistic or otherwise) feels so normalized in both Disney and Pixar, with implications for children of any gender who are watching.

In addition, vulnerability in men (especially around other men) is something that Disney and Pixar still seem to be working on. Pixar in particular has been praised in the past for creating "New Men" who are capable of valuing community and vulnerability, and while we recognize their efforts, they don't totally bear out in masculine linguistic performance. Male characters do sometimes compliment each other, but their compliments tend to be on a skill or action, often in the context of completing a task. Outside of task-based activities, male-to-male compliments are much rarer. Expressing open admiration for other male characters is avoided, and appearance compliments are completely off the table; when they're given between male characters, they're framed either as a humorous manipulation strategy, or in the worst-case scenario, as a veiled insult to their masculinity. We hope that in the future, Disney and Pixar can construct versions of masculinity that are more easily vulnerable, instead of modeling solidarity and affection only through aggressive behavior.

### Reinforcing Heteronormativity

One further question that we explored was how Disney and Pixar frame behaviors outside the gender norms. As noted throughout, both sets of films reinforce the dominance of heterosexuality. The princess films, in fact, are the epitome of heterosexuality, with their emphasis on young people choosing a romantic partner of the "opposite sex." And in Pixar we find less emphasis on romance, but what romance there is remains staunchly heterosexual, with any suggestion of queerness pushed to the very margin of the margins.

The closest we get to subversion of gender norms is in Disney's queer-coded characters, discussed at length in Chapter 8. The queer male villains in Disney not only look less gender-confirming (Li-Vollmer & LaPointe 2003), but also have a unique Quillain Language Style that purposely takes on certain elements of stereotypical Women's Language. Female villains also use this style, in a way that raises interesting questions about the difference in how male queerness and female queerness are viewed and framed. In addition, they cross into more traditionally masculine styles of using assertive and powerful language. (And as we noted earlier, because femininity is inextricably entwined with politeness in these films, female characters who fail to uphold this standard are framed as bad.) While the Quillain Language Style may be used to frame both male and female queer characters as clever and powerful, it still reinforces the othering of those who don't embrace traditional gender roles. As Li-Vollmer and LaPointe point out, the gender subversion these characters embrace is part of what makes them dangerous in the film. And ultimately, they're all defeated.

## The Question of Progress

### What Has Changed, What Stays the Same

One of the questions we are often asked is whether the Disney films in particular are "getting better." Sometimes it isn't really a question. (More of a comment, if you've ever seen that kind of thing at an academic conference.) Anyway, we're uneasy with being the arbiters of what does or does not count as progress, although we can certainly say what has changed over time and what hasn't, at least within the scope covered by our project.

### Disney

In response, at least partly, to feminist criticisms in the 1980s and early 1990s (as detailed in Chapter 2), Disney attempted to make a new and improved Princess. Did they succeed? Well, sort of. Film critics and researchers have commented on the behavioral differences between older and newer princesses. The more recent heroines *do* things, unlike the comatose Sleeping Beauty. Merida shoots a bow and arrow better than her suitors. Jasmine pole vaults into Aladdin's rooftop home. They have goals, such as Tiana's dream of owning a restaurant. They don't always marry at the end. Sometimes princesses save each other.

Do these efforts translate to linguistic shifts? Our answer: sometimes. Perhaps the most definitive "yes" we can give is with compliment topics. In analyzing compliments, we found that the proportion of skill compliments increased over time for female characters and the proportion of appearance compliments decreased, which we lauded as a positive development in Chapter 4. We see this as a linguistic manifestation of the pressure that has been on Disney since the 1990s to shift the narrative away from princesses being passive and valued for their appearance only. The shift was particularly dramatic in romantic relationships, the centerpiece of a lot of films.

We also see some promising changes in representation and in talking time. The split between male and female speech in the New Age Era is almost exactly 50–50 and some films even have female majority speech (*Brave*, *Frozen II*). It makes sense that Disney shifted these patterns because they are easy for scriptwriters and viewers to identify on the surface.

Unfortunately, most of the other linguistic patterns we tracked have not changed much at all. Female characters mitigate directives more than male characters independent of the Era of production. Male princes continue to be conversationally dominant over princesses in dyadic interactions. And the New Age Era actually has a larger gender-based discrepancy in insult usage than either previous era. Even in terms of compliment topics, little to no change has been found for male characters, despite its being the site of the biggest shift for female characters. Male characters still receive far more compliments on skill than appearance, and appearance-based compliments are treated as mockery.

We also note qualitatively that many linguistic gender stereotypes are perpetuated in the New Age films. Princesses are characterized as chatty (perhaps overly so), more emotionally intelligent than the male co-leads (not bad per se, but stereotypical), reluctant to use strong directives, apologetic for minor offenses, and so on. And humor continues to be derived from the idea that men and women are so fundamentally different that they can never hope to communicate – perhaps even more than in earlier years. In these ways, the linguistic portrayal of gender is still very much ideologically motivated, and not particularly progressive, despite the improvements Disney has presumably tried to make in their representation of women. All in all, we may just be seeing a new version of what Ross observed about the Renaissance films: a "replacement of one set of stereotypes for another" (Ross 2010, cited in Stover 2013).

### Pixar

Pixar's movies are more difficult to categorize than Disney's when it comes to the question of change or improvement, since our methodology didn't separate Pixar's movies into Eras. That being said, there are some characteristics that we can identify as being more typical of the later films. The Pixar films with the highest counts of female characters are all relatively new (*Coco*, *Finding Dory*, *Monsters University*, *Inside Out*). These films make a better attempt than older Pixar movies at including female characters in the background, and many of those characters are more intriguing and memorable than Disney's collection of mothers and domestic workers (such as the cameo by Frida Kahlo in *Coco*). The relatively recent films *Inside Out* and *Brave* are the only two Pixar films where female characters talk more than male characters, though *Finding Dory* also has a nearly equal balance of talk time. These films are also the only three with female protagonists. In this sense, Pixar, slowly, seems to be moving in the right direction. Unfortunately, three films don't do much in the face of the boys' club history of Pixar; their filmography as a whole is still overwhelmingly male, both in characters and speech representation.

As with Disney, we also see progress in the area of compliment topics. In the more recent films, especially since *Brave*, Pixar female characters receive proportionally many more compliments on their skills than on their appearance. And male characters do give and receive compliments at a higher rate than studies of real people would lead us to predict, which can be viewed as a start toward modeling more openly supportive models of masculinity. Overall, though, many of our variables, even in the newer films, continue to reinforce the discourse of gender difference, in which e.g. female characters apologize more while male characters insult each other.

In both sets of films, there is a hegemonic discourse of heterosexuality, as discussed earlier, although it could be argued that Pixar is at least trying to make progress in this area. Pixar's queer characters are not treated as deviant (in contrast with the Disney quillains), and their queerness, when it's addressed at all, is presented more matter-of-factly (Officer Specter from *Onward* is one example, at least, though the film was out of scope for this study). We definitely count that as progress. But still, these Pixar characters are represented in a few lines and a wink from the background instead of taking the main stage. Despite their flaws, we miss the drag queens of yore! Why can't Pixar (or Disney for that matter) have a flamboyant character like Maleficent or Ursula who isn't a villain? Who is beloved by all for their strength and humor (and fabulous clothing and makeup)?[7]

### Schrödinger's Princess: The Disney Time Loop

There is another serious issue with the question of progress, and it is the reason why we want to strongly temper our reports on what has and hasn't improved. To awkwardly paraphrase Faulkner, the past princesses aren't dead, they're not even past. First of all, technology continues to advance, as we have mentioned, and audiences have more ways of streaming films on all sorts of devices. With the launch of Disney+ in 2019, the entire franchise was suddenly at everyone's

---

[7] At the time of our book going to press, Amazon Prime was just announcing its new film *Cinderella*, which features Billy Porter as a stylish and enticing fairy godmother, so clearly if Disney won't do it, someone else will.

fingertips, and these days even toddlers seem to know how to work an onscreen menu.

Also, Disney has chosen a strategy of marketing and remarketing a set of characters as one idea (*Princess!* in flashing neon lights), when they actually span almost a century of cinema history. Constantly seeing them together creates what Do Rozario calls a "perpetual time loop created by the magic kingdom" (Do Rozario 2004: 36). The narrative of progress that is told by newer movies assures critically aware parents that the new princesses can actually be safely consumed. And it does seem as though that works – Newman (2018) found that parents are much more comfortable with newer films like *Frozen* and *Moana* than with older movies.

But creating a "Princess" ethos that transcends each individual movie, and, importantly, includes films from a generation of filmmakers less concerned with making a deliberate political message, blurs the lines in both directions. Older princesses can be reimagined as somehow taking on the more progressive characteristics of the newer models, while the newer princesses are drawn into a world of marketing that emphasizes traditionally feminine traits (Stover 2013). And the toys and tie-ins chosen to represent this culture aren't cookware from Tiana or swords from Mulan – instead, we find Belle's yellow ball gown, Cinderella's tiara, all these artifacts from the old gender roles that the movies promised they were leaving behind.

Basically, while each individual princess "progresses," the *Princess* as a Disneyfied abstraction is firmly anchored by the princesses of the past. Thanks to Disney+ and other media developments, *Snow White*, *Cinderella*, and *Sleeping Beauty* are arguably more salient today than they were for the latter half of the twentieth century. So in that sense, if someone were to ask us if there's progress and things are "better" with Disney, we would have to say it's kind of like Schrödinger's Princess: there's progress and no progress at the same time.

We have focused on the Disney Princess line here because so much of the critical reception and calls for being more progressive centered around that group. As for Pixar, though, many of the same caveats with respect to progress hold true. Though it may not have a single central trope like the Princesses, the Pixar franchise still clearly has its own recognizable brand. And the original *Toy Story* (1995) is as easily viewed on your device as *Toy Story 4* (2019). Pixar would have to make a lot of films with casts that are almost entirely female to ever balance out the boys' club panorama of their past.

### Behind the Scenes

Although we have focused almost entirely on what was on the screen and relatively little on how it got there, we do want to add a note here about the question of progress as it relates to hiring and other behind the scenes decisions. Disney and Pixar have a poor record of employing people other than white men as writers and directors of their movies. In terms of gender, they've each only ever had one female director (Jennifer Lee at Disney, and Brenda Chapman at Pixar, who, as we mentioned in Chapter 2, was fired partway through production). Female writers are more common, but by no means the majority, and overall the gender balance in production teams does not seem to be improving dramatically.

If we look beyond gender, one aspect that definitely has changed over time is the extent to which racial, cultural, and ethnic diversity on screen appear to be a target for these studios, especially Disney. We've discussed the mixed results of those experiments in various places, and how individual projects (such as *Pocahontas*) have been disastrous in terms of being appropriative and reproducing harmful stereotypes. At the same time, we want to note that more recent films such as *Coco* and *Moana* have creative processes that are increasingly attentive to the voices of particular cultures both on screen and behind the scenes, with better outcomes, at least in terms of academic and in-group assessments of the results. Although still imperfect, of course, we count these films as a definite area of progress.

We can't say for sure that more diverse creative teams would lead to less stereotypical language, but it certainly would bring something valuable and new to the table. Our hope would be that more diversity in hiring would lead to a richer range of representations of gender onscreen, linguistically and otherwise. Our analysis tangentially pointed out the paucity of characters outside the ideological status quo enforced by these films. In an ideal animated world, we'd see more characters who reflect the full range of human existence. In terms of gender, we'd like to see characters who are queer, in canon and performance alike, and not relegated to villainous roles. We would especially like to see queer female characters who aren't written as drag queens, and some gender-fluid or nonbinary characters. And because of how intersectionality works, gender won't be represented fairly until everything else is as well. We'd like to see more representation across genders of disabled characters, fat characters who aren't the butt of jokes, or older characters with central roles. That, we feel, would be something we could unequivocally call "progress."

### Final Thoughts

Almost everyone we've talked to about our research has expressed to us what they wish there were more of available in children's media, much like the list we provided in the previous section. The good news is that there's some clear evidence that cultural pressure from the viewing audience can help. The Disney corporation has shown that it is quite invested in looking progressive.

Social pressure for greater representation of women, and of empowering those women, has led to some changes (limited, but noticeable), and through our research, we found certain feminist talking points making headway.

We hope that our project, and others like it, will put linguistic inequalities firmly on the map when it comes to problems of gender representation. As we said at the beginning of the book, research on animated films seems to strike a chord with the public, and we're excited that this kind of work resonates with people. It would be encouraging if our analysis led audiences to challenge the status quo and ask for more, especially for historically marginalized voices, and led filmmakers to push the limits of imagination about what good representation means on screen.

Beyond what Disney or Pixar could do themselves, a trend for the future that would make us very happy is to see more research by linguists (or others using linguistic methods) on all types of media. Children's media, sci-fi films, reality TV, YouTube, whatever floats your boat. Our study has shown that a linguistic lens can be a valuable addition to the arsenal of media criticism, and that quantitative methods in particular can provide an important grounding element to otherwise qualitative work. We firmly believe that there's a world of unexplored data out there, and there's so much to be uncovered about the intricacies of how gendered discourses are reproduced in societal texts.

We also recognize once more that this one project couldn't hope to uncover all there is to know about gender in Disney. We sacrificed some level of detail, in places, in favor of looking at a large number of movies at once. We know that applying different analytical lenses based on social positionalities (e.g. ethnicity, class, disability) as a central focus, along with taking a more explicitly intersectional approach, would yield fascinating insights that we missed. We hope the techniques and perspectives in this book will provide students and others with a good starting point to do much more of this type of work.

We're excited to see where this research goes in the next few years. We hope at least some of our readers are imagining themselves shining a light on their favorite media in the interests of fostering a more thoughtful and critical audience. In the meantime, feel free to collect your belongings and exit the ride.

# References and Filmography

## References

Abe, H. (2004). Lesbian bar talk in Shinjuku, Tokyo. In S. Okamoto & J. S. Shibamoto Smith (Eds.), *Japanese language, gender, and ideology: Cultural models and real people*, 205–221. Oxford University Press.

Abedi, E. (2016). A cross-cultural comparative study of apology strategies employed by Iranian EFL learners and English native speakers. *Advances in Language and Literary Studies, 7*(5), 35–44. https://eric.ed.gov/?id=EJ1126879

Al-Yasin, N. F., & Rabab'ah, G. A. (2018). Impoliteness strategies in *The Fresh Prince of Bel-Air*: A gender-based study. *International Journal of Arabic-English Studies, 18*(1). www.ijaes.net/article/viewarticle?volume=18&issue=1&articleId=8

Anderson, H., & Daniels, M. (2016, April). Film dialogue from 2,000 screenplays, broken down by gender and age. *The Pudding*. https://pudding.cool/2017/03/film-dialogue/

Arends, H. (1994). *Snow White: The Making of a Masterpiece*. TV Is OK Productions.

Aronsson, K., & Thorell, M. (1999). Family politics in children's play directives. *Journal of Pragmatics, 31*(1), 25–48. https://doi.org/10.1016/S0378–2166(98)00050-2

Ata, R. N., Ludden, A. B., & Lally, M. M. (2007). The effects of gender and family, friend, and media influences on eating behaviors and body image during adolescence. *Journal of Youth and Adolescence, 36*(8), 1024–1037. https://doi.org/10.1007/s10964–006-9159-x

Ayres, B. (Ed.). (2003). *The emperor's old groove: Decolonizing Disney's magic kingdom*. Peter Lang.

Backman, M. (2014, September 25). Disney princesses ditch Mattel, run away with Hasbro. *CNNMoney*. https://money.cnn.com/2014/09/25/news/hasbro-frozen-disney/index.html

Barrett, R. (1998). Markedness and styleswitching in performances by African American drag queens. In C. Myers-Scotton (Ed.), *Codes and consequences: Choosing linguistic varieties*, 139–161. Oxford University Press.

(1999). Indexing polyphonous identity in the speech of African American drag queens. In M. Bucholtz, A. C. Liang, & L. A. Sutton (Eds.), *Reinventing identities: The gendered self in discourse*, 313–331. Oxford University Press.

(2017). *From drag queens to leathermen: Language, gender, and gay male subcultures*. Oxford University Press.

Barrier, M. (2003). *Hollywood cartoons: American animation in its golden age.* Oxford University Press.

Bataineh, R. F. (2004). *A cross-cultural study of the speech act of apology in American English and Jordanian Arabic.* Doctoral dissertation, University of Pennsylvania.

Bataineh, R. F., & Bataineh, R. F. (2008). A cross-cultural comparison of apologies by native speakers of American English and Jordanian Arabic. *Journal of Pragmatics, 40*(4), 792–821. https://doi.org/10.1016/j.pragma.2008.01.003

Bell, E. (1995). Somatexts at the Disney Shop: Constructing the pentimentos of women's animated bodies. In E. Bell, L. Haas, & L. Sells (Eds.), *From mouse to mermaid: The politics of film, gender, and culture,* 107–124. Indiana University Press.

Bell, E., Haas, L., & Sells, L. (Eds.). (1995). *From mouse to mermaid: The politics of film, gender, and culture.* Indiana University Press.

Bellinger, D. C., & Gleason, J. B. (1982). Sex differences in parental directives to young children. *Sex Roles, 8*(11), 1123–1139. https://doi.org/10.1007/BF00290968

Benor, S. B. (2009). Do American Jews speak a "Jewish language"? A model of Jewish linguistic distinctiveness. *Jewish Quarterly Review, 99*(2), 230–269. https://doi.org/10.1353/jqr.0.0046

(2011). Mensch, bentsh, and balagan: Variation in the American Jewish linguistic repertoire. *Language & Communication, 31*(2), 141–154. https://doi.org/10.1016/j.langcom.2010.08.006

Blum-Kulka, S. (1990). You don't touch lettuce with your fingers: Parental politeness in family discourse. *Journal of Pragmatics, 14*(2), 259–288. https://doi.org/10.1016/0378-2166(90)90083-P

Boothe, D. (1989). *Treasures untold: The making of The Little Mermaid.* www.youtube.com/watch?v=XdMMg6OSn1Q

(1992). *A diamond in the rough: The making of Aladdin.* www.youtube.com/watch?v=afqrFqn7PJg

(1995). *The making of Pocahontas.* www.youtube.com/watch?v=-78sG39u-3g

Breaux, R. M. (2010). After 75 years of magic: Disney answers its critics, rewrites African American history, and cashes in on its racist past. *Journal of African American Studies, 14*(4), 398–416. https://doi.org/10.1007/s12111-010-9139-9

Brooks, D. E., & Hébert, L. P. (2006). Gender, race, and media representation. In B. J. Dow & J. T. Wood (Eds.), *The SAGE handbook of gender and communication,* 297–317. SAGE.

Brown, P., & Levinson, S. C. (1978). Universals in language usage: Politeness phenomena. In E. N. Goody (Ed.), *Questions and politeness: Strategies in social interaction,* 56–311. Cambridge University Press.

(1987). *Politeness: Some universals in language usage.* Cambridge University Press.

Bruni, F. (1995, June 19). Cartooning history Disney attempts to avoid insult or offense in first feature based on a historical figure. *The Spokesman-Review.* www.spokesman.com/stories/1995/jun/19/cartooning-history-disney-attempts-to-avoid/

Brydon, S. G. (2009). Men at the heart of mothering: Finding mother in *Finding Nemo. Journal of Gender Studies, 18*(2), 131–146. https://doi.org/10.1080/09589230902812448

Bucholtz, M. (1999). "Why be normal?": Language and identity practices in a community of nerd girls. *Language in Society, 28*(2), 203–223. https://doi.org/10 .1017/S0047404599002043

Bucholtz, M., & Hall, K. (2004). Theorizing identity in language and sexuality research. *Language in Society, 33*(4), 469–515. www.jstor.org/stable/4169370

Burnett, F. H. (1905). *A little princess*. Wyatt North Publishing.

Butler, J. (2011). *Gender trouble: Feminism and the subversion of identity*. Routledge.

Byerly, C. M., & Ross, K. (2008). *Women and media: A critical introduction*. John Wiley & Sons.

Calder, J. (2019). From sissy to sickening: The indexical landscape of/s/in SoMa, San Francisco. *Journal of Linguistic Anthropology, 29*(3), 332–358.

Campbell-Kibler, K., Podesva, R., Roberts, S., & Wong, A. (Eds.). (2001). *Language and sexuality*. University of Chicago Press.

Cameron, D. (2005). Language, gender, and sexuality: Current issues and new directions. *Applied Linguistics, 26*(4), 482–502. https://doi.org/10.1093/applin/ ami027

(2007). *The myth of Mars and Venus*. Oxford University Press.

(2016, July 28). Sorry, but it's complicated. *Language: A feminist guide*. https:// debuk.wordpress.com/2016/07/28/sorry-but-its-complicated/

Cameron, D., Frazer, E., Harvey, P., Rampton, M. B. H., & Richardson, K. (1992). *Researching language: Issues of power and method*. Routledge.

Case, S. (1995). Gender, language and the professions: Recognition of wide-verbal repertoire speech. *Studies in Linguistic Sciences, 25*, 149–189.

Champlin, C. (1989, December 5). Diving into the "Little Mermaid" sexism issue. *Los Angeles Times*. www.latimes.com/archives/la-xpm-1989-12-05-ca-310-story.html

Chapman, B. (2012, August 14). Stand up for yourself, and mentor others. *New York Times*. www.nytimes.com/roomfordebate/2012/08/14/how-can-women-gain-influence-in-hollywood/stand-up-for-yourself-and-mentor-others

Cheryan, S., Master, A., & Meltzoff, A. N. (2015). Cultural stereotypes as gatekeepers: Increasing girls' interest in computer science and engineering by diversifying stereotypes. *Frontiers in Psychology, 6*. https://doi.org/10.3389/fpsyg.2015.00049

Cheu, J. (Ed.). (2013). *Diversity in Disney films: Critical essays on race, ethnicity, gender, sexuality and disability*. McFarland & Company.

Coca, A. (2000). A reflection of the development of gender construction in "classic" Disney films. *Amsterdam Social Science, 3*(1), 7–20.

Cohen, A. D., & Olshtain, E. (1981). Developing a measure of sociocultural competence: The case of apology. *Language Learning, 31*(1), 113–134. https://doi .org/10.1111/j.1467-1770.1981.tb01375.x

Cook, J., & Main, W. (2008). What is a princess? Developing an animated TV program for small girls. *Australian Feminist Studies, 23*(57), 401–415.

Coupland, N., & Jaworski, A. (2004). Sociolinguistic perspective on metalanguage: Reflexivity, evaluation, and ideology. In A. Jaworski, N. Coupland, & D. Galasinski (Eds.), *Metalanguage: Social and ideological perspectives*, 15–51. Walter de Gruyter.

Coyle, J. (2017). Pixar's 'Coco' feasts on 'Justice League' at box office. *New Haven Register*. www.nhregister.com/news/article/Pixar-s-Coco-feasts-on-Justice-12384697.php

Coyne, S. M., Linder, J. R., Rasmussen, E. E., Nelson, D. A., & Birkbeck, V. (2016). Pretty as a princess: Longitudinal effects of engagement with Disney Princesses on gender stereotypes, body esteem, and prosocial behavior in children. *Child Development*, *87*(6), 1909–1925. https://doi.org/10.1111/cdev.12569

Crowther, B. (1950, February 23). The screen: Six newcomers mark holiday; Capitol's "Malaya" has Tracy and Stewart in leads – Two imports offered Walt Disney's feature-Length "Cinderella," at the Mayfair. *New York Times*. www.nytimes.com/1950/02/23/archives/the-screen-six-newcomers-mark-holiday-capitols-malaya-has-tracy-and.html

(1959, February 18). Screen: "Sleeping Beauty". *New York Times*. www.nytimes.com/1959/02/18/archives/screen-sleeping-beauty.html

Culpeper, J., Short, M., Short, M., & Verdonk, P. (1998). *Exploring the language of drama: From text to context*. Psychology Press.

Davies, J. (2003). Expressions of gender: An analysis of pupils' gendered discourse styles in small group classroom discussions. *Discourse & Society*, *14*(2), 115–132. https://doi.org/10.1177/0957926503014002853

Davis, A. M. (2006). *Good girls and wicked witches: Women in Disney's feature animation*. John Libbey Publishing.

DeButts, M. (2012, September 10). Pixar and feminism. *AC Voice*. https://acvoice.wordpress.com/2012/09/10/pixar-and-feminism/

Decker, J. (2010). *The portrayal of gender in Disney-Pixar's animated films*. Lap Lambert Academic Publishing.

Desmond, R., & Danilewicz, A. (2010). Women are on, but not in, the news: Gender roles in local television news. *Sex Roles*, *62*(11), 822–829.

Desta, Y. (2017). Pixar's had a problem with women for decades. *Vanity Fair*. www.vanityfair.com/hollywood/2017/11/pixar-john-lasseter-boys-club

Deutschmann, M. (2003). *Apologising in British English*. Umeå Universiteit.

Dicker, R. C. (2016). *A history of US feminisms*. Basic Books.

Do Rozario, R.-A. C. D. (2004). The Princess and the Magic Kingdom: Beyond nostalgia, the function of the Disney Princess. *Women's Studies in Communication*, *27*(1), 34–59. https://doi.org/10.1080/07491409.2004.10162465

Doohan, E.-A. M., & Manusov, V. (2004). The communication of compliments in romantic relationships: An investigation of relational satisfaction and sex differences and similarities in compliment behavior. *Western Journal of Communication*, *68*(2), 170–194. https://doi.org/10.1080/10570310409374795

Dundes, L. (2001). Disney's modern heroine Pocahontas: Revealing age-old gender stereotypes and role discontinuity under a façade of liberation. *The Social Science Journal*, *38*(3), 353–365. https://doi.org/10.1016/S0362–3319(01)00137-9

Dutka, E. (1992, January 19). MOVIES: Ms. Beauty and the Beast: Writer of Disney Hit Explains Her 'Woman of the '90s'. *Los Angeles Times*. www.latimes.com/archives/la-xpm-1992-01-19-ca-544-story.html

Dynel, M. (2013). Impoliteness as disaffiliative humor in film talk. In M. Dynel (Ed.), *Developments in Linguistic Humour Theory*, 105–144. John Benjamins.

(2015). The landscape of impoliteness research. *Journal of Politeness Research*, *11*(2), 329–354. https://doi.org/10.1515/pr-2015-0013

Ebert, R. (1989, November 17). *The Little Mermaid movie review*. www.rogerebert.com/reviews/the-little-mermaid-1989

(2003, May 30). *Finding Nemo movie review & film summary*. www.rogerebert.com/reviews/finding-nemo-2003

Eckert, P. (2014). The problem with binaries: Coding for gender and sexuality. *Language and Linguistics Compass, 8*(11), 529–535. https://doi.org/10.1111/lnc3.12113

Eckert, P., & McConnell-Ginet, S. (1992). Think practically and look locally: Language and gender as community-based practice. *Annual Review of Anthropology, 21*(1), 461–488.

(2013). *Language and gender*. Cambridge University Press.

Edelsky, C. (1981). Who's got the floor? *Language in Society, 10*(3), 383–421. https://doi.org/10.1017/S004740450000885X

Eder, D. (1990). Serious and playful disputes: Variation in conflict talk among female adolescents. In A. D. Grimshaw (Ed.), *Conflict talk: Sociolinguistic investigations of arguments in conversations*, 67–83. Cambridge University Press.

England, D. E., Descartes, L., & Collier-Meek, M. A. (2011). Gender role portrayal and the Disney Princesses. *Sex Roles, 64*(7), 555–567. https://doi.org/10.1007/s11199-011-9930-7

Engle, M. (1980). Language and play: A comparative analysis of parental initiatives. In H. Giles, W. P. Robinson, & P. Smith (Eds.), *Language: Social psychological perspectives: Selected papers from the First International Conference on Social Psychology and Language held at the University of Bristol, England, July 1979*, 29–34. Elsevier.

Ervin-Tripp, S. (1976). Is Sybil there? The structure of some American English directives. *Language in Society, 5*(1), 25–66. https://doi.org/10.1017/S0047404500006849

Fägersten, K. B. (Ed.). (2016). *Watching TV with a linguist*. Syracuse University Press.

Finklea, B. W. (2016). Nurturing New Men and polishing imperfect fathers via hetero- and homosocial relationships in Pixar films. In R. A. Lind (Ed.), *Race and gender in electronic media: Content, context, culture*, 89–104. Routledge.

Fishman, P. M. (1978). Interaction: The work women do. *Social Problems, 25*(4), 397–406. https://doi.org/10.2307/800492.

Forgacs, D. (1992). Disney animation and the business of childhood. *Screen, 33*(4), 361–374. https://doi.org/10.1093/screen/33.4.361

Forman-Brunell, M., & Eaton, J. (2009). The graceful and gritty princess: Managing notions of girlhood from the New Nation to the New Millennium. *American Journal of Play, 1*(3), 338–364. https://eric.ed.gov/?id=EJ1068986

Foster, G., Tatalovich, N. C., & Hayashi, C. (2005, January 25). *Disney consumer products*. https://web.archive.org/web/20060323155139/https://licensing.disney.com/Login/displayContent.do?layout=fftDetail&fftId=disney_princess

Foucault, M. (1972). *The archeology of knowledge*. Tavistock.

Frueh, T., & McGhee, P. E. (1975). Traditional sex role development and amount of time spent watching television. *Developmental Psychology, 11*(1), 109.

Gammage, M. M. (2015). *Representations of black women in the media: The damnation of black womanhood*. Routledge.

Gill, R. (2007). Postfeminist media culture: Elements of a sensibility. *European Journal of Cultural Studies, 10*(2), 147–166. https://doi.org/10.1177/1367549407075898

Gillam, K., & Wooden, S. R. (2008). Post-princess models of gender: The New Man in Disney/Pixar. *Journal of Popular Film and Television, 36*(1), 2–8. https://doi.org/10.3200/JPFT.36.1.2-8

Giroux, H. A. (1999). *The mouse that roared: Disney and the end of innocence.* Rowman & Littlefield.

(2001). *Breaking in to the movies: Film and the culture of politics.* Wiley.

Giroux, H. A., & Pollock, G. (2010). *The mouse that roared: Disney and the end of innocence* (updated and expanded edition). Rowman & Littlefield.

Gleason, J. B., & Greif, E. B. (1987). Sex differences in parent–child interaction. In S. U. Philips, S. Steele, & C. Tanz (Eds.), *Language, gender, and sex in comparative perspective,* 189–199. Cambridge University Press.

Goodwin, M. H. (1980). Directive-response sequences in girls and boys task activities. In S. McConnell-Ginet, R. Borker, & N. Furman (Eds.), *Women and language in literature and society,* 157–173. Praeger.

(1988). Cooperation and competition across girls' play activities. In J. Coates (Ed.), *Language and gender: A reader,* 121–146. Blackwell.

(1990). *He-said-she-said: Talk as social organization among Black children.* Indiana University Press.

(2001). Organizing participation in cross-sex jump rope: Situating gender differences within longitudinal studies of activities. *Research on Language and Social Interaction, 34*(1), 75–106. https://doi.org/10.1207/S15327973RLSI3401_4

(2011). Cooperation and competition across girls' play activities. In J. Coates & P. Pichler (Eds.), *Language and gender: A reader* (2nd edition), 89–111. Wiley-Blackwell.

Goodwin, M. H., & Cekaite, A. (2013). Calibration in directive/response sequences in family interaction. *Journal of Pragmatics, 46*(1), 122–138. https://doi.org/10.1016/j.pragma.2012.07.008

Grabe, S., Ward, L. M., & Hyde, J. S. (2008). The role of the media in body image concerns among women: A meta-analysis of experimental and correlational studies. *Psychological Bulletin, 134*(3), 460–476. https://doi.org/10.1037/0033-2909.134.3.460

Grady, C. (2017). Is *Beauty and the Beast* "a tale as old as Stockholm syndrome"? Depends how you read it. *Vox.* www.vox.com/culture/2017/3/23/15000768/beauty-and-the-beast-feminist-stockholm-syndrome

Green, L. J. (2002). *African American English: A linguistic introduction.* Cambridge University Press.

Griffin, S. (2000). *Tinker Belles and Evil Queens: The Walt Disney Company from the inside out.* NYU Press.

Haas, L. (1995). Eighty-six the mother: Murder, matricide, and good mothers. In E. Bell & L. Sells (Eds.), *From mouse to mermaid: The politics of film, gender, and culture,* 72–85. Indiana University Press.

Hanscom, M. (2006, May 20). Is Pixar a 'boys only' club? https://michaelhans.com/eclecticism/2006/05/20/is-pixar-a-boys-only-club/

Harris, T. M., & Hill, P. S. (1998). "Waiting to Exhale" or "Breath(ing) Again": A search for identity, empowerment, and love in the 1990s. *Women and Language,* 21, 9–20.

Harvey, K. (2000). Describing camp talk: Language/pragmatics/politics. *Language and Literature*, *9*(3), 240–260. https://doi.org/10.1177/096394700000900303

(2002). Camp talk and citationality: A queer take on 'authentic' and 'represented' utterance. *Journal of Pragmatics*, *34*(9), 1145–1165. https://doi.org/10.1016/S0378–2166(01)00058-3

Heldman, C., Narayanan, S., Cooper, R., Conroy, M., Giaccardi, S., Cooper-Jones, N., . . . Young, A. (2021). *See Jane 2020 TV Report*. The Geena Davis Institute on Gender in Media. https://seejane.org/research-informs-empowers/2020-tv-historic-screen-time-speaking-time-for-female-characters/

Helmsing, M. (2016). "This is no ordinary apple": Learning to fail spectacularly in the affective pedagogy of Disney's diva villains. In J. Sandlin & J. Garlen (Eds.), *Disney, culture, curriculum*, 59–72. Routledge.

Herbert, R. K. (1990). Sex-based differences in compliment behavior. *Language in Society*, *19*(2), 201–224. https://doi.org/10.1017/S0047404500014378

Herman, D. (2016, December 2). How the story of Moana and Maui holds up against cultural truths. *Smithsonian Magazine*. www.smithsonianmag.com/smithsonian-institution/how-story-moana-and-maui-holds-against-cultural-truths-180961258/

Herrett-Skjellum, J., & Allen, M. (1996). Television programming and sex stereotyping: A meta-analysis. *Annals of the International Communication Association*, *19*(1), 157–186.

Herring, S. (2003). Gender and power in on-line communication. In J. Holmes & M. Meyerhoff (Eds.), *The handbook of language and gender*, 202–228. John Wiley & Sons.

Hine, B., Ivanovic, K., & England, D. (2018). From the sleeping princess to the world-saving daughter of the chief: Examining young children's perceptions of 'old' versus 'new' Disney Princess characters. *Social Sciences*, *7*(9), 161. https://doi.org/10.3390/socsci7090161

Hine, B., England, D., Lopreore, K., Skora Horgan, E., & Hartwell, L. (2018). The rise of the androgynous princess: Examining representations of gender in prince and princess characters of Disney movies released 2009–2016. *Social Sciences*, *7*(12), 245. https://doi.org/10.3390/socsci7120245

Holmes, J. (1986). Compliments and compliment responses in New Zealand English. *Anthropological Linguistics*, *28*(4), 485–508. www.jstor.org/stable/30028355

(1988). Paying compliments: A sex-preferential politeness strategy. *Journal of Pragmatics*, *12*(4), 445–465.

(1989). Sex differences and apologies: One aspect of communicative competence. *Applied Linguistics*, *10*(2), 194–213. https://doi.org/10.1093/applin/10.2.194

(1990). Apologies in New Zealand English. *Language in Society*, *19*(2), 155–199. https://doi.org/10.1017/S0047404500014366

(1998). Complimenting: A positive politeness strategy. In J. Coates & P. Pichler (Eds.), *Language and gender: A reader*, 100–120. Wiley-Blackwell.

(2013). *Women, men and politeness*. Routledge.

(2011). Complimenting: A positive politeness strategy. In J. Coates & P. Pichler (Eds.), *Language and gender: A reader* (2nd edition). Wiley-Blackwell.

Holmes, L. (2009, June 1). Dear Pixar, from all the girls with Band-Aids on their knees. *NPR*. www.npr.org/2009/06/01/104780204/dear-pixar-from-all-the-girls-with-band-aid-on-their-knees

Hopkins, C. (2008, June 28). *Vast public indifference.* www.vastpublicindifference.com/

James, D., & Drakich, J. (1993). Understanding gender differences in amount of talk: A critical review of research. In D. Tannen (Ed.), *Gender and conversational interaction,* 281–312. Oxford University Press.

Jarvey, P. (1989). Mermaid may look familiar: Ariel, new Disney character is a conglomeration of faces. *Telegram & Gazette.*

Jeffords, S. (1995). The curse of masculinity: Disney's *Beauty and the Beast.* In E. Bell, L. Haas, & L. Sells (Eds.), *From mouse to mermaid: The politics of film, gender, and culture,* 161–173. Indiana University Press.

Johnson, S., & Milani, T. M. (2009). *Language ideologies and media discourse: Texts, practices, politics.* A&C Black.

Jones, K. (1992). A question of context: Directive use at a Morris team meeting. *Language in Society, 21*(3), 427–445. https://doi.org/10.1017/S0047404500015517

Jucker, A. H., & Taavitsainen, I. (2008). *Speech acts in the history of English.* John Benjamins.

Junn, E. N. (1997). *Media portrayals of love, marriage & sexuality for child audiences: A select content analysis of Walt Disney animated family films.* https://eric.ed.gov/?id=ED407118

Kampf, Z. (2009). Public (non-)apologies: The discourse of minimizing responsibility. *Journal of Pragmatics, 41*(11), 2257–2270. https://doi.org/10.1016/j.pragma.2008.11.007

Kathlene, L. (1994). Power and influence in state legislative policymaking: The interaction of gender and position in committee hearing debates. *The American Political Science Review, 88*(3), 560–576. https://doi.org/10.2307/2944795

Kelley, J. C. (2013). *Queering conversation: An ethnographic exploration of the functional properties of camp-based language use in US gay men's interactions.* https://escholarship.org/uc/item/6db6x71k

Kelly, A. (1988). Gender differences in teacher–pupil interactions: A meta-analytic review. *Research in Education, 39*(1), 1–23. https://doi.org/10.1177/003452378803900101

Keltner, D., & Ekman, P. (2015, July 3). The science of 'Inside Out.' *New York Times.* www.nytimes.com/2015/07/05/opinion/sunday/the-science-of-inside-out.html

Kendall, S. (2004). Framing Authority: Gender, face, and mitigation at a radio network. *Discourse & Society, 15*(1), 55–79. https://doi.org/10.1177/0957926504038946

    (2008). Creating gendered demeanors of authority at work and at home. In J. Holmes & M. Meyerhoff (Eds.), *The handbook of language and gender,* 600–623. John Wiley & Sons.

Kiesling, S. (2001). Playing the straight man: Displaying and maintaining male heterosexuality in discourse. In J. Coates, & P. Pichler (Eds.), *Language and gender: A reader,* 275–285. Wiley-Blackwell.

Kiesling, S. F. (2005). Homosocial desire in men's talk: Balancing and re-creating cultural discourses of masculinity. *Language in Society, 34*(5), 695–726. www.jstor.org/stable/4169463

King, C. R., Lugo-Lugo, C. R., & Bloodsworth-Lugo, M. K. (2010). *Animating difference: Race, gender, and sexuality in contemporary films for children.* Rowman & Littlefield.

Kochman, T. (1983). The boundary between play and nonplay in Black verbal dueling. *Language in Society, 12*(3), 329–337. www.jstor.org/stable/4167425

Kottke, J. (2009, February 25). Pixar: No chicks allowed. *Kottke.Org.* https://kottke .org/09/02/pixar-no-chicks-allowed

Kramarae, C. (1981). *Women and men speaking: Frameworks for analysis.* Newbury House.

Labov, W. (1972). *Language in the inner city: Studies in the Black English vernacular.* University of Pennsylvania Press.

Lakoff, R. (1973). Language and woman's place. *Language in Society, 2*(1), 45–79. https://doi.org/10.1017/S0047404500000051

Lang, C. (2016, December 6). Pixar's upcoming movie "Coco" will feature all-Latino cast. *Time.* https://time.com/4592610/pixar-coco-movie-all-latino-cast/

Lauzen, M. M., & Dozier, D. M. (2002). You look mahvelous: An examination of gender and appearance comments in the 1999–2000 prime-time season. *Sex Roles, 46*(11), 429–437. https://doi.org/10.1023/A:1020417731462

Lazar, M. M. (2009). Entitled to consume: Postfeminist femininity and a culture of post-critique. *Discourse & Communication, 3*(4), 371–400. https://doi.org/10 .1177/1750481309343872

Leaper, C., & Ayres, M. M. (2007). A meta-analytic review of gender variations in adults' language use: Talkativeness, affiliative speech, and assertive speech. *Personality and Social Psychology Review, 11*(4), 328–363. https://doi.org/10 .1177/1088868307302221

Letts, W. (2016). Camp Disney. In J. C. Garlen & J. A. Sandlin (Eds.), *Disney, culture, and curriculum,* 178–190. Routledge.

Li-Vollmer, M., & LaPointe, M. E. (2003). Gender transgression and villainy in animated film. *Popular Communication, 1*(2), 89–109. https://doi.org/10.1207/ S15405710PC0102_2

Liberman, M. (2013, February 22). An invented statistic returns. *Language Log.* https:// languagelog.ldc.upenn.edu/nll/?p=4488

Liebert, R. M., & Sprafkin, J. (1988). *The early window: Effects of television on children and youth* (3rd edition). Pergamon Press.

Lippi-Green, R. (1997). Teaching children how to discriminate: What we learn from the Big Bad Wolf. In *English with an accent: Language, ideology, and discrimination in the United States,* 79–103. Psychology Press.

  (2012). *English with an accent: Language, ideology and discrimination in the United States* (2nd edition). Routledge.

Livia, A., & Hall, K. (1997). *Queerly phrased: Language, gender, and sexuality.* Oxford University Press.

Macdonald, M. (1995). *Representing women: Myths of femininity in the popular media.* E. Arnold.

Maltz, D., & Borker, R. (1982). A cultural approach to male–female miscommunication. In J. E. Goodman, J. M. Robinson, & L. Monaghan (Eds.), *Language and social identity,* 168–185. Cambridge University Press, 1982.

Manes, J. (1983). Compliments: A mirror of cultural values. In N. Wolfson & J. Manes (Eds.), *Sociolinguistics and language acquisition,* 96–102. Newbury House.

Mann, S. L. (2011). Drag queens' use of language and the performance of blurred gendered and racial identities. *Journal of Homosexuality, 58*(6–7), 793–811.

Marling, K. A. (1999). Are Disney movies really the devil's work? *Culturefront*, *8*(3–4), 25–28.

Martin, K. A., & Kazyak, E. (2009). Hetero-romantic love and heterosexiness in children's G-rated films. *Gender & Society*, *23*(3), 315–336. https://doi.org/10.1177/0891243209335635

Maslin, J. (1989, November 15). Review/Film; Andersen's "Mermaid," by way of Disney. *New York Times*. www.nytimes.com/1989/11/15/movies/review-film-andersen-s-mermaid-by-way-of-disney.html

Mateo, J., & Yus, F. R. (2013). Towards a cross-cultural pragmatic taxonomy of insults. *Journal of Language Aggression and Conflict*, *1*(1), 87–114. https://doi.org/10.1075/jlac.1.1.05mat

McConnell-Ginet, S. (2002). Queering semantics: Definitional struggles. In K. Campbell-Kibler, R. Podesva, S. Roberts, & A. Wong (Eds.), *Language and sexuality: Contesting meaning in theory and practice*, 137–160. CSLI.

McDiarmid, E., Gill, P. R., McLachlan, A., & Ali, L. (2017). "That whole macho male persona thing": The role of insults in young Australian male friendships. *Psychology of Men & Masculinity*, *18*(4), 352–360. https://doi.org/10.1037/men0000065

McGhee, P. E., & Frueh, T. (1980). Television viewing and the learning of sex-role stereotypes. *Sex Roles*, *6*(2), 179–188. https://doi.org/10.1007/BF00287341

McLeod, D. (2016). *Unmasking the quillain: Queerness and villainy in animated Disney films*. Dissertation, University of Wollongong. https://ro.uow.edu.au/theses/4802

Mills, S. (2002). Rethinking politeness, impoliteness, and gender identity. In L. Litosseliti & J. Sunderland (Eds.), *Gender identity and discourse analysis*, 69–89. John Benjamins.

Mills, S., & Mullany, L. (2011). *Language, gender and feminism: Theory, methodology and practice*. Routledge.

Mock, R. (1999). Female Jewish comedians: Grotesque mimesis and transgressing stereotypes. *New Theatre Quarterly*, *15*(2), 99–108. https://doi.org/10.1017/S0266464X00012793

Moretti, M., & Odgers, C. (2002). Aggressive and violent girls: Prevalence, profiles and contributing factors. In R. R. Corrado, R. Roesch, S. D. Hart, & J. K. Gierowski (Eds.), *Multi-problem violent youth: A foundation for comparative research on needs, interventions and outcomes*, 116–129. IOS Press.

Morgan, M. (1999). No woman no cry: Claiming African American women's place. In M. Bucholtz, A. C. Liang, & L. A. Sutton (Eds.), *Reinventing identities: The gendered self in discourse*, 27–45. Oxford University Press.

(2021). More than a mood or an attitude: Discourse and verbal genres in African-American culture. In S. S. Mufwene, J. R. Rickford, G. Bailey, & J. Baugh (Eds.), *African-American English*, 277–312. Routledge.

Motion Picture Association of America. (1930). *Motion Picture Association of America. Production Code Administration records*. Margaret Herrick Library. Academy of Motion Picture Arts and Sciences. www.asu.edu/courses/fms200s/total-readings/MotionPictureProductionCode.pdf

Motschenbacher, H., & Stegu, M. (2013). Queer linguistic approaches to linguistics: Introduction. *Linguistics and Society*, *24*(5), 519–535.

Mullany, L. (2008). "Stop hassling me!" Impoliteness, power, and gender identity in the professional workplace. In D. Bousfield & M. A. Locher (Eds.), *Impoliteness in language: Studies on its interplay with power in theory and practice*, 231–251. Walter de Gruyter.

(2011). Im/politeness, rapport management and workplace culture: Truckers performing masculinities on Canadian ice-roads. In F. Bargiela-Chiappini & D. Z. Kádár (Eds.), *Politeness across cultures*, 61–84. Palgrave Macmillan.

Murphy, J. (2019). I'm sorry you are such an arsehole: (Non-)canonical apologies and their implications for (im)politeness. *Journal of Pragmatics, 142*, 223–232. https://doi.org/10.1016/j.pragma.2018.05.014

Musker, J. (2009). *Magic in the Bayou: Making of the Princess and the Frog*. www.youtube.com/watch?v=rbCafZe4pzE

Newman, M. J. (2018). My little princess: Exploring mothers' experiences of their daughter's parasocial relationships with Disney princesses. *Visual Inquiry, 7*(2), 141–151. https://doi.org/10.1386/vi.7.2.141_1

Nikolas, A. (2014, April 23). The pro-gay message hidden in every Disney film. *The Atlantic*. www.theatlantic.com/entertainment/archive/2014/04/its-not-just-frozen-disney-has-always-been-subtly-pro-gay/361060/

Nosowitz, D. (2016, September 26). Why linguists are fascinated by the American Jewish accent. *Atlas Obscura*. www.atlasobscura.com/articles/why-linguists-are-fascinated-by-the-american-jewish-accent

Nowakowski, K. (2017 January). For princesses, the question remains: Who's the fairest? *National Geographic*. www.nationalgeographic.com/magazine/article/explore-disney-princess-ability-versus-beauty

Nugent, F. (1938). One touch of Disney; and New York surrenders to the genial warmth of his "Snow White" fantasy. *New York Times*. www.nytimes.com/1938/01/23/archives/one-touch-of-disney-and-new-york-surrenders-to-the-genial-warmth-of.html

O'Meara, J. (2016). What "the Bechdel Test" doesn't tell us: Examining women's verbal and vocal (dis)empowerment in cinema. *Feminist Media Studies, 16*(6), 1120–1123. https://doi.org/10.1080/14680777.2016.1234239

Ogiermann, E. (2008). On the culture-specificity of linguistic gender differences: The case of English and Russian apologies. *Intercultural Pragmatics, 5*(3), 259–286. https://doi.org/10.1515/IPRG.2008.013

Orenstein, P. (2006, December 24). What's wrong with Cinderella? *New York Times*. www.nytimes.com/2006/12/24/magazine/24princess.t.html

Pandey, A. (2001). "Scatterbrained apes" and "mangy fools": Lexicalizations of ideology in children's animated movies. *Simile: Studies in Media & Information Literacy Education, 1*, 1–14. https://doi.org/10.3138/sim.1.3.003

Parisi, C., & Wogan, P. (2006). Compliment topics and gender. *Women and Language, 29*(2), 21–28. https://search.proquest.com/openview/54265f7fa21c91ae4b7ef3a45c9abece/1?pq-origsite=gscholar&cbl=31040

Pearson, B. (1988). Power and politeness in conversation: Encoding of face-threatening acts at church business meetings. *Anthropological Linguistics, 30*(1), 68–93. www.jstor.org/stable/30028924

Phipher, M. (1994). *Reviving Ophelia: Saving the selves of adolescent girls*. Ballantine Books.

Pilliere, L. (2013). Dr House and the language of offense. In D. Jamet & M. Jobert (Eds.), *Aspects of linguistic impoliteness*, 60–74. Cambridge Scholars Publishing.

Podesva, R. J. (2007). Phonation type as a stylistic variable: The use of falsetto in constructing a persona. *Journal of Sociolinguistics, 11*(4), 478–504. https://doi.org/10.1111/j.1467-9841.2007.00334.x

Pols, M. (2012, June 22). Why Pixar's "Brave" is a failure of female empowerment. *Time.* https://ideas.time.com/2012/06/22/why-pixars-brave-isa-failure-of-female-empowerment/

Pomerantz, A. (1978). Compliment responses: Notes on the co-operation of multiple constraints. In J. Schenkein (Ed.), *Studies in the organization of conversational interaction*, 79–112. Academic Press.

Popp, D., Donovan, R. A., Crawford, M., Marsh, K. L., & Peele, M. (2003). Gender, race, and speech style stereotypes. *Sex Roles, 48*(7), 317–325. https://doi.org/10.1023/A:1022986429748

Porsgaard, M. R. (2019). Semitic stereotypes. *Leviathan: Interdisciplinary Journal in English, 5*, 33–45. https://doi.org/10.7146/lev.v0i5.115496

Putnam, A. (2013). Mean ladies: Transgendered villains in Disney films. In J. Cheu (Ed.), *Diversity in Disney films: Critical essays on race, ethnicity, gender, sexuality and disability*, 147–162. McFarland.

Quaglio, P. (2009). *Television dialogue: The sitcom Friends vs. natural conversation.* John Benjamins.

Queen, R. (2005). "How many lesbians does it take . . ." *Journal of Linguistic Anthropology, 15*(2), 239–257. https://doi.org/10.1525/jlin.2005.15.2.239

(2015). *Vox popular: The surprising life of language in the media.* John Wiley & Sons.

Rees-Miller, J. (2011). Compliments revisited: Contemporary compliments and gender. *Journal of Pragmatics, 43*(11), 2673–2688.

Rickford, R. J. (2000). *Spoken soul: The story of black English.* John Wiley & Sons.

Rideout, V., & Robb, M. B. (2020). *The Common Sense census: Media use by kids age zero to eight.* Common Sense Media.

Ringrose, J. (2006). A new universal Mean Girl: Examining the discursive construction and social regulation of a new feminine pathology. *Feminism & Psychology, 16*(4), 405–424. https://doi.org/10.1177/0959353506068747

Robinson, T. (2016, June 16). Finding Dory review: It isn't about family, it's about living with disability. *The Verge.* www.theverge.com/2016/6/16/11952182/finding-dory-review-finding-nemo-sequel-pixar

Romano, N. (2020, June 1). Pixar's "Out" team on short's "astonishing" impact: "We're so hungry to see ourselves." *EW.Com.* https://ew.com/movies/pixar-out-lgbtq-short/

Rosenthal, C. S. (1998). *When women lead: Integrative leadership in state legislatures.* Oxford University Press.

Schumann, K., & Ross, M. (2010). Why women apologize more than men: Gender differences in thresholds for perceiving offensive behavior. *Psychological Science, 21*(11), 1649–1655. https://doi.org/10.1177/0956797610384150

Searle, J. R. (1975). A taxonomy of illocutionary acts. In K. Gunderson (Ed.), *Language mind, and knowledge*, 344–368. University of Minnesota Press.

Scott, A. O. (2016, June 15). Review: In 'Finding Dory,' a forgetful fish and a warm celebration of differences. *New York Times*. www.nytimes.com/2016/06/17/ movies/finding-dory-review-pixar.html?_r=0

Selisker, S. (2015). The Bechdel Test and the social form of character networks. *New Literary History*, *46*(3), 505–523. https://doi.org/10.1353/nlh.2015.0024

Siegler, D. M., & Siegler, R. S. (1976). Stereotypes of males' and females' speech. *Psychological Reports*, *39*(1), 167–170. https://doi.org/10.2466/pr0.1976.39.1.167

Smith, S., & Cook, C. (2008). *Gender stereotypes: An analysis of popular films and TV*. The Geena Davis Institute on Gender in Media. https://seejane.org/wp-content/ uploads/GDIGM_Gender_Stereotypes.pdf

Smith, S. L., Choueiti, M., Pieper, K., et al. (2019). *Inequality in 1,300 popular films: Examing portrayals of gender, race/ethnicity, LGBTQ and disability from 2007 to 2019*. Annenberg Foundation. https://assets.uscannenberg.org/docs/aii-inequality_ 1300_popular_films_09-08-2020.pdf

Spender, D. (1980). Talking in class. In D. Spender, S. Elizabeth, & P. Mahoney (Eds.), *Learning to lose: Sexism and education*. Women's Press.

Stoll, J. (2021, January 13). *Walt Disney revenue worldwide*. Statista. www.statista .com/statistics/273555/global-revenue-of-the-walt-disney-company/

Stover, C. (2013). Damsels and heroines: The conundrum of the post-feminist Disney Princess. *LUX: A Journal of Transdisciplinary Writing and Research from Claremont Graduate University*, *2*(1). https://doi.org/10.5642/lux.201301.29

Sugimoto, N. (1997). A Japan–US comparison of apology styles. *Communication Research*, *24*(4), 349–369.

Sung, C. C. M. (2012). Exploring the interplay of gender, discourse, and (im)politeness. *Journal of Gender Studies*, *21*(3), 285–300. https://doi.org/10.1080/09589236 .2012.681179

Swann, J. (2003). Schooled language: Language and gender in educational settings. In J. Holmes & M. Meyerhoff (Eds.), *The handbook of language and gender*, 624–644. John Wiley & Sons.

Tannen, D. (1996). *Gender and discourse*. Oxford University Press.
    (2009). New York Jewish conversational style. *International Journal of the Sociology of Language*, *30*, 133–149. https://doi.org/10.1515/ijsl.1981.30.133

Tanner, L. R., Haddock, S. A., Zimmerman, T. S., & Lund, L. K. (2003). Images of couples and families in Disney feature-length animated films. *The American Journal of Family Therapy*, *31*(5), 355–373. https://doi.org/10.1080/ 01926180390223987

Tanny, J. (2017). "A bad, bold, big-nosed, biblical brother": Refashioning the funny Jew in post-World War Two America. *Journal of Modern Jewish Studies*, *16*(1), 100–117. https://doi.org/10.1080/14725886.2016.1199412

Tiggemann, M., & Boundy, M. (2008). Effect of environment and appearance compliment on college women's self-objectification, mood, body shame, and cognitive performance. *Psychology of Women Quarterly*, *32*(4), 399–405. https://doi.org/10.1111/j.1471-6402.2008.00453.x

Towbin, M. A., Haddock, S. A., Zimmerman, T. S., Lund, L. K., & Tanner, L. R. (2004). Images of gender, race, age, and sexual orientation in Disney feature-length animated films. *Journal of Feminist Family Therapy*, *15*(4), 19–44. https://doi.org/10.1300/J086v15n04_02

Tunzelmann, A. von. (2008). Poverty, alcoholism and suicide – but at least the natives can paint with all the colours of the wind. *The Guardian*. www.theguardian.com/film/2008/sep/10/pocahontas

Turandot, J. (2020, September 15). How to be an assertive woman. *WikiHow*. www.wikihow.com/Be-an-Assertive-Woman

U.S. Department of Health and Human Services, U.S. Public Health Service, Substance Abuse and Mental Health Services Administration (1997). *Girl Power! Have You Got It?* Center for Substance Abuse Prevention.

Vargas, J. A. G. (1999). Who is the Puerto Rican Woman and how is she? Shall Hollywood respond? In M. Meyers (Ed.), *Mediated women: Representations in popular culture*, 111–132. Routledge.

Vine, B. (2004). *Getting things done at work: The discourse of power in workplace interaction*. John Benjamins.

Weigel, M. M., & Weigel, R. M. (1985). Directive use in a migrant agricultural community: A test of Ervin-Tripp's hypotheses. *Language in Society, 14*(1), 63–79. https://doi.org/10.1017/S0047404500010940

West, C. (1990). Not just 'doctors' orders': Directive–response sequences in patients' visits to women and men physicians. *Discourse & Society, 1*(1), 85–112. https://doi.org/10.1177/0957926590001001005

Wiersma, B. (2000). *The gendered world of Disney: A content analysis of gender themes in full-length animated Disney feature films*. Dissertation, South Dakota State University. https://openprairie.sdstate.edu/etd/1906

Wilde, S. (2014). Repackaging the Disney Princess: A post-feminist reading of modern-day fairy tales. *Journal of Promotional Communications, 2*(1), 132–153.

Wodak, R. (1996). Power, discourse, and styles of female leadership in school committee meetings. In D. Corson (Ed.), *Discourse and power in educational organizations*, 31–54. Hampton Press.

Wohlwend, K. E. (2009). Damsels in discourse: Girls consuming and producing identity texts through Disney Princess play. *Reading Research Quarterly, 44*(1), 57–83. https://doi.org/10.1598/RRQ.44.1.3

Wolfson, N. (1984). Pretty is as pretty does: A speech act view of sex roles. *Applied Linguistics, 5*(3), 236–244. https://doi.org/10.1093/applin/5.3.236

Wooden, S. R., & Gillam, K. (2014). *Pixar's boy stories: Masculinity in a postmodern age*. Rowman & Littlefield.

Yin, J. (2011). Popular culture and public imaginary: Disney vs. Chinese stories of Mulan. *Javnost – The Public, 18*(1), 53–74. https://doi.org/10.1080/13183222.2011.11009051

Zaslow, E. (2009). *Feminism, inc.: Coming of age in girl power media culture*. Springer.

Zeisler, A. (2008). *Feminism and pop culture*. Basic Books.

Zimman, L. (2014). Transmasculinity and the voice: Gender assignment, identity, and presentation. In T. M. Milani (Ed.), *Language and Masculinities*, 217–239. Routledge.

## Filmography

Bancroft, T., & Cook, B. (1998). *Mulan*. Walt Disney Studios Motion Pictures.

Bird, B. (2004). *The Incredibles*. Pixar Animation Studios.

(2007). *Ratatouille*. Pixar Animation Studios.

Chapman, B., & Andrews, M. (2012). *Brave*. Walt Disney Studios Motion Pictures.

Clements, R., & Musker, J. (1989). *Little Mermaid*. Buena Vista Pictures.

(1992). *Aladdin*. Walt Disney Studios Motion Pictures.

(1997). *Hercules*. Walt Disney Studios Motion Pictures.

(2009). *The Princess and the Frog*. Walt Disney Studios Motion Pictures.

(2016). *Moana*. Walt Disney Studios Motion Pictures.

Dindal, M. (2000). *Emperor's New Groove*. Walt Disney Studios Motion Pictures.

Docter, P. (2001). *Monsters, Inc*. Pixar Animation Studios.

(2009). *Up*. Pixar Animation Studios.

(2015). *Inside Out*. Pixar Animation Studios.

Fee, B. (2017). *Cars 3*. Pixar Animation Studios.

Geronimi, C., et al. (1950). *Cinderella*. Walt Disney Studios Motion Pictures.

(1959). *Sleeping Beauty*. Walt Disney Studios Motion Pictures.

Goldberg, E., & Gabriel, M. (1995). *Pocahontas*. Walt Disney Studios Motion Pictures.

Hand, D., et al. (1937). *Snow White*. Walt Disney Studios Motion Pictures.

Howard, B., & Greno, N. (2010). *Tangled*. Walt Disney Studios Motion Pictures.

Lasseter, J. (1995). *Toy Story*. Pixar Animation Studios.

(1998). *A Bug's Life*. Pixar Animation Studios.

(1999). *Toy Story 2*. Pixar Animation Studios.

(2006). *Cars*. Pixar Animation Studios.

(2011). *Cars 2*. Pixar Animation Studios.

Lee, J., & Buck, C. (2013). *Frozen*. Walt Disney Studios Motion Pictures.

(2019). *Frozen II*. Walt Disney Studios Motion Pictures.

Minkoff, R., & Allers, R. (1994). *Lion King*. Walt Disney Studios Motion Pictures.

Molina, A., & Unkrich, L. (2017). *Coco*. Pixar Animation Studios.

Reitherman, W. (1967). *Jungle Book*. Walt Disney Studios Motion Pictures.

Reitherman, W., Geronimi, C., & Luske, H. (1961). *101 Dalmatians*. Walt Disney Studios Motion Pictures.

Scanlon, D. (2013). *Monsters University*. Pixar Animation Studios.

Sohn, P. (2015). *Good Dinosaur*. Pixar Animation Studios.

Stanton, A. (2003). *Finding Nemo*. Pixar Animation Studios.

(2016). *Finding Dory*. Pixar Animation Studios.

Trousdale, G., & Wise, K. (1991). *Sleeping Beauty*. Walt Disney Studios Motion Pictures.

Unkrich, L. (2010). *Toy Story 3*. Pixar Animation Studios.

# Index

age, 11, 20, 151, 157
aggravation (strategy), 107–121
*Aladdin* (franchise)
    Aladdin (character), 31, 61–64, 69–70, 87,
        101–102, 149, 164, 181, 201, 206–207,
        215
    *Aladdin* (film), 6, 16, 31–33, 51–54, 69, 152,
        180–181
    Jafar (character), 31, 70–71, 178–188, 200
    Jasmine (character), 29–31, 61, 71, 94, 101,
        149, 181, 206, 215
Al-Yasin, Noor, 8, 135
Anna (character). *See Frozen* (franchise)
apologies (speech act), 2, 19, 106, 112, 126,
    129, 155–172, 206, 212, 217
Ariel (character). *See Little Mermaid, The*
    (franchise)
Aurora (character). *See Sleeping Beauty*
    (franchise)
authority, xi, 39, 90, 109, 119–130, 209–212
    cultural, 3
    domestic, 117, 124–127
    hierarchal, 122, 129
    institutional, 112, 119–125, 210
    royalty, 121

Bataineh, Ruba, 156–161, 169
Bataineh, Rula, 156–161, 169
*Beauty and the Beast* (franchise)
    Beast, The (character), 149, 202, 208–214
    *Beauty and the Beast* (1991), 28, 54, 63, 71,
        148–149, 168, 209
    Belle (character), 28–30, 94, 140, 149, 168,
        202, 208, 213, 218
    Gaston (character), 71–72, 140, 149, 168, 208
    LeFou (character), 177
Bell, Elizabeth, 7, 24–26
Belle (character). *See Beauty and the Beast*
    (franchise)
bimbettes (character type), 52, 71–73
binomial test, 50–57, 82–83, 111, 136–139,
    160–161

body type, 20, 32, 182, 197
bonding. *See* inoffensive intent
boys' club, Pixar as, 42
*Brave* (franchise)
    Brave (character), 142–143
    *Brave* (film), 34–41, 48–63, 89, 96, 101,
        121, 126, 142–143, 150–152, 205–217
    Elinor (character), 54, 121, 126–127, 150,
        210
    Fergus (character), 89, 101, 126–127
    Merida (character), 40, 57, 101, 150, 163,
        177, 205–207, 215
Brown, Penelope, 77, 106–108, 155
Bucholtz, Mary, 12–15, 178, 202
*Bug's Life, A* (franchise)
    Atta (character), 57, 63, 97, 121–123, 130,
        146, 169
    *Bug's Life, A* (film), 62–63, 69–70, 121–123,
        207
    Flik (character), 63, 97, 116–123, 164, 169
Burnett, Frances, 24

Cameron, Deborah, 155, 159
*Cars* (franchise)
    *Cars* (film), 57, 62, 89, 99–102, 146–151,
        209
    *Cars 2* (film), 57–63, 96–102
    *Cars 3* (film), 57–63, 145–151, 211
    Cruz (character), 57, 63, 145–146, 151–154,
        211
    Lightning McQueen (character), 42, 63,
        87–89, 99–102, 145–146, 150, 164
    Mater (character), 87, 99, 164
    Sally (character), 57, 146
character frequency, 86
    gender, 17
children, 1–20, 31, 37–42, 77, 102–104, 107,
    121, 130, 148, 173–175, 200–203,
    209–210, 219
    gender roles, 4–12, 87, 214
    media habits, 2–4
    research on, 6–10, 41, 46, 108

Printed in Great Britain
by Amazon

13073816R00149